Lifelong Learning

Lifelong learning has developed considerably as a distinct area of study within education in recent years. This is not least because numerous governments and noted educational strategists have become very vocal supporters of new ways of learning throughout all stages of life.

This richly detailed and considered examination of current thinking in lifelong learning brings together new writing from worldwide experts in the topic, including Professors Norman Longworth and Jack D. Mezirow, to offer a broad-ranging picture of the position to date. Also including a thoughtful historic preface from Professor Peter Jarvis, the book provides a critical summary of current developments in understanding adult learning and the societal context in which they are located.

Across the different contributions and sections of the book, four clear themes are developed:

- Adult learning is distinctly different from learning in childhood.
- Learning is more than a cognitive activity in that it includes an affective dimension as well as contextual influences.
- Lifelong learning has implications for the purpose and processes of learning in educational institutions.
- There are subordinate discourses of lifelong learning that need to be aired and can enrich our understanding of what it means.

Everyone engaged in lifelong learning, including students undertaking courses of study in this field and undergraduate and postgraduate students in a variety of professional areas, will find this material essential reading.

Dr Peter Sutherland is Lecturer in Education at the Institute of Education, University of Stirling.

Dr Jim Crowther is Senior Lecturer in Higher and Community Education at the University of Edinburgh.

Lifelong Learning

Concepts and contexts

Edited by Peter Sutherland and Jim Crowther

Routledge
Taylor & Francis Group

LONDON AND NEW YORK

First published 2006 by Routledge
2 Park Square, Milton Park, Abingdon, Oxon OX14 4RN

Simultaneously published in the USA and Canada
by Routledge
29 West 35th Street, New York, NY 10001

Routledge is an imprint of the Taylor & Francis Group

Typeset in Baskerville by
GreenGate Publishing Services, Tonbridge
Printed and bound in Great Britain by
Biddles Ltd, King's Lynn

British Library Cataloguing in Publication Data
A catalogue record for this book is available from the British Library

Library of Congress Cataloging in Publication Data
Lifelong learning : concepts and contexts / Peter Sutherland and Jim
Crowther.
        p. cm.
    Includes bibliographical references and index.
    ISBN 0-415-35372-6 (hardback : alk. paper) 1. Continuing education.
I. Sutherland, Peter. II. Crowther, Jim.

LC5215.L496 2006
374–dc22
2005011157

ISBN10: 0-415-35372-6

ISBN13: 978-0-415-35372-4

Contents

Illustrations   vii
List of contributors   viii
Foreword by Peter Jarvis   xiv
Acknowledgements   xvi

Introduction   1

1   Introduction: 'the lifelong learning imagination'   3
    PETER SUTHERLAND AND JIM CROWTHER

PART I
Perspectives on adult and lifelong learning   13

2   What is special about adult learning?   15
    KNUD ILLERIS

3   An overview on transformative learning   24
    JACK MEZIROW

4   Managing change and transition: a psychosocial   39
    perspective on lifelong learning
    LINDEN WEST

5   The application of the ideas of Habermas to adult   48
    learning
    MARK MURPHY AND TED FLEMING

6   A troubled space of possibilities: lifelong learning   58
    and the postmodern
    RICHARD EDWARDS AND ROBIN USHER

PART II
Institutions and issues for lifelong learning   69

7   Realizing a lifelong learning higher education institution   71
    SHIRLEY WALTERS

8 Towards a responsive work-based curriculum for non-traditional students in higher education 82
JOHN BAMBER

9 Changing to learning cultures that foster lifelong learners 94
ROSE EVISON

10 An analysis of the relations between learning and teaching approaches 108
KEITH TRIGWELL

11 Lifelong learning: the role of emotional intelligence 117
TINA GOODWIN AND SUSAN HALLAM

12 A comparison of Piaget's and Biggs's conceptions of cognitive development in adults and their implications for the teaching of adults 127
PETER SUTHERLAND

13 Academic study as a social practice 138
CHRISSIE BOUGHEY

14 Self-regulation: a multidimensional learning strategy 146
MARTHA CASSAZZA

PART III
Informal and community contexts for learning 159

15 (Mis)recognizing lifelong learning in non-formal settings 161
JOHN PRESTON

16 Social movements, praxis and the profane side of lifelong learning 171
JIM CROWTHER

17 Learning cities, learning regions, lifelong learning implementers 182
NORMAN LONGWORTH

18 Literacy as social practice: travelling between the everyday and other forms of learning 196
YVON APPLEBY AND MARY HAMILTON

19 Lifelong learning in the community: social action 207
ROD PURCELL

20 Work and learning: implications for lifelong learning in the workplace 218
HITENDRA PILLAY, LYNN WILSS AND GILLIAN BOULTON-LEWIS

21 Making a space for adult education in mental health: the Outlook Project experience 230
FIONA DOWIE AND MATTHEW GIBSON

Index 243

Illustrations

Figures

14.1	Theory, research, principles and practice model	150
19.1	Reflection–Vision–Planning–Action cycle	211
21.1	Medical model of disability	233
21.2	Social model of disability	234
21.3	Shifting identity: from patient to student	239

Tables

7.1	Characteristic elements of the Cape Town Statement	73
10.1	Examples of items from the approaches to teaching inventory (ATI)	112
10.2	Correlation between teachers' approach to teaching and students' approach to learning variables	113
12.1	Piaget's stages of cognitive development	128
12.2	Biggs's levels of observed learning outcomes	130
12.3	Biggs's (1995) hierarchical forms of knowledge	131
12.4	Biggs's 3P's model of learning	133
12.5	Differences between Piaget's and Biggs's models	134
17.1	The TELS Learning Cities indicators	186
17.2	From education and training to lifelong learning	191–4
20.1	Conceptions of work, and variations by older and younger workers	222
20.2	Conceptions of learning at work, and variations by older and younger workers	223
20.3	Age, workplace and level of education for workers	224
21.1	Outlook and other service providers	236

Contributors

Yvon Appleby is a Research Fellow at Lancaster University Research Centre. She has been working on the Adult Learners' Lives project, a three year ethnographic study, for the National Research and Development Centre. This research links literacy, numeracy and language learning in classes (both college and in community settings) and what adults use and learn in their everyday lives. Yvon previously worked as an adult community educator developing and supporting creative approaches to learning in ex-coalfield communities and areas of urban regeneration.

John Bamber is a Lecturer in Community Education at the University of Edinburgh. He was a youth worker and local authority manager before taking up his present post. He is a programme co-ordinator for the professional graduate diploma in community education and for the part-time route to the BA in community education. His research interests include widening access, work-based learning, teaching and learning in HE, youth work and group work.

Chrissie Boughey is a graduate of St Andrews University, Scotland. She worked as a teacher of English as a foreign language in Spain, Britain and a number of countries in the Middle East before moving to South Africa in 1988. In South Africa, her work has focused on the use of mainstream subject teaching to develop language and her research on challenging dominant approaches to language teaching, and in providing alternatives to the constructions of students' 'problems' which result from them. She is now director of a centre which contributes to the development of academic staff as professional educators in higher education at Rhodes University in Grahamstown but maintains her interest in language/literacy development through research and through the supervision of a number of doctoral candidates who are all working in the field of New Literacy Studies.

Gillian Boulton-Lewis is Research Professor in the Faculty of Education at the Queensland University of Technology. She has made a significant contribution to the field of learning and teaching across the lifespan and in a range of content and contextual areas. Her research interests have focused on cognitive development in children and the implications of this for learning mathematics, learning and teaching in secondary as well as higher education, learning opportunities for children in child care, conceptions of learning for indigenous Australian university students and learning in the workplace.

Martha Cassazza is Dean of the College of Arts and Sciences at National-Louis University in Chicago, Illinois. She is a regular contributor to professional journals in the field: *Journal of Developmental Education, Learning Assistance Review*, and *Research in Developmental Education*. She has co-authored two books with Sharon Silverman (and has two more in press) which have had a positive impact on developmental education, are cited throughout the research literature, and are useful references for developmental educators: *Learning Assistance and Developmental Education: A Guide for Effective Practice* (1996) and *Learning and Development* (2000).

Jim Crowther is Senior Lecturer in Higher and Community Education at the University of Edinburgh. He was formerly a tutor and organizer of adult basic education in the city of Edinburgh between 1982 and 1990. He has extensive experience of teaching and training activities over a twenty-year period. He is the co-founder of the International Popular Education Network. He has also co-edited a number of other books: *Popular Education and Social Movements in Scotland Today* (1999), *Powerful Literacies* (2001) *Renewing Democracy in Scotland: an Educational Source Book* (2002) and *Popular Education: Engaging the Academy* (2005). All of these have been published by the National Institute of Adult Continuing Education (NIACE).

Fiona Dowie is an Adult Education Worker with the Outlook Project, part of the City of Edinburgh Community Education Service. Fiona studied Community Education at Moray House Institute of Education in Edinburgh and graduated in 1997. She has worked in a variety of educational roles within adult education. For the past seven years she has worked in the Outlook Project, developing wide ranging adult education services for people who use mental health services. She has a particular interest in inclusive education and challenging the notion of 'mainstream' education. Fiona has provided input on adult education and mental health to lectures in the Department of Higher and Community Education, Edinburgh University and regularly supervises students on placement.

Richard Edwards is Professor of Education at the University of Stirling. He is the recently retired editor of *Studies in the Education of Adults*. He has written and researched extensively in the area of adult education and lifelong learning, in particular drawing on poststructuralist and postmodernist perspectives. He has written and edited a number of books. His most recent book, with Robin Usher, Katherine Nicoll and Nicky Solomon, is *Rhetoric and Educational Discourse: Persuasive Texts?*

Rose Evison is a consultant. Since 1973 she has been an independent psychological practitioner working with industrial and commercial organizations and helping professionals. Her initial concern with improving teaching and learning methods widened into facilitating strategies and activities that help organizations and individuals to change. She regards herself as a scientist-practitioner, linking theory and research to her working situations and researching the effectiveness of change strategies. She specializes in developing supportive environments for learning. She is the founder of Change Strategies, which provides a service for both individuals and organizations. She is a Chartered Occupational Psychologist and an honorary Lecturer at Glasgow Caledonian University.

Ted Fleming is Acting Head of the Department of Adult and Community Education at the National University of Ireland, Maynooth. He has published articles and research reports on mature students in university, access issues in higher education for disadvantaged students and early school leaving. With Mark Murphy he co-wrote *College Knowledge: Power, Policy and the Mature Student at University* (1998) and is a regular contributor to *The Adult Learner: The Journal of Adult and Community Education in Ireland*, writing on civil society, democracy and the challenges for public policy. His area of interest is critical social theory and he has published 'Habermas on civil society, life-world and system: unearthing the social in transformation theory', *Teachers College Record on-line*. Ted received his MA and EdD from Teachers College, Columbia University, New York.

Matthew Gibson is a husband, stepfather and grandfather who has worked in the voluntary sector for seven years with adults with learning difficulties, mental health recoverers and carers. In addition he is an active member of the Workers' Education Association and is involved in delivering induction and training for both members and staff on the history and purpose of the WEA. He has also been involved in the work of the Scottish Civic Forum in creating opportunities for local people to discuss policy issues in the Scottish Parliament. For the past eighteen months he has worked with the Outlook Project which offers adult education opportunities to people using mental health services. He is a Christian and is developing men's work and work with the homeless community in his local church.

Tina Goodwin moved to the educational sector in 1990 after an initial career in law and engineering. Her early research studies focused on the psychology of student motivation. Her PhD studies at the Institute of Education, University of London attracted a three-year fully funded award from the Economic and Social Research Council. As a research assistant and officer she has also undertaken research on the effectiveness of information and communication technology as a learning tool for basic skills learners on behalf of the University for Industry, and a laptop initiative evaluation on behalf of

DfEE/Basic Skills Agency. She has presented at conferences and published articles relating to her own research interests on adult student drop-out, motivation and feelings and emotions and contributed to publications on basic skills and information and communication technology research projects.

Susan Hallam is the current Chairperson of the British Psychological Society's Education Section and Treasurer of the British Educational Research Association. She is an Institutional Auditor for the Quality Assurance Agency. She is a Professor at the Institute of Education, University of London.

Mary Hamilton is Professor of Adult Learning and Literacy in the Department of Educational Research at Lancaster University, UK. Her main areas of interest are in adult and continuing education: policy issues and public representations of literacy; comparative perspectives, especially across industrialized societies; processes of informal adult learning and issues of access and transition for mature students. She is founder member of the national network Research and Practice in Adult Literacy (RAPAL) and a core member of the Lancaster Literacy Research Group.

Knud Illeris is Professor of Lifelong Learning at Learning Lab Denmark at the University of Education in Copenhagen. He is the author of *The Three Dimensions of Learning* (2002), published by NIACE and *Learning in the Workplace* (2004) and *Adult Education and Adult Learning*, both published by Roskilde University Press in Denmark.

Norman Longworth is one of the world's leading authorities on lifelong learning in general and learning cities and learning communities in particular. He is Visiting Professor of Lifelong Learning at the University of Stirling and at Napier University. His previous books include *Lifelong Learning in Action: Transforming Education in the 21st Century* (2003), *Making Lifelong Learning Work: Learning Cities for a Learning Century* (1999) and *Lifelong Learning: New Visions, New Implications, New Roles – for Industry, Government, Education and the Community for the 21st Century* (1996) (with Keith Davies).

Jack Mezirow is an Emeritius Professor of Adult Education at Teachers College, Columbia University in New York City. He initiated a doctoral programme to enhance transformative learning. His research interests include adult learning theory, democratic citizenship and social change. His books include (with colleagues) *Learning as Transformation* (2000), *Transformative Dimensions of Adult Learning* (1992) and *Fostering Critical Reflection in Adulthood* (1991). He has been a consultant on adult literacy and community development for UNESCO, UNICEF, and other international organizations.

Mark Murphy is a Lecturer at the Institute of Education at Stirling University where he is Director of the Teaching Qualification in Further Education course. He is an authority on Habermas and is currently working on a book on this German critical social theorist. His other main interests include university adult education, educational sociology, critical theory and education, political economy of post-compulsory education and international adult education. He has numerous publications in the field of adult and higher education and his work has involved him in adult educational debates in Ireland, Scotland and the United States.

Hitendra Pillay is Associate Professor in the Faculty of Education at the Queensland University of Technology. His interest in human learning has led to a diverse research portfolio that includes research in the areas of adult education, industry based training, learning and cognition, spatial problem solving, technology based learning environments, and conceptions of work and conceptions of learning in the workplace. In recent years he has also worked on educational reform in developing countries.

John Preston is Senior Lecturer in Citizenship and Education at the University of East London. John previously worked as a lecturer in FE and adult education and as a researcher at the Institute of Education. His research interests are in learning and community engagement, equity and social cohesion and inequalities in HE participation. He is currently interested in ways in which 'whiteness' and 'class' are being used in lifelong learning policies to re-shape the purposes of post-compulsory and adult education. John is the co-author of *The Benefits of Learning: The impact of education on health, family life and social capital* (with Tom Schuller *et al.*).

Rod Purcell is a Lecturer specializing in Community Learning and Development with the Department of Adult Education at the University of Glasgow. He has a background in geography and has interests in models of sustainable development.

Peter Sutherland is Lecturer in Education at the University of Stirling in Scotland. He specializes in lifelong learning in both his teaching and his research. He teaches courses on adult learning at both under-graduate and post-graduate level. His research includes editing *Adult Learning: A Reader* which was published by Kogan Page. One of his current research projects is investigating the perception of lectures by both lecturers and students. Another is investigating the feedback provided by lecturers to their students.

Keith Trigwell is Reader in Higher Education in the Institute for the Advancement of University Learning at the University of Oxford. He has published numerous articles on university teaching and learning and is co-author with Michael Prosser of the book *Understanding Learning and Teaching* (1999). His current research is concerned with relations between research and student learning, indicators of variation in approaches to teaching, the influence of perceived teaching environments on teaching and of perceived learning environments (including teaching) on student learning.

Robin Usher is Professor of Education at RMIT University in Melbourne, Australia. His most recent book, with Richard Edwards, Katherine Nicol and Nicky Solomon is *Rhetoric and Educational Discourse: Persuasive Texts?*

Shirley Walters is actively involved in South Africa and internationally in the promotion of lifelong learning within higher education and in the broader society. She is currently the founding Director of the Division for Lifelong Learning that is mandated to assist the University of the Western Cape attain its lifelong learning mission. She is Professor of Adult and Continuing Education. She has been appointed by the National Minister for Education to chair the South African Qualifications Authority, which was established to be a leading instrument to facilitate access, redress and development through the National Qualifications Framework. In the broader community, she is the chairperson of a regional consortium of civil society, government, business and educational organizations that has implemented an annual month-long Learning Cape Festival which is part of a provincial strategy to develop a learning region. She continues to campaign for those on the margins of society and was co-founder of a non-governmental organization, the Women's Hope Education and Training (WHEAT) Trust, which helps poor women to further their work in communities through adult education and training.

Linden West is Reader in Education in the Department of Educational Research at Canterbury Christ Church University College, UK. He has worked for the Workers' Educational Association, for Local Education Authorities, including heading an Adult Basic Education Unit, and in broadcasting. His books include *Beyond Fragments* (about adult learner motivation) and *Doctors on the Edge* (about stress and subjective learning). He co-ordinates the Biographical and Life History Research Network of the European Society for Research on the Education of Adults (ESREA) and is a member of the Society's Steering Committee. Linden is also a qualified psychoanalytic psychotherapist and uses some of the ideas from this aspect of his work in thinking about processes of adult learning. Linden's current research is on families and their learning. He is also completing a study of a work-based teacher training programme – Teach First – in London and derived from an American initiative called Teach for America. Linden is interested in the nature of professional identities in a low-trust, audit culture.

Lynn Wilss is Senior Research Assistant at the School of Learning and Professional Studies, Faculty of Education, at the Queensland University of Technology in Australia. Her research focus is cognition and learning. Her recent research projects have included investigating indigenous higher education students and their conceptions of learning, learning in the workplace and concerns involved in caring for patients in palliative care.

Foreword

Peter Jarvis

It is a pleasure to be asked to write the foreword to this book on lifelong learning.

Lifelong learning is an ambiguous concept, used in a variety of ways and has a complex history within the field of education. For instance, we can trace the development of the term through a number of different routes: two are clearly significant here – an educational one and a learning one – and like many other terms having complex derivations it still carries its past with it – as it should.

Educationally, we can see that the term emerged from the idea of adult education as early as the beginning of the twentieth century. By the early 1970s and 1980s, however, the term adult education conveyed too narrow a connotation to describe accurately the developments that were occurring as the knowledge economy emerged in Western society. Consequently, three other terms appeared: the education of adults, continuing education and recurrent education. The first was probably too close to the term adult education and the third was too radical, and neither gained wide currency. Consequently, the rather nondescript term of continuing education came to the fore. Even its definition was disputed! From what did it continue? It could either mean education that continued after one reached school leaving age or it could mean the education that continued after initial education was completed, at whatever age that might be. In any case, the point about continuing education was that it had no specified ending and so it was lifelong. Lifelong education had been something of an ideal for adult educators, an ideal referrred to in the famous 1919 Report;* Basil Yeaxlee, one of the Committee that prepared that Report, wrote the first book on lifelong education in 1929. But the idea of lifelong education received its official sanction when UNESCO adopted it in the 1970s. However, the concept of education carried with it some problems, conceptual and otherwise, which made it an inappropriate term to use for all the forms of education for adults that were beginning to arise. By the mid 1990s in Europe and elsewhere the term 'learning' was beginning to replace 'education' – and lifelong learning was beginning to be used in place of lifelong education rather than being interchangeable with it, as it was in the USA.

---

* Ministry of Reconstruction (1919) Final Report of The Adult Education Committee, Cmnd 321, London: HMSO.

By 1995, the European Community had adopted the term but, significantly, despite the adoption of the term and the establishment of a division responsible for it, it has never been used consistently by the EC. In a sense, it has always used the term rather like the use of 'education for adults' since it still has separate divisions responsible for adult education (Grundtvig), initial education and training, and higher education.

From the perspective of learning, various theories have emerged. These were about both children's learning and adults' learning and since learning is a human process, it is not surprising that learning theory has assumed something of a lifelong perspective. Yet there are few studies that have sought to compare children's learning with adult learning or with third age learning.

There are also few that have sought to compare learning processes in formal settings, like classrooms, with informal situations like social living. Perhaps we should not expect to find a learning theory that is lifelong but there is certainly a need for a comparative approach to learning theory examining children's, adults' and older adults' learning processes and drawing rigorous comparisons. At the same time, we do have studies of the learning process that span adulthood and these have tended to be regarded as theories of lifelong learning.

But from the perspective of lifelong learning, there is a sense in which 'learning' has been used as a human process and it has become either an adjective or a metaphor to describe societies, regions and organizations: learning societies, and so on. But the trouble is that bodies such as societies, towns and organizations do not and cannot learn, but they can change, often as a result of some influential members of the organization or town learning and introducing changes into the procedures of their institutions. In this sense, learning has become synonymous with flexibility, and flexible and responsive organizations and towns have become known as learning organizations, cities, and so on.

Lifelong learning, then, is a complex and ambiguous term and any book that tries to examine the concepts and contexts associated with it needs to incorporate some of these perspectives. This means that such studies are necessarily broad. This book succeeds in conveying something of this breadth – it has chapters about learning theory that might be seen as lifelong; it seeks to cover a wide variety of educational settings, many of which might have been just as much at home in an adult education framework; it looks at learning regions. The book is also international in scope and draws on a variety of different academic perspectives. Because of the breadth and complexity of the subject, no single book can hope to carry prolonged discussion about the many overlapping fields of practice that might call themselves lifelong learning and, wisely, this book does not seek to do this.

This is an interesting study, opening up several different fields of lifelong learning to academic analysis and the editors are to be commended for compiling such an interesting and varied anthology.

Acknowledgements

We would like to express our appreciation to Philip Mudd and Thomas Young who commissioned this book and encouraged us in its production. We would like to express our appreciation to *Adult Education Quarterly* for allowing the revised version of Richard Edwards and Robin Usher's chapter, which was first published in this journal, to be amended and reduced for publication in this book. We would also like to record our thanks to Akiko Hemmi for technical editorial assistance and to Ian Martin and Pat Brechin for their helpful comments on the introduction to the book.

Peter Sutherland and Jim Crowther

Introduction

Chapter 1

Introduction

The 'lifelong learning imagination'

Peter Sutherland and Jim Crowther

> Ordinary men and women often feel their lives are a series of traps ...
> Underlying this sense of being trapped are the impersonal changes taking
> place in the structures of society.
>
> (C. Wright Mills 1959: 1)

The concern of C. Wright Mills in *The Sociological Imagination* is as relevant today
as when it was raised first almost fifty years ago. Global economic processes, environmental disasters, terrorism, insecurity at work and the geo-politics of conflict
have heightened our sense of uncertainty and of being trapped by forces we know
little about and which seem beyond our control. The answer that C. Wright Mills
proposed to address this problem was the 'the sociological imagination', which
would enable its possessor to make sense of their personal biographies in the context of larger historical events. The essential quality of mind it requires is the
capacity to connect 'personal troubles' with 'public issues' and to understand the
relationship between the two. This is the task and promise of the sociological
imagination. It cannot be expected, however, that this outlook will occur spontaneously. People have to learn the connections between their everyday lives and
wider public issues.

The relationship between 'the sociological imagination' and the 'lifelong learning imagination' is that the former is a useful resource for thinking about the latter.
The sociological imagination broadens our thinking about the purpose of learning
and challenges the preoccupation with narrow forms of vocational training that is
commonly promoted in lifelong learning policy and practice. We need a more
encompassing or 'rounded' view of what life involves so that we do not reduce
'learning for living' to that of 'learning for a living' (Martin 2000: 4). People need
to learn skills for work but they also need to learn to relate to others and to live in
families, communities and societies in ways that are mutually caring, beneficial and
supportive. The sociological imagination points to the connections necessary for
people to make if they are to understand their lives and the processes that shape
and influence living. Learning informed by the sociological imagination, therefore,
opens up a broader picture of what lifelong learning promises.

The promise of the 'lifelong learning imagination' is of a process that enables people to understand their personal circumstances and the habits of mind, knowledge and skills they possess. For this to be useful it has to be an ongoing process – a lifelong activity that people engage and re-engage in continually in order to improve their understanding and develop new knowledge and skills. If 'personal troubles' and 'public issues' are constantly changing, as society changes, then people need access to learning opportunities throughout their lives. The 'lifelong learning imagination' also promises that learning is an activity that takes place in many different settings, informal as well as formal. The idea that learning primarily occurs in schooling in the early years of life and is over, for most people, by eighteen years of age is clearly inadequate. The task of lifelong learning, therefore, is to change our preoccupation with formal education and the 'front end' model of learning.

The term imagination in the context of lifelong learning also implies something more than understanding the connections between 'personal troubles' and 'public issues'. Imagination implies thinking about possible alternative arrangements to those that currently exist and is, therefore, a hopeful activity of constructing in the mind, individually and collectively, what might one day become a reality for the organization of daily life. The lifelong learning imagination, in this sense, is a signifier of hope – an activity that is intrinsic to change at the personal, professional, institutional and structural levels of society. Of course this is an ambitious challenge. We are not claiming that this book can address all of these issues in a comprehensive way, but we are claiming that it offers a contribution to understanding how the lifelong learning imagination as an informed and critical activity can contribute to change.

If this is the promise of the 'lifelong learning imagination', the reality is often sadly different. Many people experience formal education as dissatisfying and labelling them as inadequate and deficient. Furthermore, the dominant discourse of lifelong learning in European and international policy seems to limit it to narrow forms of instrumental learning for job flexibility where its rewards are regressively distributed (Crowther 2004). If lifelong learning is to fulfil its promise then it also has to begin to change experiences of education in ways which make a meaningful difference to people's lives. The task of this book is to argue why this should be the case and what needs to be changed.

Origins of the book

The book was originally conceived as a companion volume to *Adult Learning: A Reader*, edited by Peter Sutherland (1998). This text concentrated on cognitive psychology and adult learning. However, conceptualizing learning in these terms is very partial and also limited as a way of thinking about 'life' and 'learning for life'. In this new book it was decided to widen the scope of the text to include relevant psychological resources as well as 'social' perspectives on adult learning. Jim Crowther has a background in adult and community education and is interested in the context, purpose and politics of adult learning and education that he has explored in books such as *Popular Education and Social Movements in Scotland Today* (1999). Hence the editors have very different backgrounds, experience and interests in adult and lifelong learning that we have attempted to bring together in a complementary and dynamic way.

The difference of interests and diversity of our experience has helped us resource, in one volume, a distinctive range of 'voices' inside and outside formal educational settings with something to say about lifelong learning. We have contributors from Australia, the USA, Ireland, South Africa and the UK – some of whom are very experienced writers and others who are new to writing. The book therefore provides material that will appeal to a wide audience of readers who can selectively dip into the text according to their interests. Alternatively, it can be read sequentially. The themes running through the text (see below) ensure some continuity, and the building and deepening of issues, so that it can be read one chapter after another with a reasonable degree of coherence.

All but one of the chapters for the book have been specially commissioned – the exception is the chapter by Richard Edwards and Robin Usher (Chapter 6) which is based on a longer text published in *Adult Education Quarterly*. These two authors have a considerable reputation in examining the challenge and consequences of postmodernism for education and we were delighted, therefore, to include this revised version of their text in this volume.

Thematic coherence

There are four clear themes which are developed across the different contributions and sections of the book. These are as follows:

- Adult learning is distinctly different from learning in childhood.
- Learning is more than a cognitive activity in that it includes an affective dimension as well as contextual influences.
- Lifelong learning has implications for the purpose and processes of learning in educational institutions.
- There are subordinate discourses of lifelong learning that need to be aired and can enrich our understanding of what it means.

The first theme takes the position that adult learning is distinctly different from learning in childhood (see in particular Knud Illeris, Chapter 2). This does not mean that there are no similarities with childhood learning or that learning in childhood has nothing to offer our understanding of adult learning (for example, see Peter Sutherland, Chapter 12). It is easy to lose sight, however, of its distinctive nature if the emphasis on the lifelong involves overlooking learning at particular stages of life. Whilst lifelong implies from birth to death the process of learning is not necessarily a uniform one. Although lifelong learning begins formally in school and pre-school we have not included material on these settings in the book.

In addition to our commitment to understanding adult learning, we are both located in departments that specialize in adult education and adult community education so we have a personal and professional inclination to maintain this focus of interest.

The second theme is that learning has to be understood in a rounded way and not merely as a cognitive process. Whilst the insights from psychological research on cognitive behaviour have a lot to offer, we need a more nuanced understanding of how learning identities are created, helped and hindered. This needs to include consideration of the social and material contexts in which learning occurs, as well as its affective and emotional dimension. In terms of context, the importance of communities and social movements as motivators of adult learning has too often been neglected in the lifelong learning literature. Also emotional feelings add another neglected but important resource for understanding adult learning and their significance is addressed in a number of the chapters in this book. We have therefore selected authors who can contribute towards our knowledge of these dimensions of adult learning and their implications for educational intervention. Furthermore, learning by its nature implies some degree of change and transformation. Any account of lifelong learning that fails to take account of its transformational dimension for individuals and collectivities neglects some of its important attributes.

The third theme addresses how lifelong learning challenges our understanding of purpose and process in formal educational institutions. Our specific interest is the implication of lifelong learning for higher education. In some respects changing formal educational institutions poses the biggest challenge for lifelong learning. Whilst it might be easy for universities to rebrand departments of adult and extra-mural education as offices of lifelong learning, such superficial change is not meaningful. Formal educational institutions consume by far the largest share of public resources for education but continue to systematically benefit a narrow cross section of society – in the UK primarily the middle classes. If higher education, for instance, is to be a real resource for those who have benefited least from education, then lifelong learning faces unprecedented challenges in reforming these institutions. The chapters in Part II address the institutional organization of higher education, curriculum issues, teaching and learning practices and study procedures that are potential sites for change.

Finally, the fourth theme is that there are subordinate discourses of lifelong learning that need to be included in the text. The dominant policy discourse focuses on lifelong learning for work and is primarily directed at individuals (see Coffield 1999). In these terms lifelong learning can be seen as a form of social control in a context where state investment in public services is declining (Griffin 1999; Martin 2003). Because this policy critique has been increasingly aired in a number of critical accounts we have not specifically included it. Instead, we have concentrated on arguments which seek to clarify what more creative and critical or, 'imaginative' approaches to lifelong learning might mean.

Organization of the text

The four broad themes (above) are reflected in the way the text is organized and presented. Part I of the book is primarily concerned with theoretical and conceptual approaches that help us think about adult learning, what it means and what influences it, as a distinct activity in the context of lifelong learning. Parts II and III focus more on the contexts and settings where this learning occurs.

Chapter 2 by Knud Illeris gives a sharp and insightful analysis as to why adult learning is distinctive. Illeris's work on synthesizing important perspectives on adult learning (in particular cognitive, emotional and contextual features) has recently come to the attention of a wider English reading audience and his work deserves to be influential. In Chapter 3 the founding father of transformative learning, Jack Mezirow, traces the origins of this concept in his own work and the way others have subsequently developed it – a fitting tribute to his main concept. His work has made a seminal contribution to adult and lifelong learning for over thirty years.

Transformative adult learning is also central to Linden West's 'psychosocial' perspective (Chapter 4) on how informal adult learning and community action can contribute to people positively 'moving on' from, in Wright Mills' terminology, their 'personal troubles' by learning new identities. In the context of globalization and its concomitant uncertainties more and more people are becoming casualties of these impersonal forces. If the emphasis in West's account is on the personal the next chapter introduces a more systematic theorization of the social dimension of lifelong learning. In Chapter 5 Mark Murphy and Ted Fleming explain the relevance of the work of Habermas for adult learning theory. They argue that his work has been neglected outside North America yet it provides a moral justification for critical social action and emancipatory educational practice for a deliberative democracy. The last account in this section, by Richard Edwards and Robin Usher (Chapter 6), draws on a postmodernist reference point to highlight how lifelong learning is changing and challenging the boundaries of educational spaces. Who controls learning, where it occurs, and what constitutes knowledge are potential sites of contestation or, in their terms, they are subject to incredulity and doubt.

Part II two focuses on institutions and issues for lifelong learning. If lifelong learning is to contribute towards social equity and progressive change it is important that universities maintain their intellectual rigour and open themselves to a wider social constituency. This is the hope and aspiration of activists and academics in South Africa. Shirley Walters (Chapter 7) documents comprehensive attempts to remodel the University of the Western Cape into a lifelong learning higher education institution in a context where, because of apartheid, black people have little experience of systematic and quality education. Whilst the setting is a distinctive one, the wider issues involved in this process of transformation have a clear relevance beyond it. Change on a micro level can also contribute to making a difference as John Bamber (Chapter 8) points out, in his account of one attempt in a traditional UK university to be more inclusive in its practice to engage non-traditional, working class students. He too argues that if lifelong learning is to be meaningful to marginalized working class adults, then the curriculum of universities needs to change. Cultural change in organizations to foster lifelong learning is at the centre of Rose Evison's work (Chapter 9). She draws on her own considerable experience as a facilitator of adult learning to address how this might occur. Her interest is in the emotional dimensions which block the process of learning and how we can develop practical strategies to address these inhibitors.

The rhetoric of lifelong learning claims to put the learner at the centre of the process of education. To go beyond rhetorical claims, teaching approaches and students' approaches to learning, and the connection between them, need to be understood. Keith Trigwell (Chapter 10) draws on a substantial body of research which compares teacher-centred approaches to student-centred ones in terms of the approach to learning they encourage in students. It is not surprising that, when asked, teachers invariably prefer their students to achieve deep level learning. The most effective teaching approach for this is one that addresses conceptual change and is student focused. Tina Goodwin and Susan Hallam (Chapter 11) examine the role of emotional intelligence in the context of teaching and learning. Interest in emotional intelligence has grown since Daniel Goleman's (1996) best selling book publicized the concept. The two authors of this chapter review what we mean by emotional intelligence and draw on recent empirical work to illustrate what can go wrong when it is ignored in teaching.

Peter Sutherland (Chapter 12) returns to the work of Piaget and Biggs, two distinguished psychologists who have primarily worked in the field of childhood learning, to compare their work and examine the messages for adult learning. From this he argues it is wrong to imply, as Piaget does, that all adults are formal operational thinkers (abstract thinkers) and that concrete operational thinking is a necessary and valued aspect of many adult roles. The final two chapters in this part focus on the nature of student study practice. Chrissie Boughey (Chapter 13), writing in a South African context, draws attention to academic study as a social practice. Simply dealing with formal aspects of student study skills with non-traditional students can easily lead to deficit discourses, which label the student negatively, but fail to see the underlying issue as one of different cultural traditions and valued practices. She provides constructive examples of how academics can begin to build bridges between their own practice and that of their students. The responsibility of teachers to facilitate student learning is also a concern of the next chapter in this part. Martha Cassazza's reference point (Chapter 14) is students in higher education in the United States and she highlights their strategies for self-regulating their learning. The major factor in this is the setting of achievable goals and regular monitoring of their attainment. Successful self-regulators are able to develop adaptive strategies to make adjustments when learning falls short of their expectations. None of this comes intuitively, however, and so, if teaching is to be effective, self-regulation has to be addressed explicitly.

In Part III, the opening account by John Preston (Chapter 15) focuses on processes of recognition and mis-recognition of lifelong learning. This chapter opens the section because it widens the aperture of our focus on social and urban movements, communities and by implication other sites such as workplaces as settings for lifelong learning with a variety of different groups of 'learners'. The essence of his argument is that recognition of lifelong learning is partly to do with class strategies of control and that ultimately, the important issue is to locate discourses of lifelong learning in the context of competing and conflicting traditions of adult learning. Jim Crowther (Chapter 16) is engaged in a similar project by examining social movements as sites for a profane version of lifelong learning. The space they create for educational engagement is, however, an ambivalent one and is influenced by the cognitive and political praxis of the movement – premodern, modernist and postmodernist movements create very different combinations and possibilities in this respect for social processes of lifelong learning.

Norman Longworth (Chapter 17) is an authority on the subject of learning cities and learning regions. He is interested in the spatial dimension of lifelong learning and the impact it is making on the organizations and institutions that occupy the territory around us. His specific interest is lifelong learning as a social and cultural activity and its potential to transform everyday spaces. Yvon Appleby and Mary Hamilton (Chapter 18) are specialists in adult literacy. Their focus is on literacy as social practice and the transitions that occur between learning literacy in formal contexts and in everyday life. If these 'carry over' from one context to another, in ways that are mutually supportive, they have important implications for literacy learning. Understanding these transitions has implications, therefore, for how to nurture and support learning in community-based adult literacy programmes.

Rod Purcell (Chapter 19), inspired by a broadly Freirean perspective and experience of techniques of participatory rapid appraisal, focuses on adult learning in social action. He argues the need to create space for a cycle of reflection, vision, planning and action, if the learning in these contexts is to be maximized and social action enhanced. He draws on examples from 'developed' and 'over-developed' societies to illustrate his argument. Hitendra Pillay, Lynn Wilss and Gillian Boulton-Lewis (Chapter 20) examine how learning in the workplace occurs and what types of learning workers engage in, particularly in the context of a globalized economy where information technologies are important and the policy emphasis is on the 'knowledge economy' and 'knowledge workers'. They argue involvement in such contexts creates opportunities for higher education. Finally, Fiona Dowie and Matthew Gibson (Chapter 21), working in the context of community care, draw upon their long experience of adult education with mental health service users. They see their role in a semi-independent voluntary organization as creating spaces for lifelong learning that are free from medical definitions and professional prescriptions which create deficit discourses of what 'patients' can do. They argue strongly for a process of empowering adults as active citizens in order for them to develop their individual and collective autonomy.

Conclusion

To return to the theme of the sociological imagination the entrapments we face tell us about ourselves. For example, the trap that catches the lobster tells us about the nature of the lobster that does not change. However, people have the unique capacity to change themselves and, in so doing, change the possibility of the same traps catching them out. If they are to be successful in this then lifelong learning is an imperative. However, what we mean by lifelong learning is open to dispute because it is an ambiguous and ambivalent term. There are texts which seek to pin it down and define it, but this is not a task we see as fruitful. Definitions can be arbitrary and artificial and it is ultimately the values and beliefs, which underpin these definitions, that are the key issues of interest. In other words, lifelong learning is a social practice and what counts is what people do with it.

The lifelong learning of educational institutions obviously dominates our understanding of what learning counts – but what goes on in such places is only one way of seeing it. Lifelong learning does occur in educational institutions and it can be improved. But it is just as likely, if not more likely, to occur outside of them. There are other 'troubled spaces of possibility' for adult learning, as Richard Edwards and Robin Usher argue (see Chapter 6).

We have made the case that the promise of the 'lifelong learning imagination' is a critical and creative approach essential for contemporary living. It is more likely that 'the lifelong learning imagination' will occur on the margins of dominant institutions and in contexts less constrained by the dominant policy discourse. This seems inevitable but it is only a starting point. To have a significant impact it will need to catalyse a critical mass of support for fundamental change in formal educational institutions and informal sites of learning. If this collection helps us think about the promise of the 'lifelong learning imagination' and how this might come about then it has achieved its purpose.

References

Coffield, F. (1999) 'Breaking the consensus: lifelong learning as social control', *British Educational Research Journal*, 24, 4: 479–99.

Crowther, J. (2004) 'In and against lifelong learning: flexibility and the corrosion of character', *International Journal of Lifelong Education*, 23, 2: 125–36.

Crowther, J., Martin, I. and Shaw, M. (eds) (1999) *Popular Education and Social Movements in Scotland Today*, Leicester: NIACE.

Goleman, D. (1996) *Emotional Intelligence: Why it Can Matter More than IQ*, London: Bloomsbury.

Griffin, C. (1999) 'Lifelong learning and welfare reform', *International Journal of Lifelong Education*, 18, 6: 431–52.

Martin, I. (2000) 'Reconstituting the agora: towards an alternative politics of lifelong learning', in T. J. Sork, V-L. Chapman and R. St Clair (eds), *Proceedings of the 41st Annual AERC 2000 International Conference*, Vancouver: University of British Columbia.

Martin, I. (2003) 'Adult education, lifelong learning and citizenship: some ifs and buts', *International Journal of Lifelong Education*, 22, 6: 566–79.

Sutherland, P. (ed.) (1998) *Adult Learning: A Reader*, London: Kogan Page.

Wright Mills, C. (1959) *The Sociological Imagination*, New York: Oxford University Press.

Part I

Perspectives on adult and lifelong learning

Chapter 2

What is special about adult learning?

Knud Illeris

Is adult learning distinctly different from learning in childhood? This question has been at the centre of many debates on the status of adult education and, in the context of lifelong learning, it clearly has significant implications. The author argues cogently in the affirmative and draws on a considerable wealth of evidence and experience to make his case. One of the key issues, which make a difference, is the need adults experience to control their learning and, where this does not occur, the end result is adults feeling at best ambivalent and at worst demotivated. The message of this chapter is that adults have to take more responsibility for their learning – and be allowed to do so! If lifelong learning is to be useful to adults it must be based on conditions that respect and support the unique requirements of adult learning.

Introduction

The last decade has seen *lifelong learning* become a key issue in international education policy. The concept basically involves the simple message that learning can and should be a lifelong occupation. This poses the fundamental question of whether the processes of learning are the same irrespective of age. For the traditional psychology of learning, there are no age-conditioned differences. Learning has been studied as a common phenomenon, for which researchers endeavoured to discover the decisive and basic learning mechanisms, and research and tests often observed animals and humans in constructed laboratory situations.

In relation to adult education, many scholars and researchers have claimed that adults' learning as a psychological function is basically similar to children's learning. This was, for instance, the underlying assumption behind the massive resistance to American Malcolm Knowles' launching of a separate discipline of 'andragogy', dealing with adult education and learning and at the same time limiting 'pedagogy' to the area of children's upbringing and schooling (e.g. Knowles 1970; Hartree 1984; Davonport 1993). More recently Alan Rogers, in connection with his very fine description of adults' learning, has deliberately maintained 'that there is nothing distinctive about the kind of learning undertaken by adults' (Rogers 2003: 7; see also Rogers and Illeris 2003).

This depends, however, on the kind of definition of learning one is referring to. In my understanding, as developed and explained in my books *The Three*

Dimensions of Learning and *Adult Education and Adult Learning* (Illeris 2002, 2004), learning always includes two integrated but very different processes: the external interaction process between the learner and the social and material environment, and the internal psychological process of elaboration and acquisition. If one sticks to the internal psychological process, as traditional learning psychology does, it is to some extent possible to claim that, independent of age differences, learning processes are fundamentally of the same kind throughout life. I shall return to this later.

If the social interaction process is seen as a necessary and integrated part of learning, the picture changes immediately. Many modern learning theorists actually do so, and some even consider learning as mainly or only a social process (Lave and Wenger 1991; Gergen 1994). It is obvious that the nature of our relationship to our social and societal environment changes considerably during life from the newborn child's total dependence to a striving for independence in youth and adulthood and, eventually, a new sort of dependence in old age. These changes strongly influence the character of the social dimension of our learning.

Children's and adults' learning

In order to see what is characteristic of adult learning, I shall start by pointing out some basic features of children's learning.

In general, learning in childhood could be described as a continuous campaign to capture the world. The child is born into an unknown world and learning is about acquiring this world and learning to deal with it. In this connection, two learning-related features are prominent, especially for the small child. First, children's learning is comprehensive and uncensored. The child learns everything within its grasp, throws itself into everything, and is limited only by its biological development and the nature of its surroundings. Second, the child places utter confidence in the adults around it. It has only those adults and the ways in which they behave to refer to, without any possibility of evaluating or choosing what it is presented with. It must, for example, learn the language these adults speak and practise the culture they practise.

Throughout childhood, the child's capturing of its surroundings is fundamentally uncensored and trusting as it endeavours, in an unlimited and indiscriminate way, to make use of the opportunities that present themselves. Of course, late modern society has led to growing complexity and even confusion of this situation as older children receive a lot of impressions from their peers and especially from the mass media, which go far beyond the borders of their own environment. But still the open and confident approach must be recognized as the starting point.

Opposite this stands learning during adulthood. Being an adult essentially means that an individual is able and willing to assume responsibility for his/her own life and actions. Formally, our society ascribes such 'adulthood' to individuals when they attain the age of 18. In reality, it is a gradual process that takes place throughout the period of youth, which, as we see it today, may last well into the twenties or be entirely incomplete if the formation of a relatively stable identity is chosen as the criterion for its completion at the mental level (which is the classical description of this transition provided by Erik Erikson 1968).

As for learning, being an adult also means, in principle, that the individual accepts responsibility for his/her own learning, i.e. more or less consciously sorts information and decides what he/she wants and does not want to learn. The situation in today's complicated modern society is after all that the volume of what may be learned far exceeds the ability of any single individual, and this is true not only concerning content in a narrow sense, but also applies to the views and attitudes, perceptions, communications options, behavioural patterns, lifestyle, etc. that may be chosen. So adults need to be selective in what they choose to learn from the various potential sources of information and options they are exposed to.

As a general conclusion it is, however, important to maintain that in contrast to children's uncensored and confident learning, adults' learning is basically selective and self-directed, or to put it in more concrete terms:

- adults learn what they want to learn and what is meaningful for them to learn;
- adults draw on the resources they already have in their learning;
- adults take as much responsibility for their learning as they want to take (if they are allowed to); and
- adults are not very inclined to learn something they are not interested in, or in which they cannot see the meaning or importance. At any rate, typically, they only learn it partially, in a distorted way or with a lack of motivation that makes what is learned extremely vulnerable to oblivion and difficult to apply in situations not subjectively related to the learning context.

This implies that learning incentives, such as for instance adult education options, consciously or subconsciously are met by sceptical questions and considerations. For example, why do 'they' want me to learn this? What can I use it for? How does it fit into my personal life perspectives?

Outside influence, whether it assumes the form of conversation, guidance, persuasion, pressure or compulsion, will always be received in the light of the individual's own experience and perspectives. If they are to change the possibilities for learning, the influences must be convincing on this basis, i.e. the adults must accept them psychologically, and must be brought to see the meaning with the education programme in question for themselves and their situation.

Learning capacity

Whereas the questions of the specific character of adult learning in general have almost been neglected by learning psychology as well as by adult education research, there is an ongoing, important discussion concerning adults' possibilities for learning, especially in the cognitive area.

The cognitive learning theory put forward by Jean Piaget in the 1930s, on the basis of extensive empirical studies, focuses on the development of learning possibilities in childhood through a number of given cognitive stages and sub-stages and thus maintains that there is a highly specific developmental course. But this structural development ends when a child at the age of 11 to 13 reaches the 'formal operational' level, which makes logical-deductive thinking possible as a supplement to the forms of thinking and learning acquired at earlier stages (see Flavell 1963).

However, Piaget's perception of this has been questioned from several quarters. On the one hand, it has been pointed out that not all adults are actually able to think 'formal operationally' in the logical sense inherent in Piaget's definition (see Sutherland this volume). Empirical research points out that in England it is actually less than 30 per cent, but at the same time it confirms that at the beginning of puberty a decisive development takes place in the possibilities for learning and thinking in abstract terms, so that, all in all, distinguishing a new cognitive phase is justified (Shayer and Adey 1981). On the other hand, it has been maintained that, at a later time, significant new cognitive possibilities that extend beyond the formally operative may develop (e.g. Commons *et al.* 1984). American adult education researcher Stephen Brookfield has summarized this criticism by pointing out four possibilities for learning which, in his opinion, are only developed in the course of adulthood: the capacity for dialectical thinking, the capacity for applying practical logic, the capacity for realizing how one may know what one knows (metacognition), and the capacity for critical reflection (Brookfield 2000).

Recent brain research seems indirectly to support Brookfield's claims. Whereas it is a well established understanding, psychologically as well as neurologically, that the brain matures for formal logical thinking in early puberty, evidence has been found that the brain centres of the frontal lobe that conduct such functions as rational planning, prioritization and making well-founded choices, do not mature until the late teenage years (Gogtay *et al.* 2004). This finding seems to provide some clarification of the differences between the capacity of formal logical and practical logical thinking and learning as well as between ordinary cognition and metacognition in adolescence and early adulthood.

At any rate, the general conclusion of all this must be that during puberty and youth a physiological and neurological maturing process takes place that makes possible new forms of abstract and stringent thinking and learning, so that an individual becomes able to operate context-independently with coherent concept systems and manage a balanced and goal-directed behaviour. Teenagers' determination to find out how things are structured and to use such understanding in relation to their own situation could be seen as a cognitive developmental bridge signifying the difference between children's and adults' ways of learning.

It is thus the longing for independence and the longing for coherent understanding of how they themselves and their environment function, and why things are the way they are, which separates adult learning from the learning of childhood. Up through the period of youth, individuals will themselves increasingly assume responsibility for their own learning and non-learning, make choices and rejections, and in this context understand what they are dealing with and their own roles and possibilities.

However, all this has been enormously complicated by the duality of late modernity between, on the one hand, the apparently limitless degrees of freedom and reams of information, and, on the other hand, far-reaching indirect pressure for control from parents, teachers, youth cultures, mass media in addition to the formal conditions for learning. The transition from child to adult has thus, in the area of learning, become an extended, ambiguous and complicated process, with blurred outlines and unclear conditions and goals.

Institutionalized learning

In practice, in our society, schools, colleges and universities have developed as the institutions where all of us have to learn a lot of stuff that we have not chosen ourselves. Therefore, adults' attitudes to formal institutions of learning and education are generally very ambivalent. On the one side, we know very well that learning can be useful and rewarding and even joyful in many ways. On the other side, institutional learning is often demanding, usually directed by others, and sometimes boring and tiresome.

Traditionally, adult education has been voluntary, and it has therefore also been the normal situation that the adults themselves have chosen the course in question. It might, therefore, be expected that the adults would themselves take responsibility for the learning provided by the course. However, two conditions complicate this. First, some ordinary conceptions and experiences of education often intrude. Even though the institutions, the teachers and the students might say otherwise, everyone in the education situation obstinately expects that the responsibility will lie with the teacher. This is what we all have experienced at school, and unconsciously we take this picture with us into adult education. Second, many participants in lifelong learning today are not there of their own volition, but because they are forced to be there, directly by authorities or employers, or indirectly because they have to learn and qualify themselves if they are to avoid the marginalized situation of the unemployed.

These complications lie behind a very complex and paradoxical situation that can be observed in most adult education courses today. On the one hand, the adult participants behave like pupils, taking no responsibility and waiting for the teacher to direct the course and tell them what to do. On the other hand, they have a very hard time accepting the lack of authority that the traditional role of pupil entails. As adults, they are used to directing their own behaviour and deciding for themselves.

Thus, when adults enter an institutionalized education programme, there is a distinct tendency for them to slip into the well-known pupil role where control and responsibility are left to the teacher. This is the least demanding role to adopt and often the teacher is also inclined to take on, and even insist upon, the traditional, controlling teacher role. It is only in the very few cases when the participants are brought to realize that they can take responsibility and use the teacher to support their own learning that the picture alters.

Defence against learning

In addition to this, in our complicated modern society, the amount one should learn far outstrips what any person can manage, and this applies not only to the content of learning but also to the options for attitudes, modes of understanding, communication possibilities, patterns of action, lifestyle and so on. Selection becomes a necessity, and, in principle adults would like to carry out and take responsibility for this selection themselves.

Thus, adults' basic desire to learn and their wish to direct and take responsibility for their own learning are strongly modified, first by the impact of their school experiences, and second by the inevitable selection which is necessarily developed into the kind of semi-automatic defence system which has been described as 'everyday consciousness' (Illeris 2002, 2003b, 2004).

The way this works is that one develops some general pre-understandings within certain thematic areas. When one meets with influences within such an area, these pre-understandings are activated so that if elements in the influences do not correspond to the pre-understandings, they are either rejected or distorted to make them agree. In both cases, the result is not new learning but, on the contrary, the cementing of already existing understanding. This is also part of the reason why adults are sceptical and often reluctant vis-à-vis everything that others want them to learn and which they themselves do not feel an urge to learn. Consciously or unconsciously, they want to decide for themselves. But, at the same time, it is easier to leave the decisions to others, to see what happens, and retain the right to protest, resist or drop out if one is not satisfied. In sum, the attitude is thus very often ambiguous and contradictory.

Responsibility for own learning

The most fundamental difference between children's learning and adults' learning is thus related to how the learning is controlled. In recent years, this matter has, however, been much debated from a somewhat different angle, i.e. the debate on 'responsibility for own learning'. In Scandinavia, this debate has especially been directed at youth education programmes, the background for this being that young people have not been as willing to learn 'what they have to learn' as was previously the case if they have not been able to see or accept the intention behind it. In so doing, young people have, in their own way, to an increasing extent assumed responsibility for their own learning or, at any rate, their own non-learning. The underlying opinion of many debaters has, however, been that young people should themselves assume responsibility for learning what somebody else has decided.

For adults, the problem is somewhat different. As a point of departure, adults clearly want to decide what they want and do not want to learn. The very nature of adulthood involves both legally and psychologically that the individual assumes responsibility for him/her self, his/her actions and opinions. This is the general situation of learning in everyday life, and thus adult learning is by nature self-directed. But when adults then enter into institutionalized learning situations, a kind of regression often takes place: they easily slip back into the pattern they know so well from their schooldays. They leave responsibility in the hands of the teacher, and the teacher is also almost always willing to assume responsibility, and even parts with it only reluctantly (see Illeris 1998).

Most adults, except perhaps the youngest, appear somehow to have acquired the perception that institutionalized learning is something that belongs to childhood and youth. When, as adults, people participate in courses and training programmes, they typically use the phrase 'going back to school', and this phrase reflects the feeling of reversion to childhood, disempowerment and perhaps even humiliation that lies just below the surface of many people who have not made a clear individual choice to be in the learning situation.

As David Boud (2003) has documented, adults in general do not like to be labelled as learners, not to say pupils. Because then it is precisely the case that others decide what the individual is to do, that the individual is stripped of the authority of an adult, and that the individual is not good enough as he or she is, because then obviously the whole thing would not have been necessary. This sentiment has deep roots, it necessarily has an impact on the learning, and teachers often tend to suppress the fact that it is so. Therefore we often hear in adult education sayings such as: 'we *are* adults, aren't we?' spoken as a sort of mantra in situations where the similarity with the submission to childhood learning becomes a little too insistent.

There is, however, no doubt that the learning progresses best when adults themselves accept decisive responsibility. But this presupposes that the framework of the education programme provides opportunities for such responsibility, i.e. that not too much has been decided and determined in advance, that the teacher consciously provides space for it, and that the content of the programme makes it fundamentally possible for adult participants to learn something which they themselves think is important and meaningful (Illeris 2003a).

Life projects and identity

Thus, the question of whether the intended learning is or may be subjectively meaningful for the adult becomes entirely decisive for adult education programmes. The answer lies in the participants' situation in life, their backgrounds and their interests. This can be a matter of very superficial, short-term interests, something that challenges their curiosity, or which is topical and perhaps provocative. But, more fundamentally, adults usually have some life projects that are relatively stable and long term, for example, a family project that concerns creating and being part of a family, a work project that concerns a personally and financially satisfying job, perhaps a leisure-time project concerning a hobby, a life project to do with fulfilment, or a conviction project that may be religious or political in nature.

These life projects are embedded in the life history, present situation and possible future perspectives of the individual and are closely related to what we call identity. It is on this basis that we design our defences so that we usually let what is important for our projects come through and reject the rest. It is also on this basis that, as the central core of our defences, we develop mechanisms to counter influences that could threaten the experience of who we are and would like to be. These matters typically comprise the fundamental premises for school-based adult education seen from the perspective of the participants. They make the participants' initial motivation quite crucial, that is the way in which they regard the study programme in relation to their life projects.

In some cases, adult education can lead to extensive, enriching development for the participants if they arrive with positive motivation and the study programme lives up to or exceeds their expectations. But studies in Danish adult education programmes show that a considerable proportion of the participants only become positively engaged in adult education if they meet a challenge that 'turns them on' at the beginning or along the way. In most cases in current adult education, the situation is that the participants only engage themselves superficially and do not learn very much, leading to the waste of a great number of human and financial resources.

What we all must realize is that the adult's way of learning is very different from the child's and that adult education must, therefore, be based on fundamentally different premises. The basic requirement is that the adult must take, and must be allowed to take, responsibility for his or her own learning. It is decisive that education programmes and teaching practice respects, supports and even demands this. We all have a great deal to learn in order to fully understand these fundamental conditions of adult learning.

References

Boud, D. (2003) *Combining Work and Learning: The Disturbing Challenge of Practice*, keynote speech given at *The CRLL Conference*, Glasgow Caledonian University, 27–29 June.

Brookfield, S.D. (2000) 'Adult cognition as a dimension of lifelong learning', in J. Field and M. Leicester (eds) *Lifelong Learning – Education Across the Lifespan*, London: Routledge/Falmer.

Commons, M.L., Richards, F.A. and Armon, C. (eds) (1984) *Beyond Formal Operations: Late Adolescent and Adult Cognitive Development*, New York: Praeger.

Davonport, J. (1993 [1987]) 'Is there any way out of the andragogy morass?' in M. Thorpe, R. Edwards and A. Hanson (eds) *Culture and Processes of Adult Learning*, London: Routledge.

Erikson, E.H. (1968) *Identity, Youth and Crises*, New York: Norton.

Flavell, J.H. (1963) *The Developmental Psychology of Jean Piaget*, New York: Van Nostrand.

Gergen, K.J. (1994) *Realities and Relationships*, Cambridge, MA.: Harvard University Press.

Gogtay, N., Giedd, J.N., Lusk, L., Hayashi, K.M., Greenstein, D., Vaituzis, A.C., Nugent III, T.F., Herman, D.H., Clasen, L.S., Toga, A.W., Rapoport, J.L. and Thompson, P.M. (2004) 'Dynamic mapping of human cortical development during childhood through early adulthood', *Proceedings of the National Academy of Sciences of the USA*, 101, 21: 8174–8179.

Hartree, A. (1984) 'Malcolm Knowles' theory of andragogy: a critique', *International Journal of Lifelong Education*, 3, 3: 203–10.

Illeris, K. (1998) 'Adult learning and responsibility', in K. Illeris (ed.) *Adult Education in a Transforming Society*, Copenhagen: Roskilde University Press.

Illeris, K. (2002 [1999]) *The Three Dimensions of Learning*, Copenhagen: Roskilde University Press/Leicester: NIACE.

Illeris, K. (2003a) 'Adult education as experienced by the learners', *International Journal of Lifelong Education*, 22, 1: 13–23.

Illeris, K. (2003b) 'Towards a contemporary and comprehensive theory of learning', *International Journal of Lifelong Education*, 22, 4: 411–21.

Illeris, K. (2004) *Adult Education and Adult Learning*, Melbourne, Florida: Krieger.

Knowles, M.S. (1970) *The Modern Practice of Adult Education – Andragogy Versus Pedagogy*, New York: Association Press.

Lave, J. and Wenger, E. (1991) *Situated Learning: Legitimate Peripheral Participation*, New York: Cambridge University Press.

Rogers, A. (2003) *What is the Difference? A New Critique of Adult Learning and Teaching*, Leicester: NIACE.

Rogers, A. and Illeris, K. (2003) 'How do adults learn? A dialogue', *Adults Learning*, 15, 3: 24–7.

Shayer, M. and Adey, P. (1981) *Towards a Science of Science Teaching*, London: Heinemann Educational.

Chapter 3

An overview on transformative learning

Jack Mezirow

Transformative learning involves learning to think critically by questioning assumptions and expectations that shape and influence what we think and do. In this chapter the founding father of transformative learning gives an overview of the development of this concept, what it means and why it matters. Some of the main criticisms of his approach to transformative learning are reviewed and, in turn, the author adds a rejoinder to his critics. The chapter also highlights the contribution of alternative perspectives on transformative learning that have expanded our understanding of its potential application in the field of adult education and lifelong learning.

Brief history

The concept of transformative learning was introduced in the field of adult education in 1978 in an article that I entitled 'Perspective transformation', published in the American journal *Adult Education Quarterly*. The article urged the recognition of a critical dimension of learning in adulthood that enables us to recognize and reassess the structure of assumptions and expectations which frame our thinking, feeling and acting. These structures of meaning constitute a 'meaning perspective' or frame of reference.

Influences in the development of this concept included Freire's 'conscientization', Kuhn's 'paradigms', the concept of 'consciousness raising' in the women's movement, the writings and practice of psychiatrist Roger Gould, philosophers Jurgen Habermas, Harvey Siegal and Herbert Fingerette and my observation of the transformative experience of my wife, Edee, as an adult returning to complete her undergraduate degree at Sarah Lawrence College in New York.

The research base for the concept evolved out of a comprehensive national study of women returning to community colleges in the United States (Mezirow 1978). The study used grounded theory methodology to conduct intensive field study of students in 12 diverse college programmes, comprehensive analytical descriptions of an additional 24 programmes and responses to a mail inquiry by another 314.

A transformative learning movement subsequently developed in North American adult education, involving five international conferences, featuring over 300 paper presentations, the publication of many journal articles, over a dozen books and an estimated 150 doctoral dissertations on transformative learning in the fields of adult education, health and social welfare.

Foundations

Habermas (1981) makes a critically important distinction between instrumental and communicative learning. Instrumental learning pertains to learning involved in controlling or manipulating the environment, in improving performance or prediction. We validate by empirically testing contested beliefs regarding the truth of an assertion – that something is as it is purported to be. Instrumental learning is involved in learning to design automobiles, build bridges, diagnose diseases, fill teeth, forecast the weather, do accounting, and in scientific and mathematical inquiry. The developmental logic of instrumental learning is hypothetical-deductive.

Communicative learning pertains to understanding what someone means when they communicate with you – in conversation, through a book, poem, art work or dance performance. To validate an understanding in communicative learning, one must assess not only the accuracy or truth of what is being communicated, but also the intent, qualifications, truthfulness and authenticity of the one communicating. Telling someone that you love them can have many meanings. We feel safer when a person prescribing medicine for us has training as a physician or pharmacist.

The purpose of communicative discourse is to arrive at the *best judgment*, not to assess a truth claim, as in instrumental learning. To do so one must access and understand, intellectually and empathetically, the frame of reference of the other, and seek common ground with the widest range of relevant experience and points of view possible. Our effort must be directed at seeking a consensus among informed adults communicating, when this is possible, but, at least, to clearly understand the context of the assumptions of those disagreeing. The developmental logic of communicative learning is analogical-abductive.

For Habermas, discourse leading to a consensus can establish the validity of a belief. This is why our conclusions are always tentative: we may always encounter others with new evidence, arguments or perspectives. Thus diversity of experience and inclusion are essential to our understanding. It is important to recognize that the only alternatives to this dialectical method of inquiry for understanding the meaning of our experience is to rely on tradition, an authority or force.

In suggesting specific ideal conditions for human discourse, Habermas has provided us with an epistemological foundation defining optimal conditions for adult learning and education. The conditions also provide a foundation for a social commitment by adult educators to work toward a society that fosters these ideals. To freely and fully participate in discourse, learners must:

a   have accurate and complete information;
b   be free from coercion, distorting self deception or immobilizing anxiety;
c   be open to alternative points of view – empathic, caring about how others think and feel, withholding judgment;

d   be able to understand, to weigh evidence and to assess arguments objectively;
e   be able to become aware of the context of ideas and critically reflect on assumptions, including their own;
f   have equal opportunity to participate in the various roles of discourse;
g   have a test of validity until new perspectives, evidence or arguments are encountered and validated through discourse as yielding a better judgment.

Transformative learning theory

Transformative learning is defined as the process by which we transform problematic frames of reference (mindsets, habits of mind, meaning perspectives) – sets of assumption and expectation – to make them more inclusive, discriminating, open, reflective and emotionally able to change. Such frames are better because they are more likely to generate beliefs and opinions that will prove more true or justified to guide action.

Frames of reference are the structures of culture and language through which we construe meaning by attributing coherence and significance to our experience. They selectively shape and delimit our perception, cognition and feelings by predisposing our intentions, beliefs, expectations and purposes. These preconceptions set our 'line of action'. Once set or programmed, we automatically move from one specific mental or behavioural activity to another, and we have a strong tendency to reject ideas that fail to fit our preconceptions.

A frame of reference encompasses cognitive, conative and affective components, may operate within or outside awareness, and is composed of two dimensions: a habit of mind and resulting points of view. Habits of mind are broad, abstract, orienting, habitual ways of thinking, feeling and acting, influenced by assumptions that constitute a set of codes. These codes or canon may be cultural, social, linguistic, educational, economic, political, psychological, religious, aesthetic and others. Habits of mind become articulated in a specific point of view – the constellation of belief, memory, value judgment, attitude and feeling that shape a particular interpretation. Points of view are more accessible to awareness, to feedback from others. An example of a habit of mind is ethnocentrism, the predisposition to regard others outside one's own group as inferior, untrustworthy or otherwise less acceptable. A resulting point of view is the complex of negative feelings, beliefs, judgments and attitudes we may have regarding specific individuals or groups with characteristics different than our own. Having a positive experience with one of these groups may change an ethnocentric point of view, but not necessarily one's ethnocentric habit of mind regarding other groups.

Transformative learning may occur in instrumental learning. This usually involves task-oriented learning. In communicative learning, as in the ethnocentric example, transformative learning usually involves critical self-reflection. However, elements of both task-oriented learning and critical self-reflection may be found in either type of learning. Habits of mind involve how one categorizes experience, beliefs, people, events, and oneself. They may involve the structures, rules, criteria, codes, schemata, standards, values, personality traits and dispositions upon which our thoughts, feelings, and action are based.

Meaning perspectives or habits of mind include the:

- *sociolinguistic* – involving cultural canon, social norms, customs, ideologies, paradigms, linguistic frames, language games, political orientations, ideologies, and secondary socialization (thinking like a teacher, doctor, policeman or an administrator), occupational or organizational cultures' habits of mind;
- *moral–ethical* – involving conscience, moral norms and values;
- *learning styles* – sensory preferences, focus on wholes or parts or on the concrete or abstract, working alone or together;
- *religious* – commitment to doctrine, spiritual or transcendental world views;
- *psychological* – theories, schema, scripts, self-concept, personality traits or types, repressed parental prohibitions, emotional response patterns, dispositions;
- *health*, ways of interpreting health problems, rehabilitation, near death experience;
- *aesthetic*, values, taste, attitude, standards, judgments about beauty and the insight and authenticity of aesthetic expressions, such as the sublime, the ugly, the tragic, the humorous, the drab.

Transformative learning theory, as I have interpreted it, is a metacognitive epistemology of evidential (instrumental) and dialogical (communicative) reasoning. Reasoning is understood as the process of advancing and assessing a belief. Transformative learning is an adult dimension of reason assessment involving the validation and reformulation of meaning structures.

The process of transformative learning involves our:

1 reflecting critically on the source, nature and consequences of relevant assumptions – our own and those of others;
2 in instrumental learning, determining that something is true (is as it is purported to be) by using empirical research methods;
3 in communicative learning, arriving at more justified beliefs by participating freely and fully in an informed continuing discourse;
4 taking action on our transformed perspective – we make a decision and live what we have come to believe until we encounter new evidence, argument or a perspective that renders this orientation problematic and requires reassessment;
5 acquiring a disposition – to become more critically reflective of our own assumptions and those of others, to seek validation of our transformative insights through more freely and fully participating in discourse, and to follow through on our decision to act upon a transformed insight.

Transformations may be *epochal* – sudden major reorientations in habit of mind, often associated with significant life crises or *cumulative*, a progressive sequence of insights resulting in changes in point of view and leading to a transformation in habit of mind. Most transformative learning takes place outside of awareness, intuition substitutes for critical reflection of assumptions. Educators assist learners to bring this process into awareness and to improve the learner's ability and inclination to engage in transformative learning.

In our study of women returning to college, transformations often follow the following phases of meaning, becoming clarified:

1   a disorienting dilemma;
2   self examination with feelings of fear, anger, guilt or shame;
3   a critical assessment of assumptions;
4   recognition that one's discontent and the process of transformation are shared;
5   exploration of options for new roles, relationships and action;
6   planning a course of action;
7   acquiring knowledge and skills for implementing one's plans;
8   provisional trying of new roles;
9   building competence and self-confidence in new roles and relationships;
10   a reintegration into one's life on the basis of conditions dictated by one's new perspective.

The two major elements of transformative learning are first, critical reflection or critical self-reflection on assumptions – critical assessment of the sources, nature and consequences of our habits of mind – and second, participating fully and freely in dialectical discourse to validate a best reflective judgment – what King and Kitchener define as that judgment involving 'the process an individual evokes to monitor the epistemic nature of problems and the truth value of alternative solutions' (1994: 12).

Issues

Emotion, intuition, imagination

Important questions have been raised by adult educators concerning transformation theory. One has to do with the need for more clarification and emphasis on the role played by emotions, intuition and imagination in the process of transformation. This criticism of the theory is justified. The process by which we tacitly construe our beliefs may involve taken-for-granted values, stereotyping, highly selective attention, limited comprehension, projection, rationalization, minimizing or denial. That is why we need to be able to critically assess and validate assumptions supporting our own beliefs and expectations and those of others.

Our experiences of persons, things and events become realities as we typify them. This process has much to do with how we come to associate them with our personal need for justification, validity and a convincing real sense of self. Expectations may be of events or of beliefs pertaining to one's own involuntary reactions to events – how one subjectively expects to be able to cope. Our expectations powerfully affect how we construe experience; they tend to become self-fulfilling prophecies. We have a proclivity for categorical judgment.

Imagination of how things could be otherwise is central in the initiation of the transformative process. As the process of transformation is often a difficult, highly emotional passage, a great deal of additional insight into the role of imagination is needed and overdue. As many transformative experiences occur outside of awareness, I have suggested that, in these situations, intuition substitutes for critical self reflection. This is another judgment that needs further conceptual development.

I have attempted to differentiate between the adult educator's role in working with learners who are attempting to cope with transformations and that of the psychotherapist by suggesting that the difference in function pertains to the degree of anxiety generated by the transformative experience. More insight into the process of transformative learning that takes place out of awareness is also in need of development.

Decontextualized learning

Another major criticism cites my emphasis on a concept of rationality that is considered an ahistorical and universal model leading to a 'decontextualized' view of learning – one that fails to deal directly with considerations and questions of context – ideology, culture, power and race-class-gender differences.

An epistemology of evidential and discursive rationality involves reasoning – advancing and assessing reasons for making a judgment. Central to this process is critical self-reflection on assumptions and critical-dialectical discourse. Of course, influences like power, ideology, race, class and gender differences and other interests often pertain and are important factors. However, these influences may be rationally assessed and social action taken appropriately when warranted.

Siegal (1988) explains that rationality is embodied in evolving traditions. As the tradition evolves, so do principles that define and assess reasons. Principles that define reasons and determine their force may change, but rationality remains the same: judgment and action in accord with reason. A critical thinker is one who is appropriately moved by reasons. Admittedly, this is an unfamiliar orientation. There are those who have always argued with great conviction that education – and indeed the very nature of learning and rationality itself – is and must be – the handmaiden of a particular ideology, religion, psychological theory, system of power and influence, social action, culture, a form of government or economic system.

This familiar habit of mind dictates that learning, adult education and rationality must, by definition, be servants to these masters. A rational epistemology of adult learning holds the promise of saving adult education from becoming, like religion, prejudice and politics, the rationalization of a vested interest to give it the appearance of cause. Transformative learning is essentially a meta-cognitive process of *reassessing reasons* supporting our problematic meaning perspectives.

Social action

A major emphasis of critics of transformation theory, as I have conceptualized it, has been its de-emphasis of social action. Adult education holds that an important goal is to effect social change. Transformation theory also contends that adult education must be dedicated to effecting social change, modify oppressive practices, norms, institutions and socio-economic structures to allow everyone to participate more fully and freely in reflective discourse and to acquire a critical disposition and reflective judgment. Transformative learning focuses on creating the essential foundation in insight and understanding essential for learning how to take effective social action in a democracy.

As Dana Villa notes in *Socratic Citizenship* (2001), one of our habitual frames of reference is to be disposed to view anything that is either cause-based, group-related or service-oriented as the core of 'good citizenship' and anything which simply dissents or says 'no' of little value. Socrates' original contribution was the introduction of critical self-reflection and individualism as essential standards of justice and civic obligation in a democracy. Socrates undermined fellow citizens' taken-for-granted habits of mind pertaining to what justice and virtue require. He sought to distance thinking and moral reflection from the restraints of arbitrary political judgment and action – to move to a disposition of critical reflection on assumptions and the citizen's own moral self-formation as a condition of public life.

Habermas (1981) suggests that critical reflection on assumptions and critical discourse, based on reflective judgment – the key dimensions of transformative learning – are characteristics of the highest level of adult morality.

Ideology critique

Adult educator Stephen Brookfield (1991) has challenged the breadth of transformative learning as I have conceptualized it. He writes:

> For something to count as a example of critical learning, critical analysis or critical reflection, I believe that the persons concerned must engage in some sort of power analysis of the situation or context in which the learning is happening. They must also try to identify assumptions they hold dear that are actually destroying their sense of well being and serving the interests of others: that is, hegemonic assumptions.
>
> (1991: 126)

For Brookfield, ideologies are pejorative 'sets of values, beliefs, myths, explanations and justifications that appear self-evidently true and are morally desirable' (1991:

129). Brookfield is not suggesting a critique of all relevant problematic ideologies – the point of view of transformation theory. He is quite specific that critical reflection as ideological critique 'focuses on helping people come to an awareness of how capitalism shapes belief systems and assumptions (i.e. ideologies) that justify and maintain economic and political inequity' (1991: 341). The ideology of capitalism 'frames our moral reasoning, our interpersonal relationships, and our ways of knowing, experiencing and judging what is real and true' (1991: 130).

Brookfield is not suggesting a critique of all relevant ideologies, the point of view of transformation theory in adult education. He is quite specific that critical reflection as ideology critique 'focuses on helping people come to an awareness of how capitalism shapes belief systems and assumptions (i.e. ideologies) that justify and maintain economic and political inequity' (1991: 341). Issues raised here are echoed in critical pedagogy.

Critical pedagogy

Critical pedagogy, and its current form of popular education in Latin America, is an adult education programme evolving from the village-based literacy work of Paulo Freire that assigns priority to a guided analysis of how ideology, power and influence specifically impact upon and disadvantage the immediate lives of the illiterate learners. The educator assists them to learn to read in the process of planning and taking an active role in collective social action to effect change. There is a praxis of transformative study and action.

For critical pedagogy the critical learner, prototypically an illiterate rural peasant, not only comes to recognize injustice but, upon this recognition, is expected to actively participate in the specific political or social action required to change it. The process and problems involved in taking informed, collective, political action in a functioning democracy are seldom addressed in the literature of critical pedagogy.

Burbules and Burk (1999) note that in critical pedagogy everything is open to critical reflection except the premises and categories of critical pedagogy itself and comment that 'there is a givenness of what a "critical" understanding should look like that threatens to become its own kind of constraint' (1999: 54). 'From the perspective of critical thinking, critical pedagogy crosses a threshold between teaching critically and indoctrinating' (1999: 55). Transformation theory in adult education, on the other hand, involves how to think critically about one's assumptions supporting perspectives and to develop reflective judgment in discourse regarding beliefs, values, feelings and self-concept. It is not primarily to think politically; for ideology critique and critical pedagogy, this is a false assumption.

Cosmology

Cosmology is the study of the universe as a rational and orderly system. In the book *Expanding the Boundaries of Transformative Learning* (2002), Edmund O'Sullivan and his colleagues at the Ontario Institute for Studies in Education at the

University of Toronto, move far beyond critical pedagogy's sole concern with the political and social dimensions of capitalism to include environmental, spiritual and self-concept issues in what he calls 'integral transformative learning'.

> Transformative learning involves experiencing a deep structural shift in the basic premises of thought, feeling and action. It is a shift of consciousness that dramatically and permanently alters our being in the world. Such a shift involves our understanding of ourselves and our self-locations; our relationships with other humans and the natural world; our understanding of the relations of power in interlocking structures of class, race and gender; our body awareness, our visions of alternative approaches to living; and our sense of the possibilities for social justice and peace and personal joy.
>
> (2002: 11)

'Transformative criticism', as conceptualized from this perspective posits a critique of the dominant culture's 'formative appropriateness' and provides a vision of an alternative form of culture and concrete indications of how to abandon inappropriate elements and to create more appropriate new cultural forms. They suggest that these elements should form a new type of integral education.

O'Sullivan *et al.*'s identification of transformative learning with movement toward the realization of a bold conception of a new cosmology moves well beyond the political focus of critical pedagogy. However, it shares the same limitation of not presenting or inviting a critical assessment of its core assumptions and categories. Such an assessment should consider the definition and validity of each of the five components designated in their definition of transformation, assumptions regarding the role of education and adult education as the principal vehicle for effecting the broad multi-dimensional transformation they envision, and how we are to understand the epistemology of transformative learning in adulthood, particularly the role of rationality, critical reflection on epistemic assumptions and of discourse in the context of this theory.

Perspectives on transformative learning

Constructivist development

Constructivist developmental psychologists believe that development involves movement through a predictable sequence of 'forms' (frames of reference or meaning systems) culminating in the development of the adult capacity, and in some adult learners, the ability and disposition to engage in the transformative processes of critical self-reflection and reflective judgment through discourse.

Robert Kegan (2000) identifies five forms of meaning making through the lifespan. These forms of mind include: the perceptual/impulsive, the concrete/opinionated, the socialized, the self authoring and the self-transforming mind that includes the capacity for self-reflection. He delineates the capabilities of adulthood: able to think abstractly, construct values and ideals, introspect, subordinate short-term interests to the welfare of a relationship, orient to and identify with expectations of groups and individual relationships of which one wishes to feel a part. It ordinarily takes two decades to develop these capacities and longer for some.

Mary Belenky and her associates (1986) identified six forms of knowing: silenced, received, subjective, separate, connected and constructed. The connected knower enters into the perspective of another and tries to see the world through his/her eyes. This is an essential dimension of transformative learning.

King and Kitchener (1994) have considerable evidence to support the assertion that it is only in adulthood that epistemic assumptions allow for true reflective thinking in a seven stage movement. Stage seven involves understanding abstract concepts of knowledge as a system; knowledge is the outcome of the process of reasonable inquiry for constructing an informed understanding. This stage is comparable to the adult capacity to effectively participate in discourse in transformation theory.

Psychic distortion

Psychiatrist Roger Gould's 'epigenetic' theory of adult development (1978) holds that traumatic events in childhood may produce prohibitions that, though submerged from consciousness in adulthood, continue to generate anxiety feeling that inhibit adult action when there is a risk of violating them. This dynamic results in a lost function – the ability to take risks, feel sexual, finish a job – that must be regained if one is to become a fully functioning adult. The most significant adult learning occurs in connection with life transitions. As adulthood is a time for regaining lost functions, the learner should be assisted to identify the specific blocked action and the source and nature of stress in deciding to take action. The learner is helped to differentiate between the anxiety that is a function of the childhood trauma and the anxiety warranted by his or her immediate adult life situation.

Gould feels that the learning to cope with ordinary existential psychological distortions can be facilitated by knowledgeable adult educators and adult counsellors as well as by therapists. He has developed an interactive, computerized programme of guided self-study for adult learners coping with life transitions. Educators and counsellors provide emotional support and help the learner think through the choices posed by the programme.

Schema therapy

As described by Bennett-Goleman (2001), schema therapy is an adaptation of cognitive psychotherapy that focuses on repairing emotional frames of reference, like maladaptive emotional habits, relentless perfectionism or the sense of emotional deprivation. Mindfulness, a Buddhist concept, defined here as a refined, meditative awareness, is combined by Bennett-Goleman with insights from cognitive neuroscience. Mindfulness may be applied by individuals to understand their patterns of emotional reactivity in workshops. Major schemas include:

> unloveability, the fear that people would reject us if they truly knew us; mistrust, the constant suspicion that those close to us will betray us; social exclusion, the feeling we don't belong; failure, the sense that we cannot succeed at what we do; subjugation, always giving in to other people's wants and demands; and entitlement, the sense that one is somehow special and sobeyond ordinary rules and limits.
>
> (2001: 11)

> Mindfulness allows one to separate specific experience from the overlay of mental and emotional reaction to it. In that space there is room to examine whether we harbour distorted assumptions, ungrounded beliefs, or warped perceptions. We can see the ways our thoughts and feelings define us as they come and go – we can see our habitual lenses themselves.
>
> (2001: 53)

As frames of reference, schemas are the way the mind organizes, retains and acts on a particular task, but they also selectively determine to what we will attend and what they deem irrelevant. When emotions intervene, schemas can determine what is admitted to awareness and can provide a plan of action in response. Schemas are mental models of experience.

Bennett-Goleman (2001) describes the process involved in challenging and changing schema thoughts:

1   Become mindful of the feeling or typical thoughts associated with the schema. Focus on your thoughts, emotions and body sensations – all clues to which the schema has become activated. Test whether you are overreacting.
2   Become aware of your schema thoughts as such and recognize they may be distortions.
3   Challenge those thoughts. Recognize how you have learned through critical self-reflection that they embody false assumptions. Validate your transformative insights by getting involved in a discourse with another who has a more realistic understanding of the subject.
4   Use empathic reframing to acknowledge the schema reality while you put into words a more accurate picture of things.

Individuation – Jungian Psychology

Patricia Cranton (1994) interprets Jung's theory of psychological type to integrate his concepts with those of transformative learning theory in adult education. Learners' psychological predispositions form one kind of habit of mind. This involves two interrelated processes: to become more aware and to understand our own nature while, at the same time, individuating ourselves from the rest of humanity as we learn who we are.

Jung describes a continuum on which one may differentiate two ways of relating to the world and of making judgments: introverted and extraverted. We make judgments either logically or analytically – to assess a problem, weigh alternatives and make a decision – or rely upon deep-seated reactions of acceptance or rejection in which logic plays no part. This differentiation between perception and judgment is close to transformation theory's differentiation between learning outside awareness through intuition and learning within awareness through critical reflection on assumptions. Psychological preferences (thinking and feeling or sensing and intuition) are habits of mind.

John Dirkx (1997) also identifies the goal of Jung's concept of individuation as the development of an individual's personality. This development involves a dialogue between ego consciousness and the content of the unconscious. Transformation involves participating in dialogue with the unconscious aspects of the psyche. This frees one from obsessions, compulsions and complexes that can shape and distort our frame of reference. The symbolic process of individuation is expressed in the form of images. Through a dialogue between the conscious and unconscious, mediated through symbols and images, learners gain insight into aspects of themselves that are outside conscious awareness but influence their sense of self as well as their interpretations and actions. These symbols and images express emotions and feelings that arise in the learning process. 'Behind every emotion there is an image' (Dirkx 1997: 249).

The content or process of formal learning evokes images realized through dialogue. In the course of this interaction, 'both content and ourselves are potentially transformed. Individuation is an ongoing psychic process. When entered into consciously and imaginatively, it provides for a deepening of awareness of the self, an expansion of one's consciousness, and engendering of soul. We become more fully who we are and we are more fully able to enter into a community of humans. In Jungian terms, this is transformation – emergence of the self' (Dirkx 1997: 251).

Dean Elias (1997) has expanded the definition of transformative learning to explicitly include the unconscious: transformative learning is the expansion of consciousness through the transformation of basic world views and specific capacities of the self: transformative learning is facilitated through consciously directed processes such as appreciatively accessing and receiving the symbolic contents of the unconscious and critically analysing underlying premises.

For additional insight into Jungian interpretations of transformative learning in the context of adult learning see Robert Boyd (1991).

Facilitating transformation learning in graduate adult education

The first graduate programme in adult education designed to foster and facilitate the concept of transformative learning was established at Teachers College,

Columbia University, in New York two decades ago. A highly selective doctoral programme, Adult Education Guided Independent Study was designed for professionals with at least five years of experience in this field of practice. Students came on campus one weekend a month and attended intensive three-week summer sessions to satisfy course requirements in two years. Dialogue continued through the Internet. To practice and analyse the process of discourse, students collaborated on most problems with colleagues around tables of six. A major emphasis was placed on the creation of effective learning communities for collaborative inquiry.

Applicants were required to write a paper that described an issue in the field, present arguments on both sides, describe the point of view each represented and describe their own point of view and analyse their own assumptions. Faculty members, who placed emphasis on identifying additional missing assumptions, carefully reviewed the papers. Extensive revisions were requested. Revisions were often returned to the applicant with a faculty analysis of additional missed assumptions, and second and often third revisions required. These exchanges were designed to force the applicant to critically examine their own habits of taken-for-granted ways of thinking and introduce the student to assumption analysis. Grading was limited to pass or incomplete. Academic standards were high. Three incompletes required that a student leave the programme.

Courses included assumption analysis, involving articles authored by adult educators, life histories, involving comparative assessment of key turning points in the lives of students meeting in groups of three, designed to encourage them to recognize that there are alternative ways of interpreting common experience; courses in ideologies, media analysis, the work of Paulo Freire and transformations through art and literature. Other courses, added over the years, focused on adult learning, research methods, adult literacy, community development and organizational development.

Methods found useful in fostering critical self-reflection of assumptions and discourse include using critical incidents, life histories, journal writing, media analysis, repertory grids, metaphor analysis, conceptual mapping, action learning, collaborative learning and John Peters' 'Action-Reason-Thematic Technique' – all described in Mezirow and Associates (1990).

Universal dimensions of adult knowing

There is a current debate over whether a learning theory must be dictated exclusively by contextual interests, as suggested by Brookfield, followers of critical pedagogy, other post-Marxist theorists and many post-modern critics.

Transformative learning theory, as I have conceptualized it, holds that cultures enable or inhibit the realization of common human interests – the ways adults realize common learning capabilities. Who learns what and the when, where and how of education are clearly functions of the culture. Transformative learning is a rational, meta-cognitive process of reassessing reasons that support problematic meaning perspectives or frames of reference, including those representing such contextual cultural factors as ideology, religion, politics, class, race, gender and others. It is the process by which adults learn how to think critically for themselves rather than take assumptions supporting a point of view for granted.

Universal dimensions of rationality and adult understanding upon which cultural or contextual influences impact – and may distort – include the following:

Adults:

- seek the meaning of their experience – both mundane and transcendent;
- have a sense of self and others as agents capable of thoughtful and responsible action;
- engage in mindful efforts to learn;
- learn to become rational by advancing and assessing reasons;
- make meaning of their experience – both within and outside awareness – through acquired frames of reference – sets of orienting assumptions and expectations with cognitive, affective and conative dimensions that shape, delimit and sometimes distort their understanding;
- accept some others as agents with interpretations of their experience that may prove true or justified:
- rely upon beliefs and understandings that produce interpretations and opinions that will prove more true or justified than those based upon other beliefs and understandings;
- engage in reflective discourse to assess the reasons and assumptions supporting a belief to be able to arrive at a tentative best judgment – as a sometime alternative or supplement to resorting to traditional authority or force to validate a judgment;
- understand the meaning of what is communicated to them by taking into account the assumptions (intent, truthfulness, qualifications) of the person communicating as well as the truth, justification, appropriateness and authenticity of what is being communicated;
- imagine how things could be different;
- learn to transform their frames of reference through critical reflection on assumptions, self-reflection on assumptions and dialogic reasoning when the beliefs and understandings they generate become problematic.

These are generic dimensions of adult understanding that may be deliberately or unconsciously enhanced or discouraged through the process of adult education. Limiting the development of these qualitative dimensions of adults learning by exclusively focusing adult education on immediate contextual issues is self-defeating. It brings to mind the old Chinese saying, 'Give a man a fish and he can eat for a day; teach him to fish and he can eat for his lifetime'.

References

Belenky, M.F., Clinchy, B.M., Goldberger, N.R. and Tarule, J.M. (1986) *Women's Ways of Knowing: the Development of Self, Voice and Mind*, New York: Basic Books.

Bennett-Goleman, T. (2001) *Emotional Alchemy*, New York: Three River Press.

Boyd, R. (1991) *Personal Transformations in Small Groups; a Jungian Perspective*, London: Routledge.

Brookfield, S. (1991) 'Transformative learning as ideology critique', in J. Mezirow (ed.) *Transformative Dimensions of Adult Learning*, San Francisco: Jossey-Bass.

Burbules, N. and Burk R. (1999) 'Critical thinking and critical pedagogy: relations, differences, and limits', in T. Popkewitz and L. Fendler (eds) *Critical Theories in Education*, New York: Routledge.

Cranton, P. (1994) *Understanding and Promoting Transformative Learning*, San Francisco: Jossey-Bass.

Dirkx, J. (1997) 'Nurturing soul in adult learning', in P. Cranton (ed.) *Transformative Learning in Action*, San Francisco: Jossey-Bass.

Elias, D. (1997) 'It's time to change our minds', *ReVision* Summer, 26, 1: 3–5.

Gould, R. (1978) *Transformation Growth and Change in Adult Life*, New York: Simon & Schuster.

Habermas, J. (1981) *The Theory of Communicative Action*, vol. 1, Thomas McCarthy (trans.), Boston: Beacon Press.

Kegan, R. (2000) 'What "form" transforms?' in J. Mezirow & Associates *Learning as Transformation*, San Francisco: Jossey-Bass.

King, P. and Kitchener, K. (1994) *Developing Reflective Judgment*, San Francisco: Jossey-Bass.

Mezirow, J. (1978) *Education for Perspective Transformation: Women's re-entry Programs in Community Colleges*, New York: Teachers College, Columbia University (available through ERIC system).

Meizrow, J. and Associates (1990) *Fostering Critical Reflection in Adulthood*, San Francisco: Jossey-Bass.

O'Sullivan, E., Morrell, A., O'Connor, M. (2002) *Expanding the Boundaries of Transformative Learning*, New York: Palgrave.

Siegal, H. (1988) *Educating Reason*, New York: Routledge.

Villa, D. (2001) *Socratic Citizenship*, Princeton, New Jersey: Princeton University Press.

Chapter 4

Managing change and transition
A psychosocial perspective on lifelong learning

Linden West

The 'psychosocial' dimension of lifelong learning is concerned with people's inner subjective world of thought and feeling combined with sensitivity to their outer world of social relationships set in a context of wider structural inequalities. The focus of interest in this chapter is on understanding how people can creatively and constructively engage with constantly changing and disruptive circumstances which undermine established identities. The 'defended self' essentially inhibits positive engagement with change. The argument is made that lifelong learning in communities is potentially a transitional space for overcoming anxieties and ambivalent feelings in order to negotiate new identities.

Introduction

I want to reflect on processes of managing change and transition, and the meaning and parameters of lifelong learning, in what has often been described as a 'postmodern', 'globalized' world in which, for many, predictable biographical trajectories have broken down. This can bring in its train new and enticing opportunities for self-experiment, free from some of the constraints of the past, but this can be accompanied by deep-seated anxieties about people's capacity to cope with the uncertainties generated. Economic liberalization and individualization mean that people, like it or not, have to take greater responsibility for the circumstances, rules and direction of their lives, while lifelong learning, in such a world, can be seen as a resource to enable individuals to respond in creative ways. People need the capacity and resources to make meaningful choices and to constantly re-orientate themselves afresh (Alheit and Dausien 2002; West 1996).

The question at the heart of this chapter is what enables individuals to remain creative, rather than paranoid, in the face of constant change and uncertainty, and compose meaningful biographies in the process. A 'psychosocial' perspective on learning and subjectivity is offered, drawing on psychoanalytical perspectives. Learning and the subject called the learner are, in this view, to be understood socially, emotionally and psychologically in an interconnected way. Social, in that basic perceptions of self, including the capacity to learn, are forged in relationships and shaped by the structuring forces of class, gender, ethnicity, etc. and the discourses of power that pervade these. Social, in the sense that adult learning often raises questions about who we are and where we belong and the implications of embracing a new community of practice. Social in that learning is rather more than a matter of cognitive processes inside people's heads but is stimulated and sustained by the social relationships in which we are embedded. Psychological in that the psyche has a life and dynamic of its own: not everyone, even in roughly similar 'objective' situations, responds in the same way to a similar experience. Some more so than others remain open and creative, or learn how to, in the face of difficulties while others retreat into defensiveness and even paranoia. There is, from a psychosocial perspective, a defended as well as a social self to consider.

An uncertain context

Whereas in previous agrarian and industrial societies, people lived according to more or less clearly defined social scripts, economic change can mean these may quickly unravel or become redundant. The new global economic order involves fund managers, banks, corporations as well as millions of individual investors, transferring massive sums of money from one part of the globe to another, at the flick of a switch. Traditional economies, communities and shared biographical expectations can fracture overnight. Moreover, it is not simply that change is choosing people, but people, as Giddens (1999) notes, are also choosing change. Under the impact of feminism and changes in the labour market, for instance, many women have sought to compose lifestyles radically different from those of their mothers, while in intimate relationships, people nowadays expect more by way of emotional fulfilment and reciprocity than would have been the case even a couple of generations ago.

Yet this is a world that appears to provoke deep uncertainties around notions of identity, at many interconnected levels. Insecurity and constant changes in working life, as Richard Sennett (1998) has observed, can have profound implications for individuals' senses of who they are. When the notion of a job for life can seem an illusion and people are told to be flexible and responsive to a constantly changing labour market, their sense of identity may become fragile and uncertain. This may, in turn, Sennett suggests, nurture feelings of detachment and estrangement from others. This may be mirrored, in turn, by the collapse of adult solidarities and trust at the level of local, geographical communities, as networks of kinship and shared biographical expectations, built around common patterns of employment, in, for instance, traditional industrial areas of Britain, have fractured. Insecurity, or at least impermanence, may also characterize interactions at a more intimate level, with increased divorce and expectations that relationships are transitory (Furedi 2001). Psychologically, this is a world that promises enticing possibilities but also brings stress and anxiety in its train. While some people – the highly individualized, who are critically engaged with modernizing tendencies and concentrated in higher social groupings – may to an extent thrive in the new order (Field 2000), most people, even in relatively well-paid work, can struggle, at times, with feelings of impermanence. And if most individuals crave some degree of work security, they are told, in the neo-liberal mantra, that this is illusion in a cut-throat competitive world (Elliot and Atkinson 1998).

Ulrich Beck (1997) has observed that individuals face such insecurities, and what may be the constant disembedding and re-embedding of ways of life, at a time when the welfare state has retreated and many people, especially on the margins, have lost faith in national governments and corporations, as well as conventional politics, to address their concerns. The political agenda, in this view, is dominated by a pervasive neo-liberal consensus, in which responsibility and risk have shifted from the collective level to individuals and families. Here is a world where those most marginalized and buffeted by economic and cultural transformations, and suffering most intensely, are held to be personally responsible for their plight and morally and financially cajoled into taking jobs, however short-term, unskilled and low paid, or into training, however purposeless. Learn, or lose benefits; 'upskill', or lose your job in what some suggest has become a morally authoritarian environment (Coffield 1999). 'Lifelong learning', in these terms, when servicing the narrow economic agendas of the powerful, becomes part of the problem rather than the solution.

Yet lifelong learning – in a biographical, lifewide and, sociologically speaking, reflexive sense – has become essential to individual and collective well-being in a more fragmented, individualized and unpredictable culture: one in which we often need to learn our way – at a personal as well as more collective level – through a range of difficulties, dislocations and conflicting claims and prescriptions, without confident reference to familial templates or uncontested knowledge (Field 2000). I suggest, in such a world, that relationships – cultivated in learning and more widely – and the building of new kinds of social networks and solidarities, through, for instance, informal community-based learning, can be important in helping people forge new, more confident identities, in healthy interaction with others. This can include political agency, especially for marginalized peoples, enabling them to talk back to power, via new forms of political engagement. I want to illuminate such processes by reference to what I term 'auto/biographical' research.

Auto/biographical research

I have been exploring, over a period of time, the narratives of marginalized adults and young people struggling to compose and recompose their biographies in difficult, demanding social and economic conditions, including managing redundancy and dealing with depression (West 1996). The intention has been to engage those at the heart of change processes in collaborative as well as more dialogical forms of enquiry. Auto/biographical research emphasizes how we draw on others to make sense of our narratives as well as vice versa but also how research, inspired by feminist approaches, can become a kind of shared enquiry in which researcher and researched learn together (Stanley 1992; West 1996, 2001). In fact, researching the lives of many adult learners and young people has made me increasingly realize how much, in asking questions of others – about learning, managing change and the struggle for some agency in life – I was asking questions of myself.

I will use two case studies (distinct but also illustrating some common themes across the research) to illuminate what I term a psychosocial perspective on life-long learning. The emotions, especially anxiety, in this view, are fundamental to learning and managing change. Anxiety, especially around threats to the self, can generate a whole range of defensive manoeuvres, often unconscious, included in adult learning. These manoeuvres focus themselves around, for instance, our capacities to cope, or whether we are good enough, or are acceptable to, or even deserve to be accepted by, others. Such a perspective is radically different from linear notions of self development, especially in the North American literature of adult education, that tend to assume that primitive anxiety and our need for others are transcended in the impetus towards self-actualization.

Two case studies

Jim was a working-class man who entered an Access to higher education programme in a further education college. He was part of a longitudinal, in-depth study of learner motivation that involved up to seven cycles of narrative interviews over a period of four years (West 1996). He lived in Thanet, on the furthermost edge of South East England, a place of economic insecurity, pockets of intense poverty, and a fragile, casualized labour market. Jim was made redundant on many occasions. His story is one of ambivalence towards learning, but also of taking risks and finding greater agency at the sharp and painful edge of the new economic order. His narrative of learning and rebuilding a career evolved, over a period, to encompass the central role of relationships in enabling him to compose a new, more confident identity from the fragments of the old.

'Gina' was a highly disaffected and emotionally disturbed young mum, who became dependent on hard drugs. She lived on a marginalized public housing estate in East London suffering from a range of social ills, including poverty. She participated in a community arts programme and her story likewise illuminates how supportive others, and what I term transitional space provided by the community arts, offered resources to compose a more confident biography and sense of self, however contingently. The notion of transitional space is taken from the work of Donald Winnicott (1971). This is an in-between space, as in learning, where identity may be negotiated and risks taken in relation to potentially new identities – such as becoming a learner or an artist – by engaging in different kinds of symbolic activity.

Jim: rebuilding a life through education

Jim and I shared stories, over time, as the research developed into more of a dialogue and shared exploration of processes of men managing change and transitions. Men, like Jim, in working-class communities where historic occupational structures and the biographical predictabilities have shattered, can easily become trapped in pretences of coping and psychological defensiveness, as I had done, at difficult times in my life, including dealing with changing roles, marital breakdown and in training to be a psychotherapist (West 2001). Men, especially, can struggle to handle the emotional aspects of lost status or crises in relationships, given their relative investment in public roles and how we have been taught to repress anxiety and deny vulnerability (Samuels 1993).

Jim, in fact, was managing to rebuild his biography, in the broadest sense, rather well. He was 35 when we first met, with a wife and two sons. He had a relatively successful time as a painter and decorator, which came to an abrupt end with redundancy in the middle of the 1990s recession. He felt insecure, he said, for most of his working life and knew what it was like to drift. Over three years in higher education, he trained as a radiographer, and distanced himself from his previous identity, as he grew more confident both in himself and in the prospect of making a success of his experiment. At first, in the early stages of the Access programme, he was fearful of severing ties with the building trade but this gradually changed as he progressed towards a degree.

His decision to break with the building industry and enter an Access programme, in the early interviews, troubled him greatly. He felt on the margins of two worlds, of college and a previous career, but identified more with the latter. He thought he was taking risks before he believed he could cope. He felt guilty at not providing for his family and struggled with the impact of redundancy, higher education as well as the research. He was anxious about studying and there were constant hints of needing to justify his actions to himself as well as to others. It was the apparent impossibility of finding another job that led him towards college and radical change. Had he found work in the building trade, and prospects had been reasonable, for all his reservations, he would probably have continued as before. But he tried and failed in an increasingly fragile economic environment. He might also, he said, have drifted into a career of drink and depression.

In an early interview Jim mentioned, almost in passing, that his sister had taken an Access programme and she encouraged him to do the same. Towards the end of the research the story developed and he said that he would never have started the degree, or completed it, without her support and challenge. She encouraged him and he was able to identity with her as a role model and an inspiration: quite simply she helped him believe in himself. Their relationship was central to his story about managing change, as was strengthening relationships with his two sons, which included taking them fishing. Lifelong learning is, or ought to be, about far more than instrumentalism. At one time, the relationships with his sons and wife had been peripheral but that changed. His wife entered an Access programme and they were searching to rebuild their relationship in new ways. She had educational qualifications and increasingly felt frustrated at home and in her part-time job. Negotiation included the emotional division of labour in the home. Jim was enjoying his family more and felt better about himself, although at times he could feel miserable and inadequate too. Higher education, he said, provided a space in which, over time, he could take risks, with supportive teachers and other students coming alongside. But he had also struggled to enter the space, for fear of letting go of an older identity and anxiety about his capacity to embrace a new one. Even thinking of himself as a learner in higher education had often seemed ridiculous, only a relatively short time before.

Gina: 'cottoning on' to community art

Gina lives in East London, which has been an especial casualty of globalization and neo-liberal economics (as well as, in part, a beneficiary too, in the huge growth of financial services). Since the 1970s East London has been subject to a massive process of deindustrialization, dramatized most obviously in the closure of the docks but also affecting other traditional trades and industries. Large pockets of what has been termed 'yuppification' co-exist with depressed public housing estates suffering racial violence, drug abuse and growing youth unemployment. It is a place of widespread educational under-achievement and social exclusion, poor health and poverty (Bardsley *et al.* 1998). East London symbolizes, in an acute form, the divided, unequal state of contemporary neo-liberal England.

Gina participated in a parenting and community arts project organized by a body called Theatre Venture. The aim was to engage, via outreach work, disaffected learners in the visual arts and to encourage them to progress into formal arts education or the labour market. The project was ambitious and involved recruiting groups of educationally alienated young men and women. Gina joined a series of workshops called 'Cotton on', targeted at young mothers aged 14 to 19. The focus was experiences of pregnancy and parenthood using the visual arts, including textile design, sculpture, printing, photography and video. In-depth interviews were held with Gina at an early stage of the project and towards the end while I also spent time in the workshops.

Gina told me that no one had ever really listened to her and she had felt lost and alone as a young mum. She felt pressurized to participate in education and get a job and yet also wanted to enter college. But she had her child to think of and felt confused, muddled and under pressure, from all sides. Her introduction to the centre where the workshops were based was due to the encouragement of a sympathetic health visitor. At first she was upset at leaving her daughter in the crèche but she relaxed. She changed, she said, as a result of the parenting programme. There was a time, she insisted, when she could not tolerate mess, in the home or anywhere else, and everything had to be kept in order. She had never let her baby play on the floor, in case she got dirty, while upstairs other children were 'romping about'. She was more at ease now.

She liked the centre and the peer education project, while 'Cotton on' had given her ideas for the future. Three months later, when we next met, Gina was working intensely on a sculpture:

When I was pregnant and I didn't really get very big. I made myself a little pregnant belly from a washing basket to put your washing in. I used chicken wire and plaster of Paris and painted it up funny colours. They kind of expressed my mood when I was pregnant, bit dark, dull colours, bit cold. Yes ... I don't know people who are looking at it probably won't get it, but to me it's a hangover for anger.

Pregnancy was hard and troubling, and she felt, at times, unreal since she did not look pregnant. She was depressed and 'really ill throughout'. Her mood was translated into the sculpture. She was trying, she said, 'to get across that, the darkness'. There was no head on the sculpture, either; it was a headless torso, which, she said, was deliberate. She found sculpting therapeutic: she needed, she realized, to express her feelings about the pregnancy, and of being 'a baby machine'. But she was past some of that now and the centre provided a key. She was starting to use brighter colours too, more 'yellows and reds', which symbolized feeling better about herself and more alive.

New and changing relationships were also at the heart of her story about managing change and transition. A strong relationship with a youth leader, for instance, who acted as a surrogate parent, in many and diverse ways (including being firm when Gina was in a destructive mood) as well as with an art tutor, who encouraged her 'to go for it'. Gina talked, increasingly, of wanting to learn and of enjoying engaging with others in the group. Learning even had a 'political' dimension as she described being encouraged to formulate and present a case to the local council for more single-parent friendly housing. She went for it and did well as she did in leading peer sex education programmes in schools. She felt good, empowered and enlivened but also surprised at what she was able to do, including for others. She had, on her own admission, a destructive and rebellious side, when she wanted to do nothing and disengaged from the group. Yet she was progressing in her life, in many ways. Two things were clear from her narrative: the capacity of significant others – the youth leader and art tutor, among others – to work empathically, in emotionally attuned ways, with Gina, and to contain some of her anxiety; and the importance of art, in providing precious transitional space where Gina could project painful, confused and disturbed feelings, work on them, symbolically, and, over time, transform and re-introject them in new, more life-enhancing, meaningful ways.

On managing change and transition: a psychosocial perspective

Contemporary psychoanalytic perspectives can help theorize some of the processes involved in such stories of lifewide, lifelong learning. Feminist psychoanalysis has sought to connect the social and psychological, outer and inner worlds, by paying attention to the importance of intersubjective processes (rather than innate drives) in shaping intrasubjective life, which are, in turn, moulded by wider cultural imperatives. Many feminists have been drawn to object relations theories because these are compatible with a constructivist model of human development and identity formation in which culture and society penetrate to the core. In object relations theory the interpersonal (and by extension, culture and society) are brought into the heart of learning and struggles for self. Melanie Klein's ideas, grounded in clinical observation, have been particularly influential, not least her assertion that selves are forged out of the interplay of inner and outer worlds: most notably in the way we internalize objects – whole people or parts (most famously the breast) but also symbolic activity – and absorb these as sets of fantasized internal relationships which become the building blocks of personality (Frosh 1991). Internal life mirrors patterns in our external relationships, rather like the development of a cast of characters in a play: some characters 'out there' may stifle and abuse us and we in turn stifle and abuse others, including ourselves. But new characters and objects can enter the stage, including via lifelong learning.

In this psychosocial perspective, there is a defended as well as a social self, which has, interestingly, just begun to be recognized in the lifelong learning literature. Tara Fenwick, for instance, in applying complexity science to experiential learning, notes the potentially important contribution of psychoanalytic ideas in that analysis of learning 'should focus less on reported meanings and motivations' and more on what is happening 'under the surface of human encounters', including 'the desire for and resistance to different objects and relationships' (Fenwick 2003). Resistance can be especially strong when people feel overwhelmed, unable to cope and deeply ambivalent about themselves and their capabilities: or where they have been taught that risk taking and experiment can bring humiliation and ridicule. It may feel safer to stay on the margins, however dissatisfying, and to reject new opportunities; and even to embrace, at an extreme, fundamentalism, when the world is experienced as too dangerous and threatening.

For learners like Gina and Jim, and many others, learning can be interpreted in terms of desire and resistance to relationships and objects. Their learning – emotional, intimate, relational, biographical, imaginative as well as symbolic – involved, at times, deep resistance and ambivalence. For a person, any person, to progress requires sufficient feelings of security and encouragement to enter a transitional space, a community of practice – such as in higher education or an arts group – and to engage with others and symbolic activity. We need to be able to perceive self, however fleetingly – in the eyes of others as well as ourselves – in new ways, in processes of becoming, and to manage the anxieties generated: whether as a learner in higher education, a radiographer, a budding artist or political activist. We have to tolerate the ambivalence of moving from the safety of the periphery towards a more central space in which we are able to let go, sufficiently, of self-preoccupation and absorb ourselves in the creative moment.

From a psychoanalytic perspective, primitive anxiety is never fully transcended and can be reactivated, sometimes intensely, at moments of change and transition, especially for those who have been taught they are of little consequence. In clinical settings, the capacity of the therapist to contain anxiety and process ambivalent feelings as well as projections (that the therapist does not care) and feed these back in intelligible and digestible forms, lies at the heart of progression. Similar dynamics can operate, informally, in lifelong learning too, in many and different spaces but they often remain unrecognized and implicit. Significant others as well as symbolic activity can help people manage their anxieties and ambivalent, messy and muddled feelings. New dialogic, empathic and emotionally literate relationships are central to enabling the Ginas and Jims of the world, in fact all of us, to feel more understood, supported but also challenged in the transitional spaces of life. Yet, as stated, insufficient attention is paid to these intimate, intersubjective dimensions of lifelong learning and their psychological implications. Therein lies the 'psychosocial' challenge in considering lifelong learning to be lifewide as well; remembering the emotionally fragile, yet often-heroic humanity, which lies at its heart, especially in a world where nothing, sometimes, seems secure.

References

Alheit, P. and Dausien, B. (2002) 'Lifelong learning and biographicity', in A. Bron and M. Schemmann (eds) *Social Science Theories in Adult Education Research, Bochum Studies in International Adult Education*, Munster: LIT, 3: 211–41.

Bardsley, M., Baker, M., Bhan, A., Farrow, S., Gill, M., Jacobson, B. and Morgan, D. (1998) *The Health of Londoners, A Public Health Report for Londoners*, London: Kings Fund.

Beck, U. (1997) *The Reinvention of Politics. Rethinking Modernity in a Global Social Order*, Cambridge: Polity Press.

Coffield, F. (1999) 'Breaking the consensus: lifelong learning as social control', *British Journal of Educational Research*, 25, 4: 479–99.

Elliot, L. and Atkinson, D. (1998) *The Age of Insecurity*, London: Verso.

Fenwick, T. (2003) 'Reclaiming and re-embodying experiential learning through complexity science', *Studies in the Education of Adults*, 35, 2: 123–41.

Field, J. (2000) *Lifelong Learning and the New Educational Order*, Stoke-on-Trent: Trentham Books.

Frosh, S. (1991) *Identity Crisis*, London: Macmillan.

Furedi, F. (2001) *Paranoid Parenting*, London: Allen Lane.

Giddens, A. (1999) *Runaway World: How Globalisation is Reshaping Our Lives*, London: Profile Books.

Samuels, A. (1993) *The Political Psyche*, London: Routledge.

Sennett, R. (1998) *The Corrosion of Character: The Personal Consequences of Work in the New Capitalism*, New York: Norton.

Stanley, L. (1992) *The Auto/biographical I. The Theory and Practice of Feminist Research*, Manchester: University Press.

West, L. (1996) *Beyond Fragments, Adults, Motivation and Higher Education: A Biographical Analysis*, London: Taylor and Francis.

West, L. (2001) *Doctors on the Edge: General Practitioners, Health and Learning in the Inner-City*, London: Free Association Books.

Winnicott, D. (1971) *Playing and Reality*, London: Routledge.

Chapter 5

The application of the ideas of Habermas to adult learning

Mark Murphy and Ted Fleming

Adult educators outside of North America have largely ignored the contribution of Habermas's work for a critical pedagogy of adult learning. The authors seek to explain and explore his social and political theory for developing a morally justified critique for emancipatory practice in adult education. This imperative arises not simply because of the incursion of the 'system world' into the 'lifeworld' but also to transform the former with values of care, ethics and democratic principles. The impact of Habermas can be seen in adult education which focuses on civil society as a site of struggle for decolonizing the lifeworld. Habermas has also had an impact on adult educators like Jack Mezirow who have been particularly influenced by his analysis and search for a discursive democracy and, because of their integral connections, a learning society too.

Introduction

Jürgen Habermas has had a major impact on the development of social and political theory for fifty years and is generally regarded as the contemporary embodiment of the critical theory tradition of the Frankfurt School. He is a vocal public intellectual recovering the progressive traditions from Kant and the Enlightenment and is, according to Bernstein, 'the philosopher of democracy' (1991: 207).

He studied in Göttingen, Bonn and Zurich and was assistant to Adorno (1956–1959) at the Frankfurt Institute for Social Research. *The Structural Transformation of the Public Sphere* (Habermas 1989), published in 1962, prompted his appointment as Professor at Heidelberg and later, while at Frankfurt, he published *Knowledge and Human Interests* (1971). His most famous works are *The Theory of Communicative Action* (two volumes, 1984, 1987) and *Between Facts and Norms* (1996).

In a tribute to Marcuse, he asserted; 'I know wherein our most basic values are rooted – in compassion, in our sense for the suffering of others' (Habermas 1985: 72). Habermas in his critical social theory outlines the reason for this moral position. His quest is to ensure that the emancipatory possibility of critical theory is reasonable, well grounded and a firm foundation for 'the public political struggles for a more just social form of life' (Matuštík 2001: xix).

Habermas and adult education

In terms of theory, compared to the ideas of Foucault and other postmodern thinkers, the influence of Habermas on the field of education has been muted. Certainly his influence has been witnessed in such diverse fields as industrial training (O'Donnell 1999), nursing and dental education (Duffy and Scott 1998; Ekstrom and Sigurdsson 2002; Whipp et al. 2000), educational administration (Harris 2002; Ryan 1998), teacher education (Conle 2001) and open and distance education (Sumner 2000). His influence, however, has never really reached critical mass level in the discourses of the wider educational profession.

This situation changes somewhat when the field of adult education is examined, more specifically in North American adult education, where Habermas has gained more widespread acceptance. Having said that, it is only relatively recently that the application of his work has become more visible and widespread. In a comprehensive survey by Ewert (1991) of English language articles (from 1972–1987) that cite Habermas, Mezirow was the only adult educator making reference to him. Mezirow has been rightly credited with bringing Habermas to the attention of adult education (Connolly 1996), and an increasing number of authors have expressed an interest in applying his ideas to the field, for instance, as a grounding for critical pedagogy (Morrow and Torres 2002).

Before an overview of Habermas and his impact on adult education is outlined, it is necessary to provide at least a brief synopsis of some key ideas present in his work.

Habermas, reason and colonization

Habermas is widely viewed, sometimes disparagingly, as a theorist of the 'grand narrative', in that he has developed a broad and comprehensive analytical framework within which to understand processes of social change. In this way, he can be placed in the tradition of sociological thinkers such as Emile Durkheim, Max Weber and Talcott Parsons. He should also be associated with the other sociological tradition of Karl Marx, who, while also an unashamed grand theorist, sought to develop a class-based theory of society to challenge the conventional 'bourgeois' sociology of the time. Habermas has sought to develop and extend the ideas of Marx and Weber as well as Horkheimer and Adorno's (1972) *Dialectic of Enlightenment* (1972) in his attempt to understand social change and conflict in the twentieth century.

In continuing the work of the Frankfurt School, Habermas has explicitly focused on new forms of social conflict that are not necessarily based on social class. In this regard, he has endeavoured, most notably in his famous work *The Theory of Communicative Action (TCA)*, to reconstruct the ideas of the above-mentioned theorists in order to provide what he considers to be a more effective 'diagnosis of the times'. The two volumes of the *TCA* cover a vast range of complex and interrelated lines of theoretical analysis, in keeping with the intention of

Habermas to develop a comprehensive 'grand' theory. As a result the two-volume set is a highly abstract and difficult work to follow.

Whilst not wishing to oversimplify the ideas contained in the *TCA*, a useful and appropriate way of engaging with the central thesis of this vast opus is by outlining the manner in which Habermas has sought to adapt and reconstruct Max Weber's 'loss of freedom' thesis, most famously epitomized in the 'iron cage' metaphor to denote modern state forms of bureaucracy. Weber argued that the process of capitalist modernization, alongside the disenchantment or secularization of religious worldviews, witnessed the inevitable institutionalization of what he referred to as instrumental rationality, i.e. a utilitarian form of reason focused on outcomes rather than the processes involved in achieving these outcomes. According to Weber, this process of rationalization would inevitably lead to a nightmarish iron cage world of bureaucracy, in which the imperatives of the state, over the heads of its citizens, became all pervasive.

While finding much agreement with Weber's analysis and diagnosis, the analysis of Habermas differs in two fundamental respects. First, Habermas agues that Weber mistakenly equated modernization with rationalization, or put another way, Weber incorrectly conflated instrumental rationality with rationality per se. As a result, Weber is forced to view reason *itself* as the iron cage, a belief central to the argument outlined in Horkheimer's and Adorno *Dialectic of Enlightenment*. Instead, Habermas argues that modernization and rationalization are not one and the same thing, and that there exists another form of rationality – communicative rationality oriented to processes of mutual understanding – that is not necessarily tied into modernization processes.

Second, where Weber appropriates an *action* theory of society, one formulated from the perspective of acting subjects, Habermas instead utilizes a two-level concept of society, which allows for both an action-theoretic and a systems theoretic analysis of the process of societal rationalization. Here, he introduces the concepts of the *lifeworld* – denoting the background consensus of our everyday lives, the vast stock of taken-for-granted definitions and understandings of the world that give coherence and direction to our lives (Welton 1995) – and the system – the aspect of society where imperatives of technical efficiency and bureaucracy have precedence, i.e. the state administrative apparatus (steered by power) and the economy (steered by money).

By reconstructing Weber's iron cage thesis in these two respects, Habermas is able to explore the core issue at the heart of the *TCA* – namely, 'the question of whether, and if so, how, capitalist modernization can be conceived as a process of one-sided rationalization' (Habermas 1984: 140). His answer to this question is that, yes, capitalism has ushered in a process of one-sided (instrumental) rationalization, and has done so via the state and the market overstepping their own functional boundaries and 'colonizing' the lifeworld. Political and economic imperatives, the two main manifestations of instrumental rationality in Habermasian terms, have more and more reduced the potential of communicative rationality to guide and shape decisions and actions that affect the core activities of the lifeworld, namely socialization, cultural reproduction and child-rearing. Put a different way, the pursuit and maintenance of state political agendas, alongside the ability of capitalism to exploit new avenues for wealth creation, have resulted in more and more decisions affecting the lives of citizens being based on the 'bottom line' of power/money.

This argument constitutes Habermas's diagnosis of the times, and while certainly not an overtly Marxist or revolutionary take on critical theory, has clearly provided enough food for thought to be adopted by some in the field of adult education. What follows is a brief account of two key forms of this appropriation, the first focusing on the capacity of *civil society* to provide a vehicle for de-colonizing the lifeworld, and the second more strongly focused on the learning potential associated with Habermas's notion of discursive democracy.

Civil society, democracy and adult education

Some adult educators have seized on the more overtly political aspects of Habermasian sociology. One such author is Michael Collins (1995), a relentless critic of instrumental rationality in adult learning. He builds on Habermas's explanation of how coercive aspects of modern life prevent people from arriving at mutually agreed understandings of what is at stake in making decisions about how we should be and act in the world. The modern world and its meaning making are increasingly shaped by the imperatives of strategic action stemming from a technical rationality which runs counter to the practical and emancipatory interests of ordinary people.

A core theme among North American educators who have adapted this political side of Habermas is the connection between civil society, democracy and adult education (Welton 1995, 2001). Habermas defines civil society as

> composed of more or less spontaneously emergent associations, organizations and movements that, attuned to how societal problems resonate in the private public sphere, distil and transmit such reactions in amplified form to the public.
>
> (Habermas 1996: 367)

Key to both adult educators' and Habermas's own emphasis on civil society is the role of voluntary organizations. Voluntary organizations in civil society are comprised of citizens who seek acceptable interpretations for their social interests and experiences and who wish to exert influence on institutionalized opinion-and-will-formation. These organizations 'push topics of general interest, and act as advocates for neglected issues and under represented groups; for groups that are difficult to organize or that pursue cultural, religious or humanitarian aims ...' according to Habermas (1996: 368).

Civil society, by actively sustaining a public sphere for discourse, can insert moments of democratic accountability into the system world. Revitalizing civil society and sustaining a critical public sphere then becomes a task for critical adult education. Adult education can foster the creation of spaces where citizens can debate publicly and adopt the methodologies of discourse in pursuit of consensual agreements. This emphasis on a Habermasian version of civil society is unsurprising, as adult educators have long been involved in identifying spaces where critical learning can take place – Freire's culture circles, Mezirow's women returners of the 1970s, Flecha's literary circles – and now civil society is regarded as a prime location for learning that is free from domination by the state or economy. There are many practical examples of this in operation: Highlander (Adams and Horton 1975); popular education (Crowther, Martin and Shaw 1999); theatre of the oppressed (Boal 2000); participatory research (Chambers 1994) and training for transformation (Hope and Timmell 1999).

According to Welton (1995), in order for the field of adult education to fulfil such a role in civil society, adult learning must involve both social reproduction (enculturation) and social revolutionary learning (system-bursting and socially critical learning). As the world of power and money are a constant threat to civil society, the forces of technical control must be made subject to the consensus of acting citizens who, in dialogue, redeem the power of reflection.

It is this logic attached to civil society that has provided North American educators such as Welton and also Collins with a ready-made critique upon which to analyse the dominance of instrumental rationality in adult education. According to Welton, critical adult education has a normative mandate to preserve the critically reflective lifeworld and extend communicative action into systemic domains (Welton 1995). The public sphere is an important pedagogical site for democratic learning, where democracy as a social movement is embedded in an ongoing effort of individuals to produce a social discourse and to ponder the implications of such a discourse for social or political action.

The aim for Habermas and adult education is not to re-embed the state and the market into the lifeworld, but instead to inoculate lifeworld values of caring, ethical concerns and democratic principles into the system, and so resist and reverse colonization. Habermas provides this critique and theoretical support for adult educators, who hope and work for a more rational society: 'the social goal toward which adult education strives is one in which all members of society may engage freely and fully in rational discourse and action without this process being subverted by the system' (Mezirow 1995: 57).

It should be pointed out, however, that civil society does not occupy the position of a utopia, and is often the location for racism, sexism, and non-inclusive ideas, a counter argument acknowledged by Habermas himself, who is all too aware of the capacity of populist movements in civil society to exhibit regressive tendencies (Habermas 1996). As a result, there is also a need to constantly renew civil society.

Communicative action, discursive democracy and adult education

In terms of adult learning theory, the influence of Habermas's argument concerning rationalization and colonization can be seen most forcefully in the work of Jack Mezirow (see this volume). While in his earlier work on his famous concept of *Perspective Transformation* Mezirow drew on *Knowledge and Human Interests* (Habermas 1971) where knowledge constitutive interests suggested to Mezirow three domains of instrumental, interpersonal and emancipatory learning (Mezirow 1978). However, in keeping with Habermas's own move away from this earlier conceptual apparatus, he has recently examined both instrumental and communicative learning and redefines emancipatory learning as pertaining to both instrumental and communicative learning (Mezirow 1996a).

> Transformative learning refers to the process by which we transform our taken-for-granted frames of reference (meaning perspectives, habits of mind, mind-sets) to make them more inclusive, discriminating, open, emotionally capable of change, and reflective so that they may generate beliefs and opinions that will prove more true or justified to guide action.
>
> (Mezirow and Associates 2000: 7–8)

In further linking with Habermas, Mezirow appropriates the idea that justification of beliefs is done through collaborative discourse. The distinctive feature of discourse is that validity claims, tacitly accepted in conversations, become subject to explicit argumentation. Validity of speech actions is questioned, and disputes over truth claims are resolved through argumentation, with the sole purpose of reaching agreement on the basis of the better argument. Mezirow identifies this as the process of transformative learning (Mezirow *et al.* 2000).

According to Mezirow, the conditions of rational discourse are also ideal conditions for effective adult learning. As such, they are crucial to educational efforts to facilitate adult learning. Participants must have accurate and complete information; freedom from coercion and distorting self-deception; openness to alternative points of view; empathy with and concern for the thoughts and feelings of others; the ability to weigh evidence and assess arguments; awareness of ideas and the ability to be critically reflective of assumptions; equal opportunity to participate in the various roles of discourse and a willingness to understand and accept agreement and accept agreed best judgments as a test of validity until new outcomes from discourse are identified (Mezirow and Associates 2000).

Habermas's abstract ideal of discursive democracy is based on the abstract ideal of a 'self-organizing community of free and equal citizens' (Habermas 1996: 7). Democracy is grounded in this right to understand our experience. Community organizations, as understood by Habermas, can serve as vehicles for critical debate and discourse.

> As learners in a democracy become aware of how taken-for-granted, oppressive, social norms and practices and institutionalized cultural ideologies have restrained or distorted their own beliefs, they become understandably motivated toward taking collective action to make social institutions and systems more responsive to the needs of those they serve.
>
> (Mezirow 1996a: 11)

This reliance on Habermas leads to the statement that it is the particular function of adult educators to create communities of collaborative discourse in which distortions in communication due to differences in power and influence are minimized. As a consequence, for Ewert, 'Education is a form of rational social action' (1991: 362). Mezirow adds:

> Transformation theory advances the argument that the nature of adult learning itself mandates participatory democracy as both the means and social goal. Following Habermas, this view identifies critical reflection, rational discourse, and praxis as central to significant adult learning and the *sine qua non* of emancipatory participation.
>
> (Mezirow 1995: 66)

One learns about democracy 'by practicing it, and we all do this when we engage in rational discourse' (Mezirow 1995: 67). Basically, an adult learning group engaging in transformative learning is a democratic society, so a democratic society is a learning society. This is a different understanding of both learning and democracy than usually proposed in the literature of lifelong learning. Transformation theory grounds its argument for an emancipatory participative democracy in the very nature of adult learning (Mezirow 1995). Freedom, community and democracy are the conditions necessary for us to understand our experience.

We learn from Habermas that there is a rational justification for seeking the means for reaching decisions in a genuinely participatory democratic manner, i.e. in a way in which ethical and aesthetic considerations are not dominated by instrumental rationality. And for adult educators the quest for emancipation is rationally justified and the basis for this resides in Habermas's account of those innate learning capacities that enable us to understand each other and the world. The need to develop communicative competence becomes a task for adult education.

Mezirow makes further use of these ideas lamenting the absence of a learning theory underpinning adult literacy (Mezirow 1996b). Critical discourse assumes communicative competence:

> literacy is centrally concerned with the crucial and neglected distinction between instrumental and communicative learning, the development of critical reflection and participation in rational discourse – all essential to adult

learning. Literacy educators and evaluators have failed to locate literacy in adult learning theory. This blind side of literacy has resulted in the reductionist fallacy of developing curricula and evaluations in terms of tasks and competencies alone.

(Mezirow 1996b: 115)

This contribution of Mezirow continues the task of mining the ideas of Habermas for critique and insight that provide a grounding for a critical pedagogy for adult education.

Conclusion

Habermas, through a number of authors, has been brought to the attention of adult educators. There are, as Connolly rightly asserts, both humanistic and radical readings of Habermas's work in adult education (Connolly 1996). Connolly concludes with the assertion that references to Habermas in adult education literature are becoming increasingly compulsory if the authors are to claim some theoretical validity. He laments the inability of many in the field to engage critically with Habermas's theories. Familiarity with these ideas involves a sustained reading of a range of abstract and complex texts and relating to theorists in a range of disciplines. Few adult educators engage with these ideas or their critique.

This will promote a greater understanding both of the merits of Habermas's theory, and of the criticisms and problems of that theory; it may also suggest ways in which these criticisms could be challenged and the problems resolved. This fuller, critical understanding is essential to a valid Habermasian-informed theorization of adult education.

(Connolly 1996: 250)

Involvement in this debate by adult educators is about involvement in the critique and grounding of the discipline of adult education itself. However, while both Collins and Welton cite non-educational critiques of Habermas, they do not address these in detail. Such critiques are important because in their detailed examination of the theoretical assumptions and interpretations which inform Habermas's macro theory, they demonstrate many problematic features of the communicative project. Rorty's critique is particularly powerful as it challenges the core belief that validity-claims raised within context-bound discussions contain a moment of universal validity (Rorty 2000). As an adult educator Plumb (1995) raises the possibility that Habermas gives a better foundation for critical adult education than Freire. He nevertheless believes that postmodernist critique of Habermas raises important questions about the normative foundations of critical theory.

Finally, Brookfield (2001) in repositioning ideology critique as the Marxist underpinnings of critical theory, emphasizes the essentially socialist underpinnings of critical adult education. In his own reaction to American adult educators' resistance to Marx he forgets that Habermas too has moved on. Brookfield redeems the Marxist roots of critical theory through the filters of Gramsci, Althusser and Horkheimer but he does not complete the project and filter these ideas through the contemporary Habermas. Brookfield does not confront the distance that Habermas has moved from the original Frankfurt School and from Horkheimer in particular.

Habermas provokes adult education theorists to rediscover a critical pedagogy beyond the self-directed and competency model of past decades and also lays down a significant challenge to understand, critique and apply these ideas in such a way that adult education engages in the elaboration of these ideas and asserts its ambition to be more than applied social studies.

References

Adams, F. and Horton, M. (1975) *Unearthing Seeds of Fire*, Winston-Salem, NC.: John F. Blair Publisher.

Bernstein, R.J. (1991) *The New Constellation: The Ethical-Political Horizons of Modernity/Postmodernity*, Cambridge, MA.: MIT Press.

Boal, A. (2000) *Theatre of the Oppressed*, London: Pluto.

Brookfield, S. (2001) 'Repositioning ideology critique in a critical theory of adult learning', *Adult Education Quarterly*, 52, 1: 7–22.

Chambers, R. (1994) *Paradigm Shifts and the Practice of Participatory Research and Development (IDS Working Paper)*, Brighton, Sussex: Institute of Development Studies.

Collins, M. (1995) 'Critical commentaries on the role of the adult educator: From self-directed learning to postmodern sensibilities', in M. Welton (ed.) *In Defense of the Lifeworld: Critical Perspectives on Adult Learning*, New York: SUNY.

Conle, C. (2001) 'The rationality of narrative inquiry in research and professional development', *European Journal of Teacher Education*, 24, 1: 21–33.

Connolly, B. (1996) 'Interpretations of Jürgen Habermas in adult education writings', *Studies in the Education of Adults*, 28, 2: 241–53.

Crowther, J., Martin, I. and Shaw, M. (eds) (1999) *Popular Education and Social Movements in Scotland Today*, Leicester: NIACE.

Duffy, K. and Scott, A. (1998) 'Viewing an old issue through a new lens: a critical theory insight into the education-practice gap', *Nurse Education Today*, 18, 3: 183–89.

Ekstrom, D. and Sigurdsson, H. (2002) 'An international collaboration in nursing education viewed through the lens of critical social theory', *Journal of Nursing Education*, 41, 7: 289–94.

Ewert, G.D. (1991) 'Habermas and education: a comprehensive overview of the influence of Habermas in educational literature', *Review of Educational Research*, 61, 3: 345–78.

Habermas, J. (1971) *Knowledge and Human Interests*, Boston: Beacon Press.

Habermas, J. (1984) *Theory of Communicative Action, Vol. 1: Reason and the Rationalization of Society*, Boston: Beacon Press.

Habermas, J. (1985) 'Questions and counter questions', in R.J. Bernstein (ed.) *Habermas and Modernity*, Cambridge, MA.: MIT Press.

Habermas, J. (1987) *Theory of Communicative Action, Vol. 2: Lifeworld and System: A Critique of Functionalist Reason*, Boston: Beacon Press.

Habermas, J. (1989) *The Structural Transformation of the Public Sphere: An inquiry into a Category of Bourgeois Society*, Cambridge, MA.: MIT Press.

Habermas, J. (1996) *Between Facts and Norms: Contributions to a Discourse Theory of Law and Democracy*, Cambridge, MA.: MIT.

Harris, C. (2002) 'Imagining the good organization: educational restructuring in a coastal community', *Educational Management and Administration*, 30, 1: 65–82.

Hope, A. and Timmell C. (1999) *Training for Transformation: a Handbook for Community Workers: Books 1, 2, 3 & 4*, Rugby, Warwickshire: ITDG Publishers.

Horkheimer, M. and Adorno, T. (1972) *Dialectic of Enlightenment*, New York: The Seabury Press.

Matuštik, M.B. (2001) *Jürgen Habermas: A Philosophical-Political Profile*, Oxford: Rowman & Littlefield.

Mezirow, J. (1978) 'Perspective transformation', *Adult Education*, 28, 2: 100–10.

Mezirow, J. (1995) 'Transformation theory of adult learning', in M. Welton (ed.) *In Defense of the Lifeworld: Critical Perspectives on Adult Learning*, New York: SUNY.

Mezirow, J. (1996a) 'Adult education and empowerment for individual and community development', in B. Connolly, T. Fleming, D. McCormack and A. Ryan, (eds) *Radical Learning for Liberation*, Maynooth: MACE.

Mezirow, J. (1996b) 'Towards a learning theory of adult literacy', *Adult Basic Education*, 6, 3: 115–27.

Mezirow, J. and Associates (2000) *Learning as Transformation: Critical Perspectives on a Theory in Progress*, San Francisco: Jossey-Bass.

Morrow, R.A. and Torres, C.A. (2002) *Reading Freire and Habermas: Critical Pedagogy and Transformative Social Change*, New York: Teachers College Press.

O'Donnell, D. (1999) 'Habermas, critical theory and selves-directed learning', *Journal of European Industrial Training*, 23, 4–5: 251–61.

Plumb, D. (1995) 'Declining opportunities: adult education, culture and postmodernity', in M. Welton (ed.) *In Defense of the Lifeworld Critical Perspectives on Adult Learning*, New York: SUNY.

Rorty, R. (2000) 'Universality and truth', in R.B. Brandom (ed.) *Rorty and his Critics*, London: Blackwell.

Ryan, J. (1998) 'Critical leadership for education in a postmodern world: emancipation, resistance and communal action', *International Journal of Leadership in Education*, 1, 3: 257–78.

Sumner, J. (2000) 'Serving the system: a critical history of distance education', *Open Learning*, 15, 3: 267–85.

Welton, M. (2001) 'Civil Society and the public sphere: Habermas's recent learning theory', *Studies in the Education of Adults*, 33, 1: 20–35.

Welton, M. (ed.) (1995) *In Defense of the Lifeworld: Critical Perspectives on Adult Learning*, New York: SUNY.

Whipp, J., Ferguson, D., Wells, L. and Iacopino, A. (2000) 'Rethinking knowledge and pedagogy in dental education', *Journal of Dental Education*, 64, 12: 860–66.

Chapter 6

A troubled space of possibilities

Lifelong learning and the postmodern

Richard Edwards and Robin Usher

Adult education in the context of postmodernity may have lost some of its foundational certainties but it has also enabled a fuller range of adult learning practices to emerge. In this context lifelong learning has become a powerful resource for challenging traditional educational boundaries and institutions. Lifelong learning helps us imagine and value different sources and forms of knowledge which occur outside designated educational spaces. Who controls learning, what it means, what constitutes a curriculum are subject to 'incredulity' and doubt. In the postmodern condition of education these signal a specific attitude or approach to engage with authoritative claims to know and the canonical status of modernist knowledge claims, and the illusive search for mastery. Lifelong learning is implicated in this postmodern condition which, the authors argue, is opening up (as well as closing down) ambivalent spaces for learning.

Introduction

During the last fifteen years there has been much debate about the significance of postmodern framings for theorizing, researching and practising the education of adults. These framings have taken a variety of forms across a spectrum ranging from enthusiastic support to outright hostility. For some, the postmodern is part of the globalization of capitalist economic relations and the growth of post-industrial and consumer-oriented social formations within an information-rich environment enabled by new technologies (Harvey 1989). For others, it is a form of analysis associated with post-structuralism and deconstruction that brings to the fore the place of language and discourse and the challenging of foundational certainties in thought and action (Lemert 1997). Some view it as promoting individualism and lifestyle practices, linked to a revitalized neo-liberalism, marketized structures and a consumer society (Featherstone 1991). Others argue that it provides a space for radical and emancipatory politics associated with 'new' social movements and the bringing to the fore of issues of gender, 'race', ethnicity and sexuality, where the possibility is provided for practices free from the totalizing discourse of the traditional left (Ellsworth 1997). We ourselves have played a role in these debates (Usher and Edwards 1994), arguing for some of the ways in which postmodern framings in general and specific post-structuralist analyses can open different spaces and spaces of difference for investigation. These are suggestive of alternative, if less certain, perspectives to those embedded in neo-liberal, humanistic or radical theories of adult education. We would certainly want to argue that, at the very least, the postmodern has provided a space for the development of social imaginaries productive of a multiplicity and diversity of meanings and possibilities, through which to make sense of and engage with contemporary trends and processes, including those of lifelong learning.

However, we have also been unhappy about the nature of some of the debate to which we have contributed. There is a certain tilting at windmills, as those advocating a postmodern framing 'set up' a certain view of modernity against which to 'test' their alternative and vice versa. This is perhaps unsurprising, as the rhetorical strategies at play in academic debate can tend towards a polarization of positions rather than a subtle exploration and teasing out of the various issues within a complex, layered and sometimes unfamiliar landscape. Thus, for instance, Lyotard, who was the first to outline a specifically postmodern condition of knowledge, argued that a 'work can become modern only if it is first postmodern. Thus understood, postmodernism is not modernism at its end, but in a nascent state, and this state is recurrent' (1992: 22). This suggests a far more nuanced view of the postmodern condition than is often provided by advocates and detractors alike – a view which we ourselves would readily endorse.

The location of adult education within a postmodern landscape is a troubled one (Usher *et al.* 1997; Edwards 1997). However, for us, the important thing is that the postmodern provides a conceptual and practical space for understanding and engaging with a fuller range of adult learning practices without the privileging of certain pre-defined goals and purposes, or the positioning of certain bodies of knowledge as inherently worthwhile. It is this space that opens up possibilities for recognizing adult education as encompassing the multiplicity and diversity of adult learning practices that are such a striking characteristic of the contemporary scene and are themselves suggestive of a postmodern condition.

This is particularly the case, given that over the same period as debates about the postmodern have taken place – and not coincidentally – 'lifelong learning' has emerged as a potent way of framing policy and practice in many countries around the globe. These policies and practices have been diverse and in most countries are still in the process of development. However, there would be considerable agreement with the argument that lifelong learning is providing a strategy through which post-school education and training, including the education of adults, and potentially all education, is being and is likely to continue to be reshaped. This reshaping is often framed within discourses of modernization and renewal rather than more traditional notions of reform, itself signifying a future-orientated approach within which are embedded certain economic, political and social imaginaries. Here the shift towards a concern to encourage individuals to become lifelong learners is part of a wider shift whereby governments 'empower' their populations to become 'active citizens' and more responsible for their own life courses (Field 2000).

Under the sign of lifelong learning institutionalized education at all levels is becoming increasingly more diverse in terms of goals, processes, organizational structures, curricula and pedagogy. This both reflects and contributes to a breakdown and re-inscription, in different forms, of clear and settled demarcations between different sectors of education and between education and the lifeworld. Lifelong learning is a manifestation of and contributor to this de- and re-differentiation, now increasingly seen as a goal to be pursued by education across the board rather than by a specific sector or through a particular curriculum. This spreading epidemic of lifelong learning has meant that institutionalized education can no longer claim a monopoly over knowledge production and assessment on the grounds that it is a formally constituted field or through its role in epistemological policing. Both its authority and power are now subject to question. Once learning starts to become recognized as located in a variety and diversity of social practices outside the institutional, a greater multiplicity of activities are now seen as involving learning and hence can be deemed 'educational'.

What this implies is that lifelong learning is not simply a term for a policy or mode of provision. Additionally, and perhaps more importantly, it can be understood as a metaphor that brings to the fore the boundlessness of learning. The metaphor 'lifelong learning' alerts us to a way of imagining learning as without boundaries even though there has been a strong attempt to impose boundaries on lifelong learning practices. Simultaneously, we want to argue that this way of seeing brings out the ambivalence that locates its postmodern condition. However, what is common is that the various phenomena subsumable under the heading 'lifelong learning', located in different discourses and played out through different social practices, signifies learning that could be inside or outside educational institutions, and not necessarily bounded by what educators would traditionally define as the transmission of 'appropriate' and/or 'worthwhile' knowledge. As such, we want to suggest – echoing Lyotard's (1984) argument regarding a postmodern condition of knowledge – that lifelong learning can be viewed as a postmodern condition of education, where this implies a diversity of practices, including an enfolding within modernist educational practices.

Our intention in the rest of this chapter is to specifically address and position lifelong learning as a postmodern condition of education. First, we locate lifelong learning within the framing of the postmodern condition, in particular the analysis offered by Lyotard (1984), with its consequences for knowledge and education. We draw upon Lyotard because of our concern to relate our discussion to the significant texts of the postmodern and because of his pivotal role in framing specifically the notion of a postmodern condition. Second, drawing on work influenced by Nietzsche, a philosopher whose work is echoed in post-structuralist framings, we wish to locate lifelong learning as a contemporary challenge to the notion of 'mastery' embedded in certain modernist views of education. Here we are pointing to the problematic status of the 'newness' associated with some renditions of the postmodern, as philosophically many of the ideas have a history of their own. The final section points towards the reflexive challenges of the practices in which we are engaged, subject to the processes outlined in this chapter, even as we attempt to engage in social theory that is 'speculative, without being teleological' (Adam and van Loon 2000: 11).

The paradox of performativity and decentring

The postmodern is at one and the same time an aspect of a changed and changing contemporary world and a way of understanding those changes. Reflexively, there is the attempt to provide a discourse for the world it seeks to describe and explain, a discourse that highlights notions of decentring, ambivalence and contingency, and that interlinks with the thrust of postmodernity in a socio-cultural and economic sense. The assumption is that the contemporary world is changing in different ways and that these require alternative modes of understanding and meaning-making. The very ambivalence of these changes requires more ambivalent and modest, if rhetorically powerful, forms of understanding, particularly ones that are not enmeshed in binary modes and teleological framings.

In his work on the changing condition of knowledge, Lyotard (1984) argued that the grand narratives of modernity – the narratives of emancipation through scientific truth and social progress – no longer have the ability to compel consensus in quite the same ways as in earlier times. Whilst not rejected – an important point that is often overlooked – they are increasingly greeted with 'incredulity' and understood as masterful narratives and narratives of mastery. Their relative decline in influence and power has also thrown into doubt the subaltern narratives they have helped to shape, including the narratives that frame the modernist educational project. Modernist master signifiers then are generally seen as no longer quite as masterful – even if they remain powerful – as the effects they produce are seen not to have produced the progress and emancipation promised, or at least, too often have come at an unacceptable cost.

It is this incredulity towards modernist claims to mastery that characterizes the postmodern condition of knowledge. As such, the postmodern does not represent the passing away or the replacement of the modern, but rather a particular form of (en)counter with it. Incredulity and doubt are widespread, encompassing a questioning of any foundation or authorizing centre and thus a scepticism that certain kinds of knowledge have canonical status – that some knowledge is *intrinsically* worthwhile – whether this knowledge be conservative or critical. The authority invested in certain groupings – the universities, scientific communities, professional bodies, government – is often treated with suspicion and scepticism. There is a diversification of modes, centres and sources of knowledge production and of social actor positions. The result is less certainty as to what constitutes authoritative discourse and who can speak authoritatively on and as a subject. Even as some governments look to the research community to provide them with evidence to inform policy and practice, those communities are less capable of giving clear messages or directions. This questioning of foundations and authorizing centres is itself a form of decentring.

In this situation, lifelong learning becomes a significant technology – of production, power, self and sign system (Foucault 1988) – helping to bring about the very uncertainty to which it is positioned as a response. However, as well as functioning as a technology, lifelong learning needs to be located in the contemporary 'society of signs' (Edwards and Usher 1999). The significance of signifying practices in contemporary society involves forms of learning that barely feature in mainstream discourses of a learning society. Traditional forms of and rationales for pedagogy are subverted by, for instance, the spread of electronically mediated networks of learning. Who controls learning and indeed what constitutes a curriculum, a learning text and a classroom become ever more problematic and contested. Lifelong learning is a way of framing and concretizing this multiplicity and diversity, even whilst at the same time contributing to it.

Postmodern incredulity and the decentring of authoritative knowledge positions have paradoxical educational consequences. On the one hand, they contribute to an erosion of the liberal curriculum and curiosity-driven research. There is an emphasis on learning and knowledge production oriented to what Lyotard (1984) termed 'performativity' – learning that seeks to optimize the efficiency and effectiveness of the economic and social system. On the other hand, however, postmodern incredulity and the decentring of knowledge results in a valuing of different sources and forms of knowledge and a corresponding devaluing of discipline-based knowledge.

With performativity, the modernist educational project of progress and emancipation is reconstructed in terms of economic modernization and 'empowerment'. The educational task becomes one of producing the knowledge specifically needed by, and those with the skills indispensable to, the dominant globalizing processes. Here, performativity is located within wider discursive practices of economic globalization, neo-liberal economics and market competitiveness. Lifelong learning becomes seen as the means of attaining and maintaining the flexibility that is considered necessary in meeting the technological and socio-economic change required. Learning is the condition of flexibility and flexibility is seen as the condition of learning. One cannot stop learning, not only in relation to work, but also in relation to life more generally. Thus, lifelong learning becomes integral to the discourses and practices of business. At the same time and in response to this context, educational institutions themselves seek to commodify and manage learning and knowledge production by becoming more business-like, corporatist and consumer-oriented. Managerial discourse and a logic of accountability, innovation and excellence come to dominate providers of learning opportunities.

However, as we have said, there is more in play here. Stronach and MacLure (1997) argue that the contemporary scene is characterized by a certain 'unruliness' of knowledge. Once knowledge is no longer an end in itself, its production and transmission ceases to be the exclusive responsibility of researchers and teachers. It becomes, as it were, 'up for grabs' epistemologically and within diverse contexts of practice. Hence its 'unruliness' – relatively undisciplined and 'without rules'. Subjects (in the sense of bodies of disciplinary and canonical knowledge) and their transmission seem less significant in relation to curriculum developments such as work-based learning, and the development of new skills and capacities such as generic and transferable skills, multi-disciplinarity, multi-literacies and transcoding. In this situation, experiential, informal and community-based learning all become legitimate sources, settings and forms of learning, including those engaged in through the consumer market. Ironically, therefore, the postmodern condition of knowledge provides a situation in which the established arguments of adult educators that lifelong learning is lifewide can take hold, even if not quite in the same ways as once would have been envisioned.

Another aspect of this paradox in the postmodern condition is traceable to the impact of the information and communications technologies (ICTs) that are such a recognized cause of this condition. Through the Internet, e-mail, CD-Roms, etc., possibilities are presented for individuals to access information, interact with it, and thus learn more flexibly and without the need to attend institutional centres or designated spaces of learning. This can result in a commodification of knowledge (Lyotard 1984) with an emphasis on delivering online learning in 'bite-sized chunks' to people's workstations when they have a moment to learn – a phenomenon found in the developing corporate universities. Here ICTs enhance the performativity of learning. However, computer-mediated-communication (CMC) can also bring people together across space and time and produce different geographies of learning, practice and politics. They provide opportunities for distributed forms of learning that are nonetheless collaborative. With the problematizing and, some would argue, breakdown in the hierarchy of, and the very distinction between, knowledge and information and with more people engaging in learning in diverse settings through ICTs and CMC, there is a further and accelerating decentring of authority and knowledge, even though in specific contexts there may be very strict rules governing what is learnt and continuing assertions of authority.

The paradox, therefore, is that the very demands of performativity have themselves contributed to 'unruliness' by subverting the very notion of knowledge as something that has to be validated by a 'scientific' epistemology. In this sense, performativity has the paradoxical result of simultaneously closing and opening possibilities. Performativity therefore – like lifelong learning and the postmodern of which it is an aspect – has multiple significations and significances. It contributes to both the strengthening and loosening of boundaries, to both an economy of the same and to an economy of difference. It is within these interlocking and inter-related economies that the lifelong learner is now (dis)located. It is these paradoxes that mark the complexity of a postmodern condition.

Without mastery?

The uncertainty of the epistemological markers for knowledge that characterizes a postmodern condition and the requirement for lifelong learning can be argued to signify a loss of mastery as a goal of education. Yet mastery is inscribed in modernist educational discourse. Education is a central modern practice, developing alongside and as part of the modern – Western, liberal, capitalist – nation state. Modernist education provides a training in certain forms of rationality, sensibilities, values and subjectivities. Through this comes a disembodying of learners with a consequent formation of bodies that inscribes a mind/body dualism in its place. Foucault (1979) points to the training of 'docile bodies' that takes place in modern disciplinary institutions, yet it is the training of the mind that is the focus of modern educational discourse. Here the more educated you are, the more rational and the more 'civilized'. The extension of education and educational opportunities is both a symbol of progress in a modern nation state and contributes to progress through the education provided. Clearly, there are discourses of lifelong learning that are still located in this educational paradigm.

Mastery of the 'subject' (in both senses) is a key educational goal. One becomes an educated person, attends finishing school, gains a Masters degree, becomes a master-craftsperson, masters a body of disciplinary knowledge and in so doing 'masters' oneself by enthroning reason and the mind. Each is a form of completion, an end to learning. Embedded in this, the very language of education, is a gendered view of knowledge and the world. In mastering a subject (knowledge), one is able to master subjects in the sense of both self and others. Even as modernist education attempts to develop the rational, the suppressed emotional and erotic embedded in its discourses continues to surface (McWilliam 1999). We can see that there are many dimensions to the notion of mastery in modernist education and, even as it points to a position of finality and closure, we can point to the oppositions and incompleteness to which it is subject. Mastery of the subject and subjects and self-mastery themselves become subject to incredulity. There is an incredulity as to the possibility of mastering and managing the modernist project, even as ever greater attempts are made to regulate, discipline and administer. Thus, the attempts at mastery – increasingly inscribed in discourses of standards and targets – only point to the inability to master.

Nor is this all entirely new. Modernity's rush to the new in the service of progress and truth has always produced uncertainty, insecurity and ambivalence. This was recognized in the classic analyses and critiques by Marx, Durkheim, Weber and many more contemporary sociological accounts. However, such accounts have often sought to find resolutions through which mastery could be reasserted and ambivalence and uncertainty overcome. In other words, implicit to the critique of modernity has been the failure to master, not that mastery itself is problematic and unobtainable.

What certain postmodern framings do is surface the ambivalence of the contemporary. These framings enable a critique of those over-arching or totalizing schemes that fabricate progress as linear and inevitable. At the same time, they also surface and problematize the exclusions and oppressions that these inscribe. Hence the growing importance of gender, race, disability, sexual orientation alongside class in adult educational discourses. There is a recognition of the productiveness of difference rather than its assertion only as a justification for oppression and exclusion. This productiveness is fundamental to Lyotard's notions of justice and paralogy – the creative destabilizing of performative language games – as oppositional to the emergence of a disciplined and disciplining society. The more interesting postmodern writing therefore seeks to critically, if sometimes playfully, engage with the messiness and complexity of the contemporary condition, part of which is the incredulity towards mastery as an achievable goal. It is this that is inscribed, if not always very obviously, in the epidemic of lifelong learning. Here the playfulness is itself a recognition of the lack of mastery in the engagement.

Lifelong learning has many significations. For educators there has been a tendency to see 'lifelong learning' only as a set of transcendental principles that they have formulated and which they relate to a set of cognitive processes inherent in all learners. By focusing only on this signification they have failed to locate lifelong learning in contemporary social developments and in so doing have not only failed to recognize its multiple significations but also failed to embrace issues of mastery. Social practices involve attempts at mastery with lifelong learning the means to achieve this. Yet in each case the search for mastery is sourced in a lack of mastery. Furthermore, lifelong learning, whilst an unavoidable activity, does not remedy this lack, but actually accentuates it further. So the lack of mastery creates the conditions for the endlessness for lifelong learning.

Thus, while there is no doubting the modernist thrust in much of the discourse, policy and practice surrounding lifelong learning, nor the powerful effects of a postmodern, performative condition, both articulate a form of certainty. However, each is premised on the uncertainty, insecurity and ambivalence that is a characteristic of a postmodern condition. Change and uncertainty seem to require lifelong learning with 'lifelong learning' itself a signifier of the uncertainty and change characteristic of this condition. Thus, rather than being a solution to the problem of change and uncertainty – a condition of mastery – lifelong learning can be therefore understood differently – as actually fuelling the uncertainty to which it is the supposed response. Lifelong learning here becomes not a condition of modernist mastery but rather of postmodernist ambivalence, of the attempt at mastery and the failure of that attempt. It is not, as many would see it, a secure ground upon which to stand, but is better understood as a process of constant travelling that is never completed and where destinations are always uncertain and constantly changing. Rather than a route to mastery, lifelong learning might be better considered a condition of constant apprenticeship (Rikowski 1999) – but one that is mobile, flexible and adaptable. Here, the traditional notion of the apprentice working towards mastery with a 'master' in the field is reconfigured, giving way to a different relationship where the masters themselves are also subject to lifelong learning and continuing (professional) development. This is not to deny the continuing need for novices to be trained by the suitably proficient. Rather what it points to is that one never masters completely and there is no end to the search for mastery. Proficiency is never final or complete. It is unsurprising therefore that continuing professional development has grown as an area of practice as postmodern incredulity has enveloped education as well as other modern institutions and practices.

Lifelong learning: a postmodern condition of education?

In this chapter, we have examined some of the contours and ravines in the landscape of the postmodern and lifelong learning. For us, lifelong learning and a postmodern condition are implicated with each other in the incredulity, performativity, decentring and lack of mastery that they manifest and to which they point. Yet there is a many-sidedness to this, not least because we do not see the postmodern and modern as polar opposites, but as layered and enfolded in complex ways.

There is a paradox here of course, as in naming lifelong learning in the way we have we are in danger of providing a universal and totalizing explanation of its significance, thereby gaining mastery of its 'true' meaning, even as we problematize such explanations. Indeed there might be said to be tension between the content of this chapter and the rhetoric through which we aim to persuade and influence. Suggesting lifelong learning is part of a postmodern condition of education is a very definite stance, despite any hedging in which we might engage. No doubt we have more to learn, as we too have not attained mastery of the subject. Lifelong learning like the analysis prompted by a postmodern condition opens up a range of spaces and as Stronach and MacLure (1997) suggest, any opening depends upon the closings that make the opening possible. We believe that in positioning lifelong learning as part of a postmodern condition of education we can engage with, and be engaged by, those openings/closings and the ambivalence and troubled possibilities they provide. Here we position ourselves with Bauman (1991) who writes that rather than, as is the case in modernity, knowledge overcoming ignorance, in a postmodern condition what we (en)counter is the growth of knowledge expanding the field of ignorance, and with each step towards the horizon new unknown landscapes appear. Lifelong learning as travel and, no doubt, travail.

Note

A longer version of this chapter was originally published as Edwards, R. and Usher, R. (2001) 'Lifelong learning: a postmodern condition of knowledge?', *Adult Education Quarterly*, 51, 4: 273–87.

References

Adam, B. and van Loon, J. (2000) 'Introduction: repositioning risk; the challenge for social theory', in B. Adam, U. Beck and J. van Loon (eds) *The Risk Society and Beyond: Critical Issues for Social Theory*, London: Sage.
Bauman, Z. (1991) *Modernity and Ambivalence*, Cambridge: Polity Press.

Edwards, R. (1997) *Changing Places? Flexibility, Lifelong Learning and a Learning Society*, London: Routledge.

Edwards, R. and Usher, R. (1999) 'A society of signs? Mediating a learning society', *British Journal of Educational Studies*, 47, 3: 261–74.

Ellsworth, E. (1997) *Teaching Positions: Difference, Pedagogy, and the Power of Address*, New York: Teachers College Press.

Featherstone, M. (1991) *Consumer Culture and Postmodernism*, London: Sage.

Field, J. (2000) 'Governing the ungovernable: why lifelong learning policies promise so much yet deliver so little', *Educational Management and Administration*, 28, 3: 249–61.

Foucault, M. (1979) *Discipline and Punish: the Birth of the Prison*, Harmondsworth: Penguin.

Foucualt, M. (1988) 'Technologies of the self', in L. Martin, H. Gutman and P. Hutton (eds) *Technologies of the Self*, Amherst: University of Massachusetts.

Harvey, D. (1989) *The Condition of Postmodernity*, Oxford: Basil Blackwell.

Lemert, C. (1997) *Postmodernism Is Not What You Think*, Oxford: Basil Blackwell.

Lyotard, J-F. (1984) *The Postmodern Condition: a Report on Knowledge*, Manchester: Manchester University Press.

Lyotard, J-F. (1992) *The Postmodern Explained to Children: Correspondence 1982–1984*, London: Turnaround.

McWilliam, E. (1999) *Pedagogical Pleasures*, New York: Peter Lang.

Rikowski, G. (1999) 'Nietzsche, Marx and mastery: the learning unto death', in P. Ainley and H. Rainbird (eds) *Apprenticeship: Towards a New Paradigm for Learning*, London: Kogan Page.

Stronach, I. and MacLure, M. (1997) *Educational Research Undone: the Postmodern Embrace*, Buckingham: Open University Press.

Usher, R. and Edwards, R. (1994) *Postmodernism and Education*, London: Routledge.

Usher, R., Bryant, I. and Johnston, R. (1997) *Adult Education and the Postmodern Challenge*, London: Routledge.

Part II

Institutions and issues for lifelong learning

Chapter 7

Realizing a lifelong learning higher education institution

Shirley Walters

Activists and scholars committed to lifelong learning for social justice and democratic citizenship have devised a framework for transforming higher education in the new South Africa. The author draws on this work, developed at the University of the Western Cape, to examine the extent to which her own institution is addressing the challenges it presents. The former context of apartheid has left a legacy where few black and poor people – particularly women – have had experience of higher education. To realize the potential of lifelong learning in an emancipatory narrative requires an awareness of issues for change for individuals and organizations. Ultimately, it involves challenging ideas and assumptions about identity, pedagogy, epistemology and power relations.

Introduction

Higher education policy in many parts of the world, at institutional, national and international levels, is peppered with references to lifelong learning. *The World Declaration on Higher Education for the Twenty-first Century: Vision and Action* (UNESCO 1999) has at least seven direct references to lifelong learning and an equal number of indirect ones. Higher education is responding to a new discourse of lifelong learning born in the 1990s. As Bourgeois *et al.* (1999: 173) state, 'the new lifelong learning combines old and abiding concerns about equity, with emphasis upon higher education as a means to equip for employment and for survival in conditions of uncertainty and loss of security in employment'. Still more recently, scepticism has grown about the official and political adoption of lifelong learning, as furthering the interests of a rampant neo-liberal economic agenda (Crowther 2004).

Within higher education there are scholars and activists who are concerned particularly with the equity and social justice dimensions of lifelong learning who are striving to realize lifelong learning higher education institutions (HEIs). They are undertaking organizational, pedagogical and political work to help move from symbolic policies of lifelong learning, that remain at the rhetorical level, to ones which become embedded practice within institutions.

This chapter explores what it means to realize a lifelong learning higher education institution by using a framework, *The Cape Town Statement on Characteristic*

Elements of a Lifelong Learning Higher Education Institution (DLL 2001) to describe and analyse what is happening in one institution. I focus on the University of Western Cape in South Africa (UWC), where I have been involved for twenty years as a champion of adult and lifelong learning, in order both to assess the value of the framework and to highlight key issues and challenges. UWC is a historically black, urban university based in South Africa, which is a middle-income country recently emerged from a protracted liberation struggle. The country's re-entry into the global economy is heightening the tensions between economic development, equity and redress. As such South Africa, and its higher education institutions, is both a mirror reflecting these processes and a lens through which to examine them. The chapter will begin with a description of the framework and will then move onto its application to UWC.

Characteristic elements of lifelong learning higher education institutions

Higher education within a lifelong learning framework and approach is quite new (Volbrecht and Walters 2000). Lifelong learning assumes multiple meanings and interpretations. It is a contested concept that is not always seen as 'a good thing'. As Taylor *et al.* (2002) state, lifelong learning is seen variously as concerned essentially with vocationalism and performativity, social control and incorporation, pluralistic complexity within a post-modern framework, personal development and growth, and radical social purpose and community development.

A group of international scholars and activists within higher education developed an organizational framework to assist them in the realization of their mission to develop lifelong learning for active and democratic citizenship. They did so at a meeting in Cape Town in 2000, co-hosted by the UNESCO Institute for Education, the Danish Pedagogical University, and UWC, to grapple with 'Lifelong learning, higher education and active citizenship'. They agreed that potentially education:

> connects individuals and groups to the structures of social, political and economic activity in both local and global contexts, and emphasizes women and men as agents of their own history in all aspects of their lives.

And the working definition of lifelong learning is that:

> it enables students to learn at different times, in different ways, for different purposes at various stages of their lives and careers. Lifelong learning is concerned with providing learning opportunities throughout life, while developing lifelong learners.

> (DLL 2001: 4)

It is concerned with both flexible, convenient, relevant provision of learning opportunities and with curricula that promote lifelong learning qualities. Lifelong learning is 'lifelong, life wide and life deep' (DLL 2001: 4). In these terms, they recognized that implementing lifelong learning assumes the need for major pedagogical, organizational and social changes.

The Cape Town Statement (DLL 2001: 6) describes six useful 'Characteristics elements' that have guided the work at UWC and elsewhere (Dunlop and Nesbit 2004). See Table 7.1 below.

These broad categories indicate a systemic awareness of the interconnections between the macro-environment, the meso-organizational context and the micro cognitive and affective learning interactions. A lifelong learning framework forces our gaze both inwards towards individual and organizational learning and outwards towards relationships in the broader society (Volbrecht and Walters 2000).

Changing the culture and the practices within higher education institutions is a daunting task. The literature which refers to the struggle to create adult-focused universities is illustrative of this. Bourgeois *et al.* (1999) argue that the 'struggle for adultification' requires a combination of 'successful actor strategies in decision- and policy-making', and 'conducive conditions related to organizational structure and context'. They too emphasize the interconnectedness of the macro, meso and micro levels both within the institution itself and reflecting the institution's place in the broader society.

Table 7.1 Characteristic elements of the Cape Town Statement

Characteristic	Description
Overarching frameworks	Overarching frameworks provide the context which facilitates an HEI to operate as a lifelong learning . institution. These are: regulatory, financial and cultural/social.
Strategic partnerships and linkages	Partnerships and linkages include the following: forming relationships internationally; forming relationships with other institutions; forming relationships within institutions; and forming relationships with other groups in society.
Research	Research is understood in a broad sense and includes working across disciplines and/or across institutions. Lifelong learning is regarded as an important and legitimate focus for research activity.
Teaching and learning	Educators encourage self-directed learning and engage with the knowledge, interests and life situations that learners bring to their education and use open and resource-based learning approaches.
Administration policies and mechanisms	Service to students is the top priority of the administration.
Student support systems and services	Learners are supported to become independent learners in various ways.

Realizing the lifelong learning mission

I turn now to a reflection of the process of realizing the lifelong learning mission at UWC with the help of the framework. Organizationally the lifelong learning mission at UWC is driven by a small cross-cutting structure, the Division for Lifelong Learning (DLL), which reports to the Academic Vice-Rector, and which is represented on the Senate Executive and other high level committees. This has been the catalyst for ongoing advocacy and implementation of the mission and is a key 'actor' in the project. While the DLL has been working from the centre to support faculties and advocate for new practices, the implementation occurs primarily in the faculties. The relationships amongst the DLL, faculties and central administration are not uncontested as debates continue about whether there is a need for a central catalytic agency, with some feeling that the lifelong learning mission has been sufficiently 'mainstreamed' and others arguing that without the DLL the mission would 'lose its way'.

Overarching frameworks

Conducive conditions are needed in order to realize a lifelong learning institution. So what are these? What are the regulatory, financial, cultural, historical, legislative frameworks which encourage or discourage the implementation of lifelong learning practices? Is there consensus on a working definition of lifelong learning?

Working definition of lifelong learning

There is no consistent or elaborated use of the term lifelong learning in the various government policy documents in South Africa. It can be interpreted at one end of a spectrum to mean continuing professional education and, at the other end, it can imply major pedagogical and organizational shifts. It can also be primarily seen as relating only to mature learners or to all learners. Within UWC, as Bourgeois *et al.* (1999) mention, the old and abiding concerns about equity and redress exist, along with those about employment and survival in conditions of uncertainty and loss of security. While the working definition from the Cape Town Statement has been adopted in official documents at UWC, the definition of lifelong learning itself is contested and is debated and discussed continuously. It cannot be assumed that there is consensus on the definition.

Cultural/Social context

Realizing lifelong learning HEIs means that organizational cultures need to change. In South Africa as elsewhere, the picture that holds many institutions captive is still that of a lecturer speaking or reading to a class of young adults. This is true too at UWC despite the fact that about 22 per cent of the 14,000 students are part-time, many work, and the majority of all students are women who are on average 27 years old, and are poor. The challenge of changing this dominant picture can be seen, for example, in the debates and practices of widening access to HEIs for 'non-traditional students' and 'non-traditional ways of learning' even where they are in the majority (Schuetze and Slowey 2000). In addition, Bourgeois *et al.* (1999) remind us of the resilience of the status accorded to 'research' as opposed to 'teaching' universities. Lifelong learning institutions by definition are concerned with learning and teaching; will they therefore by definition have lower status?

It is important to locate the decision taken in 1998 to set up the DLL to drive the lifelong learning mission in the UWC context of the time. Student numbers had been falling consistently and there were predictions of a headcount of 6000 students in 1999. Over 40 academics were retrenched in June of that year and the trade union was on strike to resist the laying off of their members. There were crisis meetings of Senate and a proposed vote of no confidence in the Rector was narrowly averted. There were major changes amongst executive leadership with several temporary appointees. It is fair to say that the institution was in crisis.

In the broader policy environment there was a flurry of activity on almost all education and training fronts, including the establishment of the South African Qualifications Authority (SAQA) and the emergence of the national skills development strategy. These held the promise of rapid growth in workplace learning possibilities and facilitation of access and flexibility in the education and training systems. Simultaneously UWC's history resonated with the institutional and national commitment to lifelong learning as it prided itself on its contribution to the liberation struggle and its distinctive academic role in helping achieve equity and social justice for the black majority.

It was at this time of crisis and national re-configuration that the DLL was set up. A major concern was to increase student numbers, while contributing to equity, and it was argued that part-time and continuing education students should be targeted, new marketing strategies implemented, and quality and types of services and support be improved. In early 1999, it was decided that the DLL was to focus initially on helping stem the tide of diminishing numbers; therefore emphasis was placed on marketing the university and on access, particularly recognition of prior learning (RPL). While the issues of improving quality were seen as crucial, the imperative of the time was student numbers.

At UWC these strategies are contributing to changing perceptions but the broader national context is critical to the creation of a conducive environment. As I describe elsewhere (Walters 2004), the *National Plan for Higher Education* prioritizes the need to broaden the social base of higher education by increasing access to higher education of workers and professionals in pursuit of multi-skilling and re-skilling, and of adult learners denied access in the past. They propose to promote RPL initiatives to increase the intake of adult learners. The major structural shifts in the economy over the last twenty-five years, the endemic shortage of high-level professional and managerial skills, and the impact of HIV/AIDS on the labour force, has ensured that there is recognition of the significant need for continuing education of workers. In addition, the inadequate numbers of school-leavers with the necessary entry requirements mean that the demands for higher education graduates in the economy have to be met by ensuring adult learners gain access. Generations of black people and women were excluded from higher education for either political or economic reasons. There has been a push from individuals, organized labour and government to ensure redress for those who were excluded from access to higher education and it is beginning to have an uneven effect (Cooper and Subotzky 2001).

While the policy rhetoric supports adult and lifelong learning there are various signals that lead to a questioning of its substantive nature. For example, it is interesting to note that while the National Plan sets participation targets for the 18–24-year-olds there are no similar targets for adult learners. There are examples of a disjuncture between the policy goal of widening access to non-traditional students and government practices.

In South Africa, while the reality has been that the historically black institutions have run extensive part-time programmes for working adults, one of the paradoxes is that it is difficult to obtain statistics on the age of students and the numbers and profiles of part-time students. This lack of data possibly reflects both the state of the statistical database of the system as a whole and also the lack of appreciation for the importance of age as a necessary social category to assist planning. At UWC over the last seven years there has been ongoing advocacy to recognize this but such data is still not presented as a matter of course. While this may be indicative of the resilience of 'youth culture' that pervades higher education, the demographic reality in the country is that 45 per cent of people are under 19 years of age and there is high youth unemployment.

The issue of age also raises the important definitional question of lifelong learning. Often lifelong learning is equated with adult learning and it does not emphasize the second part of the definition within the Cape Town Statement which relates to 'developing lifelong learners', which is critical to the education of students of all ages. At UWC there has been a tendency for advocacy of lifelong learning to be weighted towards those who are older, working and part-time students. As Candy et al. (1994) elaborated in their research, the curricula and the pedagogy used for all students either aids or hinders the possibilities for developing lifelong learners. It is therefore important to challenge the notion that lifelong learning is only relevant to 'older', 'mature' or 'non-traditional' learners.

Financial frameworks

In several countries, there is the paradoxical situation that there is acceptance of lifelong learning as a preferred approach, but the national frameworks for funding and student loan schemes work against part-time or older learners, and by implication, women. The main student financing schemes tend to discriminate against some groups of non-traditional students and modes of study. Examples are the age ceilings in countries such as Germany, where generally students above 30 are no longer eligible for financial support. After campaigning for access by part-time students, the South African financial aid system opened to them in 2003. There is an assumption in many institutions that adults will be able to afford the fees. With unemployment in South Africa running at approximately 40 per cent, plus the neo-liberal economic policies that pass costs of health and education increasingly to the 'consumers', this is patently not the case. The limited financial support for part-time students is a major disincentive and no doubt influences successful completion of courses by students.

In South Africa the new funding formula for higher education is currently being introduced. We therefore have not yet experienced its impact directly. However, it is anticipated that certain features of the system may well work against part-time learners. There are indications that the Department of Education will limit the time to complete degrees and the norm they will use will relate to full-time students. In addition, they may be capping numbers in terms of headcount rather than full-time equivalency, which will dissuade enrolment of part-time and therefore adult learners. The fiscal constraints could well produce practices that seriously compromise the implementation of the lifelong learning policy.

In summary, the higher education environment in South Africa may not be particularly conducive to the realization of lifelong learning for 'non traditional' or older learners within the higher education system given the demographic profile, the traditional focus on younger learners and high status accorded to research institutions. However, the legacy of apartheid continues to highlight the political necessity of giving access to black women and men of all ages. The economy also demands that sufficient students are produced with the capabilities of 'lifelong learners'. This highlights the importance of ensuring that lifelong learning is not equated entirely with adult learning. Lifelong learning as part of the ongoing struggle for social justice within a highly unequal society, which is challenged by the HIV/AIDS pandemic, also continues to be promoted by activists. UWC has its historical roots in these traditions and this, against various other odds, contributes to an enabling environment on the one hand. On the other, however, the university finds itself severely constrained financially and will be seriously influenced by the way in which the funding formula is interpreted.

Strategic partnerships and linkages

The Cape Town Statement describes a lifelong learning HEI as well networked and having backwards, forwards and sideways linkages, back to schools, forward to continuing professional education, and out into communities, workplaces and families. It encourages mobility and interactions amongst different types of institutions and sectors (Candy *et al*. 1994). There is pressure from business and parts of government on higher education to transform to be more 'responsive' to its external environments. There are calls for partnerships to be developed between HEIs and various sectors in society at local, regional, national or international levels.

At UWC there are a range of innovative practices which connect the institution to 'the real world' in curricula terms and which build relationships with communities within civil society, business, labour, or government. One innovative institution-wide strategy has been its high profile involvement in the promotion of the Western Cape Province as a learning region. This promotes the culture of life-long learning in the community at large (see Longworth this volume). It has both provided exposure for UWC as a lifelong learning advocate and it has brought it into closer relationships with government, other educational institutions, and civil society. UWC has been a leading proponent of the Learning Cape Festival that has helped to propel the initiative and promote lifelong learning on and off campus (Walters and Etkind 2004).

There are of course many different relationships with local, national and international organizations, sectors or movements, but the question is which of these are essential for the realization of a lifelong learning HEI concerned with equity and social justice?

Research

In the Cape Town Statement research is understood in a broad sense and includes working across disciplines and/or across institutions. Lifelong learning is regarded as an important and legitimate focus for research activity in its own right. This would include ongoing institutional research. The framework foregrounds particular notions of knowledge and knowledge production and begs the question as to what of the institution's research profile is particularly pertinent to its definition as a lifelong learning institution.

At UWC these debates have not yet been held. The most obvious aspects, which have been identified and monitored, relate to the study of lifelong learning more broadly, to policy, institutional and advocacy research. This aspect of the framework needs further elaboration.

Teaching and learning

The lifelong learner is central in the conception of a lifelong learning HEI. As the Cape Town Statement says, the institution focuses on curricula to support holistic, self-directed learning. It is concerned to ensure that student support, teaching and learning, and administrative mechanisms service this need appropriately and effectively. According to the findings of Candy *et al.* (1994) a lifelong learner would exhibit qualities or characteristics, for example, a repertoire of learning skills, information literacy, and so on.

Both staff and students would be encouraged to be lifelong learners, hence staff and student development is pivotal. A learning culture within the institution that recognizes informal, non-formal and formal learning would be encouraged. Candy *et al.* (1994) argue that the attainment of these qualities derives from, amongst others, the methodologies that are used and the relevance of curricula to real life problems.

Teaching and learning in South Africa, as in many parts of the world, struggle to be recognized within higher education as a central concern. It is the research profile of institutions that brings status. It is teaching and learning that are most in need of concerted attention if HEIs are to be transformed into quality lifelong learning institutions. UWC is no different. As a visiting colleague said, he found a paradox amongst many progressive academics in South Africa: 'Everyone wanted to talk about transformation, about redress, about restructuring, but almost no one evinced much interest in what actually went on in the classrooms even on their own campuses' (Wolff 2003: 7).

Recently at national level, the Higher Education Quality Committee has identified teaching and learning as a key area of focus. This may help give legitimacy to the struggles of activists and scholars within institutions who have been working hard to raise the status of teaching and learning. These activities are at the core of lifelong learning, therefore a key question is how can we ensure that quality curricula, methodologies, staff and student development practices and delivery strategies, can encourage students and staff to be effective lifelong learners? While it is beyond the scope here, there is much to learn from the academic and staff development literature (Volbrecht 2001).

Administration policies and mechanisms

When new policies are to be implemented, there is a truism that 'the devil is in the detail' and that transformation is dependent on changing administrative procedures and practices, which are social constructions that maintain a particular 'picture' of the institution. There are many examples where policies are contradicted by regulations or daily practices. Within HEIs there are many practices or procedures that conserve the institution and its culture.

At UWC we have experience over the last seven years of trying to obtain greater recognition for adult learners, part-time learners, learners accessing the institution through continuing education or resource-based learning, or through recognition of prior learning. We have used a marketing strategy focused both inwards and outwards, as part of these efforts. But in order to make headway on transforming systems, the Vice Chancellor, the Registrar as the head of administration, and other executive leadership are pivotal. A developmental agency, which works across the institution, with leadership and faculties, also seems critical. There needs to be the political will to drive change at both the institutional and national levels. At the institutional level progress has been made within micro-organizational practices to align to the lifelong learning mission. It requires constant vigilance and intervention to align policies with procedures.

Student support systems and services

Lifelong learners require appropriate guidance, counselling and support at their different ages and stages of life and careers in order for them to become successful learners. In many instances services are geared to full-time young students even though, as at UWC, an average student is a woman aged 27 years old. Questions about the range of services and their appropriateness to the full range of students need to be asked. Should counselling services, for example, assist with marital or child rearing issues; with mid-career changes; with unemployment and its effects; with financial management? Do we understand how adult learners mobilize support for themselves and what they need from the institution to assist them?

At UWC where the climate has historically been politically charged, often students' support has been framed largely in political rather than pedagogical and developmental terms. This has limited the possibilities for quality student development and support, which is integral to good teaching and learning practices. However, there has not been in-depth questioning of what student development and support may mean for part-time and older learners. The full-time students are very much the norm. The climate is beginning to shift as concerns with quality provision to part-time students are being raised and it is not possible, because of expense, to duplicate services. This is forcing the institution to begin to pose the questions about what quality alternatives may be.

In closing

Realizing a lifelong learning higher education institution requires clear political will at the national, organizational and individual levels. This is because organizational changes at the macro, meso and micro levels are so intertwined. As Bourgeois *et al.* (1999: 199) state, there needs to be a combination of 'successful actor strategies in decision- and policy-making', and 'conducive conditions related to organizational structure and context'. This is illustrated in the UWC case where it both affects and is affected by its environment.

Change is needed from international and national policies, through institutions, into the learning/teaching relationships. The framework within the Cape Town Statement provides a very useful way of unpacking what lifelong learning within an HEI may mean 'on the ground'. It identifies that major changes are needed on all levels and it emphasizes the critical need to read the context in an ongoing way to assess whether or not conducive conditions prevail. Several of the characteristic elements do need to be developed further in order to make them of greater practical value within varying contexts.

The Cape Town Statement suggests by implication that realizing a lifelong learning HEI may also entail the creation of a new discourse in which lifelong learning, rather than, for example, that of 'academic development', 'adult education' or 'continuing education', is the dominant frame and this entails important shifts in identity, epistemology and power relations, including the complex interplay amongst them (Volbrecht 2001). The working definition of lifelong learning also requires continuous negotiation. The strong impetus internationally to equate lifelong learning mainly to market needs ensures that there is constant political and pedagogical work to realize practices that emphasize both micro pedagogical relationships and their link to macro socio-economic and political locations of the institutions and actors.

Lifelong learning within an emancipatory narrative is concerned with social justice and active democratic citizenship amongst groups who are 'marginalized' within particular societies. In many instances the opportunities for 'non-traditional students' to participate mean that, for example, women and black, rural, working class, older or physically disabled people are gaining access to learning opportunities and acquiring lifelong learning capacities. Realizing a lifelong learning higher education institution is therefore very much about organization, pedagogy and politics, which requires, as Bourgeois *et al.* (1999) argue, a combination of successful actor strategies and conducive conditions related to organizational structure and context.

References

Bourgeois, E., Duke, C., Guyot, J.L. and Merrill, B. (1999) *The Adult University*, Buckingham: Open University Press/SRHE.

Candy, P., Crebert, R.G. and O'Leary, J. (1994) *Developing Lifelong Learners through Undergraduate Education*, Canberra: Australian Government Publishing Services.

Cooper, D. and Subotzky, G. (2001) *The Skewed Revolution. Trends in South African Higher Education: 1988–1998*, Education Policy Unit, UWC: Bellville, South Africa.

Crowther, J. (2004) 'In and against lifelong learning: flexibility and the corrosion of character', *International Journal of Lifelong Education.* 23, 2: 123–36.

Division for Lifelong Learning (2001) *The Cape Town Statement on Characteristic Elements of a Lifelong Learning Higher Education Institution*, University of Western Cape: Bellville, South Africa.

Dunlop, C. and Nesbit, T. (2004) 'Reaching higher ground: An analysis of effective principle and practices of lifelong learning in higher education institutions', Paper presented at the *AERC Conference*, University of Victoria, Canada.

Schuetze, H. and Slowey, M. (eds) (2000) *Higher Education and Lifelong Learners*, London: RoutledgeFalmer.

Taylor, R., Barr, J. and Steele, T. (2002) *For a Radical Higher Education. After Postmodernism*, Maidenhead: Open University Press/SRHE.

UNESCO (1999) *The World Declaration on Higher Education for the Twenty-first Century: Vision and Action*, Paris: UNESCO.

Volbrecht, T. and Walters, S. (2000) 'Re-imagining a picture: higher education in lifelong learning', *Adult Education and Development*, IIZ/DVV, 271–91.

Volbrecht, T. (2001) *Plot and Practice. A Narrative Enquiry into Academic Development, Language Policy and Lifelong Learning as Frameworks for Literacy Development at University of Western Cape*, Doctoral Thesis, South Africa: UWC.

Walters, S. (2004) 'Researching access in a rapidly changing context: experiences from higher education in South Africa', in M. Osborne, J. Gallacher and B. Crossan (eds) *Researching Widening Access to Lifelong Learning*, London: RoutledgeFalmer.

Walters, S. and Etkind, R. (2004) 'Developing a learning region: what can learning festivals contribute?', Paper presented at the *AERC Conference*, University of Victoria, Canada.

Wolff, P. (2003) 'Tertiary education in the New South Africa: a lover's complaint', unpublished paper presented to an HEQC seminar, UWC.

Chapter 8

Towards a responsive work-based curriculum for non-traditional students in higher education

John Bamber

Lifelong learning should have implications for the way in which institutions operate and the focus of this chapter is how a degree programme, in a traditional university, has combined work-based learning and normal course study mode in ways which are particularly attuned to the experiences of non-traditional, working class, adult students. If widening participation is to be a reality and the class structure of higher education transformed there is a need to develop, it is argued, a more responsive curriculum that allows students to be active learners involved in the construction of knowledge which is relevant and meaningful.

Introduction

This chapter focuses on the learning experiences of one small group of work-based, non-traditional students, in higher education (HE). Work-based learning involves a hybrid mixture of studying at the workplace in addition to study in an educational institution. It would be wrong to imply that non-traditional students form a homogenous group but broadly they may be mature, come from low participation neighbourhoods and lower social classes, are often the first ones in their family to attend university, lack conventional academic entry requirements to HE, or come from communities and groups that may be disadvantaged on grounds, for example, of ethnicity or disability.

The argument of this chapter builds on previous empirical and theoretical research (Bamber *et al.* 1997; Bamber and Tett 1999, 2000), which found that ensuring integrative learning experiences requires a two-way process of change and development from both non-traditional students and institutions. It is written at a time when 'widening participation initiatives tend to focus on raising the aspirations of the working class rather than changing educational cultures' (Tett 2004: 253). In this view the student is deemed inadequate and must be helped to gain access to, and thereafter fulfil the requirements of, the 'unproblematic' institution. This is challenged by a structural perspective, which takes account 'not only of people's shifting class identities but also the role of the educational institution itself in creating and perpetuating inequalities' (Archer, cited in Tett 2004: 253). It is argued that institutions must seek to redress the malign effects of structural factors on performance and at the heart of any redress is a responsive curriculum; one that embodies an understanding of the difficulties faced by non-traditional students and is supportive of their situation (see also Walters this volume).

Examining the design and effect of curriculum goes to the core of what it means to participate in higher education. It is known, for example, that only 'academic' students spontaneously use higher-order learning processes such as critical thinking (Biggs 1999). In a responsive curriculum, course content, tasks, activities, and the vehicles for assessment would be 'constructively aligned' (Biggs 2003) to support higher order learning. Work Based Learning 1 – Professional Development (WBL1), created for first year part-time students undertaking a BA degree in Community Education, can be seen as an example of such a curriculum. Supported by an electronic learning frame, the course requires students to learn by critically reflecting on aspects of their practice. It embodies the characteristics of work-based learning elaborated by Raelin (in Gray 2001: 4) whereby the process:

> Centres around reflection on work practices, involves reviewing and learning from experience and is more than acquiring knowledge and a set of technical skills.
>
> Views learning as arising from action and problem-solving within a working environment, incorporating live projects and challenges to individuals and organizations.
>
> Sees the creation of knowledge as a shared and collective activity, one in which people discuss ideas and share problems and solutions.
>
> Requires the acquisition of new knowledge and the acquisition of meta-competence – learning to learn.

WBL1 is premised on the idea that learning is holistic and situated (Seely Brown and Duguid 1996). As such it addresses emotional, behavioural, existential, contextual and collective aspects of learning.

The research involves triangulating information from various sources including individual interviews, focus groups and textual data (e.g. student assignments). As Lillis (2001) states, the accounts of 'non-traditional' students are important in that they are often the participants who experience dissonance with prevailing academic practice and are easily able to problematize its 'given' status. The analysis also draws on the concepts of 'valid knowledge' and 'special attention' in relation to the student experience (Torbert in Reason 1994 and Meyer 2003). These concepts help to identify and explain learning in terms of 'ontological shift – a change in the way of being as a person' (Treleavan 1994: 160). This reflects changes in the construction of identities and sense of possible futures (Rossiter 2003), which has a beneficial impact on the journey through higher education. When students learn to learn in this way, they are developing the meta-competence that has ineluctable and positive consequences for lifelong and life-wide learning.

Policy and the institutional context

Since 1995 widening access for non-traditional students has become a global phenomenon (Schuetze and Wolter 2000). Over the last ten years or so there has been a mounting interest in developing educational opportunities in the United Kingdom leading to the recent White Paper on *The Future of Higher Education* (DfES 2003). The seminal Dearing Report devoted a chapter to the issue of widening participation, and states that:

> Increasing participation in higher education is a necessary and desirable objective of national policy over the next 20 years. This must be accompanied by the objective of reducing the disparities in participation in higher education between groups and ensuring that higher education *is responsive* to the aspirations and distinctive abilities of individuals.
>
> (DfES 1997: 101 [emphasis added])

From just over 800,000 in 1987, there are now over two million students in HE in the UK (HEFCE 2004). Such overall figures, however, mask the fact that the move to a mass system has been achieved by differential enrolment with the skilled, semi-skilled and manual classes still seriously under-represented (Gilchrist *et al.* 2003). Furthermore, those who do participate from the lower socio-economic groups and minority ethnic communities are concentrated in the former polytechnic sector (Hutchings and Archer 2001). The 'elite' university in this research is no exception to the rule in that 90 per cent of its entrants are young and around 10 per cent are from lower socio-economic groups. Mature, part-time students with no previous experience of HE and from low participation neighbourhoods, amount to just 2 per cent of all first-degree entrants.

The nature and genesis of WBL 1

Work Based Learning 1 contributes 40 out of the 360 credits needed to obtain a professionally endorsed degree. The students cover the same learning outcomes and course content as their full-time counterparts but take one extra year to complete the degree. It involves attendance at university one day per week, which favours part-time students with work and/or domestic commitments. The students study with their full-time counterparts and they are also taught separately.

WBL1 is divided into four sections, each of which covers a major aspect of professional life. Each section has two parts, and each part addresses one learning outcome through an extended exercise. Associated resources accompany each exercise, together with an 'issues' component highlighting problematic or controversial aspects of the course content. The assessment requires the completion of eight exercises and there are three essays to complete. The students are formed into 'learning clusters' with four or five other participants and the course culminates in seminars organized by the clusters. The course content can be elaborated as follows:

Professional practice

- Assessing competence using a competence framework.
- Preparing learning objectives for the designated placement period.

Personal practice

- Managing time effectively.
- Setting work related goals and developing action plans.

Reflective practice

- Learning from experience at work.
- Applying action learning at work.

Collaborative practice

- Making effective presentations.
- Organizing effective seminar activities.

Professional practice lays the foundation for the course by inviting students to identify their developmental needs. In exercise one they analyse their professional knowledge, skills and understanding using a competence framework from the professional field. Raising awareness itself is not a sufficient basis for change and the students are further required to address identified gaps and weaknesses in exercise two, where they set specific learning objectives for the placement period that runs in tandem with WBL1.

Personal practice continues the focus on self-development by concentrating in exercise three on time management. The premise is that poor use of available time leads to under-performance, which in turn means that employing agencies will not meet their objectives and those who could benefit from the agency's work will be prevented from doing so. Good use of time cannot be separated from having a clear and meaningful set of work objectives. Exercise four takes up this idea by familiarizing students with the notion of personal action planning involving monitoring, evaluating and reviewing.

Reflective practice introduces the idea that professionals develop through constructive and critical engagement with the realities of the practice situation. Exercise five invites students to examine the process of their own learning in terms of the experiential learning cycle (Kolb 1984). Exercise six introduces the notions of action learning (Revans 1984), reflective practice (Schön 1983) and critical thinking (Brookfield 1987). This exercise marks a significant juncture in the course by involving students in a learning cluster where they engage in a process of collective and collaborative learning. The premise is that professionals must be able to learn from and co-operate with colleagues as they seek to continuously improve practice.

Collaborative practice extends the theme of co-operating with colleagues by focusing on the sharing of ideas in public forums. The basic premise is that communicating ideas effectively is an essential ingredient in promoting critical discourse about the resolution of practice problems in any given context. Exercise seven concentrates on the fundamentals of presenting effectively. Finally, exercise eight is based on the premise that professional activity takes place within a community of professionals who are collectively committed to improving practice. A fundamental aspect of being professional, therefore, is actively participating in this collective process of development. The exercise requires the student groups to run and participate in a seminar event based on issues that they have found important as a result of their engagement with the course.

The course is stored on a CD, which students download onto their computer at home or at work. It is not necessary to be on-line but they can make use of hyperlinks to websites if the Internet is available. The course combines weekly face-to-face meetings with distance approaches in a structured learning process incorporating an integral resource-base of content materials. It is an example of what Nichols (2003) describes as mixed-mode, blended or resource-based learning.

Course participants and research findings

The 22 students involved in this study range between the ages of 21 and 50. The four men and 18 women comprise the full cohort, which recruits once every four years. Employment in the group is varied with some in full-time, permanent positions whilst others work on a paid part-time basis or have voluntary commitments. All work at least ten hours per week in the associated field of practice. Entry to the part-time programme puts a high premium on relevant experience with candidates having a variety of qualifications. Most have a Higher National Certificate or some other evidence of recent study of equivalent status. An arrangement with the University's Centre for Lifelong Learning meant that a number with no qualifications could gain entry to the programme by taking accredited courses. Few had the standard entry qualifications and where this was the case these had been obtained many years ago. The students are white British with most coming from Scottish manual working class backgrounds.

Torbert's notion of 'valid knowledge' (cited in Reason 1994) has strong explanatory power in relation to the content and process of learning. The development of valid knowledge involves participants in learning about and changing fundamental conceptions of themselves, education and their world. Often these are unconscious, tacit and taken-for-granted and brought into awareness by the process of learning. Meyer (2003) suggests that individuals require valid knowledge of four 'territories' of human experience involving the following:

- *Purposes* in terms of an intuitive or spiritual knowledge of desired goals and objects worthy of attention, and how these might change over time.

- *Strategy* in terms of the intellectual or cognitive knowledge of the theories underpinning choices.
- *Behavioural choices* that are open and which depend on awareness of self and the skills possessed.
- Knowledge of the *outside world* and of the consequences of behaviour.

Whilst these categories interpenetrate and interact they can be used separately to analyse and explain students' learning experiences. Their learning can be discussed in terms of becoming critical and being professional (purposes); learning to learn and collective learning (strategy); authority and control (behavioural choices); 'creating waves' and dealing with reactions (knowledge of outside world). These are elaborated below.

Purposes: becoming critical and being professional

The movement in this territory was towards embracing the nature of learning in higher education. This can be seen in the growing importance attached by the students to the development of critical thinking. For them this capacity meant questioning deeply held assumptions and seeing the bigger picture, for example, in organizational, policy-related, political or ideological terms. It meant appreciating the nature, value and place of propositional knowledge in developing their capacity for critical thinking. The most consistent comment was the students' sense of a greater criticality in their approach to professional development. The following quote is representative:

> The main area of learning in the frame is developing critical thinking. Engaging with case studies, learning about experiential learning theory and action learning theory, is very important to our professional development and confidence.
>
> (A female)

At the very least, the shift signals a definite psychological adjustment towards HE with an increasing acceptance of the value and utility of this type of learning for their personal and academic development. This was closely linked to a growing understanding that being professional is less about having a qualification that permits entry to certain, higher status and better paid jobs, and more about gaining proper 'distance' from those being served, acting on the basis of principles, theorizing, arguing a case and exercising the authority inherent in a given role.

Strategy: learning to learn and collective learning

Student change in this territory was demonstrated in newfound approaches to learning. Initial responses reflected deep concerns about finding the time to engage with the course in, and amongst other, out-of-university commitments.

Instead of a sense of 'freedom to work when and where you wanted', the lack of a formal structure (in contrast to attending lectures) initially resulted in feelings of uncertainty and in some cases panic at the 'uncontrollability' of this part of their lives. Linking into the above were questions about preferred learning styles, and the expectations of a learning situation – which, until experienced, could be unknown and daunting. By the end of the course opinions had changed. The following comment is typical:

> I was very sceptical of WBL1 as I looked at it as open learning and I have never been any good at that! I find it difficult to be motivated and I know a lot of the other students did as well. I think after the initial exercises were completed I realized that I was going to get something out of it and that I was actually learning. More specifically I was learning more about me – both professionally and personally.
>
> (B female)

In exercise five the students learned how to interrogate their work experience using Kolb's (1984) learning cycle. In exercise six they learned to generate fresh questions about practice through action learning (Revans 1984):

> This exercise [action learning] brought our critical thinking to the group, where we could actively engage in critical dialogue. There was so much learning that took place during the set's meetings, i.e. people, personalities, how people work etc, what challenges they face in their practice. This was very interesting, and it definitely dulled the feeling of isolation.
>
> (A female)

Through such exercises an appreciation of and commitment to collective learning developed, partly out of the need to counter the isolation that is endemic to part-time study, a situation compounded for some with the introduction of the unfamiliar technology associated with WBL1. The extent to which they grasped collective learning as a strategy for development, however, is not explained solely as a reaction to isolation. The strength of their commitment in this direction was a result of conscious choices and the strong desire for more personal authority and control in and over their own learning. This movement is further explained under the category of behaviour.

Behavioural choices: authority and control

Many students reported a significant behavioural shift after the time management and action planning exercises. These resulted in a greater awareness of how they had previously operated in an unthinking way, reacting to immediate demands. This realization brought forth commitments to more focused activity set around their own priorities in terms of work, personal lives and study. As one student commented in relation to work, 'Before doing this course I had little control in my work but I had just accepted this without realizing it' (K female). Students could see how they were too busy and how a lack of organization meant that they were not concentrating efforts on their priorities. Not being asked to think about the wider organizational and policy context of their work in the past had meant it wasn't considered. They were now more likely to allocate time to forward plan and to identify and stick to priorities linked to the wider objectives of their organization. Students also described how they applied the time management principles in their personal lives. How, for example, domestic arrangements had changed so that some household tasks were more equally shared with children and partners.

The group exercises were demanding in their own ways and also had repercussions in terms of authority and control over learning. As one said:

> I initially enjoyed working in a group for exercises five, six, seven and eight. However it began to feel a bit too much by the end of the seminar, although this was probably my steepest learning of the whole eighteen months ... and made me realize that I must take more responsibility for my own learning.
>
> (C female)

It is clear that the students felt more able to take account of their own principles, to stand back and to make decisions with confidence. As a result, there were consequences for their relationships in various spheres and their learning about this can be explained in the next category of knowledge of the outside world.

Knowledge of outside world: creating waves and dealing with reactions

Change in this territory was evident when students became more critical of their own work, about practice in their agency, about study and the university environment and about their own personal lives. It was generally acknowledged that the course gave workplace discussions with line managers and colleagues a new legitimacy. Becoming critical, however, had wide-ranging consequences, as the following comment makes clear:

> Due to the development of critical thinking in my action learning set, we wanted to challenge wider structural inequalities, as well as challenge professional colleagues. It wasn't just about being critical of our jobs, or ourselves, but of the wider structure and the bureaucracy that affects our practice. Being engaged in collective dialogue made us want to challenge the system.
>
> (A female)

Critical questions created tensions with colleagues in the workplace where practices taken for granted were suddenly scrutinized and challenged. In some instances this led to changing relationships with colleagues who were threatened by the student's attitude. It was noted, for example, that line managers could take issues personally where these appeared to involve the line manager themselves. There was a potential, therefore, for the learning from the exercises to lead to conflict if not sensitively handled. An important part of this behavioural learning was a growing appreciation of the need to challenge in ways that did not gratuitously offend colleagues or unnecessarily trigger defensive and aggressive reactions. The students were keenly aware of the need for support in work and other situations. They acknowledged how, for example, the requirement in exercises one and two to engage with a 'critical friend' who would challenge the student in a supportive way, brought a rigour to their self-assessments and also gave extra legitimacy to the learning process.

From despair to delight: special attention and possible selves

The main finding from the enquiry is that the students' stories indicate 'ontological shift – a change in the way of being as a person' (Treleaven 1994: 160). Not every student moved in exactly the same direction, to the same extent and at the same time. The reality was more complex, and too detailed to recount here, but it is still possible to see an overall pattern, a general trend. The shift can be explained in terms of the changing nature and intensity of the students' response to the course, signalling the development of a 'special attention', which sees, embraces, and corrects incongruities among the four territories (Torbert cited in Reason 1994). It is a moment-to-moment consciousness, which heightens the possibilities and potential inherent in situations. This is not a cyclical model of learning emphasizing the dialectic of action and reflection. Rather it is a peculiar quality of consciousness or discipline in which action and reflection interpenetrate and are simultaneous.

The following list portrays the often hostile and negative impressions of the students during the initial period of engagement with WBL1. There was:

- frustration with technology and high levels of stress;
- dislike of the distance-learning element;
- preference for face-to-face contact and lectures;
- subversion of the technology by printing everything off;
- a sense that the exercises were boring;
- judgement that the exercises were too open ended (students didn't know when enough was enough for completion);
- complaint about apparent lack of links between exercises and formal assessments;
- a debilitating sense that the experience was isolating;
- lack of motivation to engage with the process;
- frustration that the cluster groups had not started early enough;
- a sense of a lack of clarity about the purpose of it all;
- difficulties with competition for access to the computer at home.

By the end, however, the initial despair had turned to delight. Students drew favourable comparisons with conventional modes of delivery in other parts of their degree programme:

> It's not as hoity toity! It uses plain language and we don't need to reach for a sociology dictionary!
>
> (D female)

> It seems more real to me because it's less theory based and it relates directly to my practice and to my work.
>
> (E female)

> The point of it's obvious and it's possible to see how it can help practice.
>
> (F female)

> The pace was more relaxed and less pressured although I didn't feel this with the first couple of exercises.
>
> (G female)

> The exercises were excellent!
>
> (H male)

In the end their engagement with WBL1 was positive and intense. In one focus group it was suggested that the extent of the commitment came down to personality factors. No doubt this had a bearing but the level of commitment across the group also points to other influences. It is significant that the cohort is composed of highly motivated mature students. Some had been waiting for a long time to undertake higher education and when the opportunity came it was grasped with both hands. It was important to demonstrate their abilities to tutors and also to a wider audience of colleagues who can be sceptical, and to family and friends. These may appear to be negative factors but they are powerful motivators and it is clear that from a teaching and learning point of view such factors are valuable assets in higher education settings.

In the students' accounts the development of critical thinking and new conceptions of professionalism were both a product and cause of fresh questions. The questions triggered and resulted from simultaneous changes in strategic approaches to learning and to behaviour in practice and personal settings. There is a connection here to the concept of 'possible selves' (Rossiter 2003). New possible selves can emerge when learners are encouraged to try on differing identities through, for example, the kind of experiential and action learning activities featured in WBL1. If the possible self is too 'close' to the current conception, little development will occur. If it is too 'distant' then development is not seen as possible because it is not seen as attainable. The experience of WBL1 appears to indicate that profound shifts in ways of knowing can occur when learners see desirable alternatives or extensions to current identities. A future orientated and realistic self-concept can, therefore, be a motivating and organizing factor in transformational learning.

Conclusion: towards a responsive curriculum

Although the part-time route is spread over four years, the participants have had to deal with all the problems associated with intensive courses such as having less time to read and reflect, and stressful workloads (see Sims and Woodrow 1996). Their circumstances are a far cry from those of the traditional, younger, single, middle-class students whose conditions, though they have undoubtedly worsened in the past two decades, are still good by comparison. In the end, class is not an abstract concept but is real and operative in the daily lives of these students. For this group higher education has been difficult to gain access to and will be exceedingly hard to survive. In relation to under-represented groups these wider structural aspects need to be taken into account in terms of course development.

Notwithstanding a number of reservations and problems, it would appear that the particular form of learning embodied in WBL1 enabled the students to engage intensively and productively with degree level studies. This finding echoes the idea that non-traditional students seek 'a different kind of relationship around meaning making in academia' (Lillis 2001: 54). The concepts of 'valid knowl-edge', 'special attention' and 'possible selves' help to reveal how the curriculum encouraged students to develop an 'internally persuasive discourse' (Lillis 2001: 49), in which they were active learners receiving, interacting with and reshaping knowledge as they wrestled with real-life, personally meaningful situations. The concepts also help to show how emergent insights and understandings begin to impact on other aspects of their academic, working, personal and social lives. The change and movement described in this paper speak to the true meaning of par-ticipation, which is diminished when students can only engage superficially with the teaching and learning processes on offer. Treleaven (1994) uses the metaphor of fire to explain this phenomenon, with 'embers' from the learning starting 'flames' at some distance from it. The development of such a capacity is, of course, highly relevant to any consideration of lifelong and life-wide learning.

References

Bamber, J. and Tett, L. (1999) 'Opening the doors of higher education to adults: a case study', *International Journal of Lifelong Education*, 18, 6: 465–75.

Bamber J. and Tett, L. (2000) 'Transforming the learning experiences of non-traditional stu-dents: a perspective from higher education', *Studies in Continuing Education*, 22, 1: 57–75.

Bamber, J., Tett, L., Hosie, E. and Ducklin, A. (1997) 'Resistance and determination: work-ing class adults in higher education', *Research in Post-Compulsory Education*, 2, 1: 17–28.

Biggs, J. (1999) *Teaching for Quality Learning at University*, Buckingham: Open University Press/SRHE.

Biggs, J. (2003) *Aligning Teaching and Assessment to Curriculum Objectives*, Learning and Teaching Support Network Generic Centre, York: Institute of Learning and Teaching.

Brookfield, S. (1987) *Developing Critical Thinkers*, Oxford: Oxford University Press.

DfES (1997) *Higher Education in the Learning Society – The Report of the National Committee of Inquiry into Higher Education*, London: HMSO.

DfES (2003) *The Future of Higher Education* (White Paper), London: DfES.

Gray, D. (2001) *A Briefing on Work-based Learning* (Assessment Series No 11), York: Learning and Teaching Support Network.

Gilchrist, R., Phillips, P. and Ross, A. (2003) 'Participation and potential participation in UK higher education', in L. Archer, M. Hutchings and A. Ross (eds) *Higher Education and Social Class: Issues of Exclusion and Inclusion*, London: RoutledgeFalmer.

HEFCE, (2004) *Higher Education in the United Kingdom*, Guide January (Revised), Bristol: HEFCE.

Hutchings, M. and Archer, L. (2001) '"Higher than Einstein": constructions of going to university among working class non-participants', *Research Papers in Education*, 16, 1: 61–9.

Kolb, D.A. (1984) *Experiential Learning – Experience as the Source of Learning and Development*, New Jersey: Prentice-Hall.

Lillis, M.T. (2001) *Student Writing: Access, Regulation, Desire*, London and New York: Routledge.

Meyer, J. (2003) 'Four territories of experience: a developmental action inquiry approach to outdoor-adventure experiential learning', *Academy of Management Learning and Education*, 2, 4: 352–63.

Nichols, M. (2003) 'A theory for elearning', in *Educational Technology and Society*, 6, 2: 1–10, available at http://ifets.ieee.org/periodical/6-2/1.html (accessed 1.6.04).

Reason. P. (ed.) (1994) *Participation in Human Inquiry*, London: Sage Publications.

Revans, W.R. (1984) *The Origins And Growth Of Action Learning*, London: Chartwell Blatt.

Rossiter, M. (2003) 'Possible selves and adult learning', CRLL Conference Proceedings, *Experiential-Community-Workbased: Researching Learning Outside the Academy*, Glasgow, 383–90.

Schön, D.A. (1983) *The Reflective Practitioner: How Professionals Think in Action*. London: Temple Smith.

Schuetze, H.G. and Wolter, A. (2000) 'Higher Education and Non-Traditional Students in Industrialised Countries – Developments and Perspectives'. Unpublished paper, ESREA Access Network Conference, 25–26 September, Barcelona.

Seely Brown, J.S. and Duguid, P. (1996) 'Towards a unified view of working, learning and innovation', in M.D. Cohen and L.S. Sproull (eds), *Organisational Learning*, London: Sage.

Sims, L. and Woodrow, M. (1996) *Fast and Flexible: the AIRS Experience*, Bristol: HEFCE.

Tett, L. (2004) 'Mature working-class students in an "elite" university: discourses of risk, choice and exclusion', *Studies in the Education of Adults*, 36, 2: 252–64.

Treleaven, L. (1994) 'Making a space: a collaborative inquiry with women as staff development', in P. Reason (ed.) *Participation in Human Inquiry*, London: Sage Publications.

Chapter 9

Changing to learning cultures that foster lifelong learners

Rose Evison

The focus of this chapter is on how the learning of adults is interfered with by emotional blocks from their childhood. Overcoming these necessitates changing the learning culture, of both groups and individuals, if lifelong learning is to happen. Methods for doing this depend on increasing social bonding in groups, and developing supportive rather than judgmental inner coaches. Evison argues that shame and pride are key emotions in this process. In order to remove the threats that produce shame and trigger blocks it is crucial that positive emotions dominate the culture. Core processes are those like laughing and active relaxation that reset body and mind to learning mode. Equally vital are activities that generate pride and increase emotional resilience such as celebrating achievements.

Introduction

This chapter explores current learning cultures drawing on research but, equally importantly, on considerable experience over forty years of facilitating learning – including teaching in schools, training teachers in higher education, working in people development with organizations and facilitating personal growth groups for helping professionals and the general public. It also presents a theory of emotions that underpins the strategies and behaviours that facilitate learning and summarizes strategies for changing to cultures that foster lifelong learners. In addition, existing cultures that are difficult to change are listed.

Learning can mean achieving formal educational goals, developing useful skills from life experiences or undergoing conditioning processes. My own working definition is that learning is the process by which individuals add to their repertoires of skills and knowledge by purposive activity in any arena of life. Whilst this covers any step forward in a task, any new awareness, any addition to knowledge or any increase in skill, it excludes conditioning processes.

Developmental psychologists have demonstrated that the learning ability of humans is superior to all other known species. The innate nature of this ability correlates with the evolutionary development of neurological controls over movement (Porges 2001). So humans are born with highly effective learning abilities and function as lifelong learners unless such abilities are damaged. Lifelong learners take all possible opportunities to learn without being put off by difficulties. They perceive failures as providing information about what does not work.

The term culture is used here to refer to the relationship climate and norms within a group. A learning culture exists whenever there are learning objectives for participants e.g. in classrooms, lecture theatres, practical classes, training courses, small group situations and all dyad work with learning objectives. Such learning situations have *learning facilitators* with titles like teacher, trainer, coach or mentor. Both learning cultures and learning facilitators can be effective or ineffective. Furthermore, individuals have an internal learning culture, formed by the way they talk to themselves during learning tasks. Such self-talk acts as an *inner coach* facilitating or interfering with the *inner learner*.

Learning cultures do not exist in isolation, they are embedded in organizational cultures and influenced by the internalized cultures participants bring with them: the professional cultures of the learning facilitators and the previous learning cultures of the learners. Such contextual cultures have strong influences and can support or interfere with learning cultures.

Blocks to learning occur in current learning cultures

The need to develop lifelong learners arises from the experience that many children and adults appear unable or unwilling to learn, indicating damage to their learning abilities. Such damage shows up when adults list things about themselves they would like to change. Typically such lists comprise thoughts, feelings, and behaviours where the individuals are stuck. Even though motivated, they find changing very hard. Using this exercise over many years with thousands of people, Evison discovered that everyone makes rigid responses some of the time, regardless of how talented and successful they are. Such rigid responses are called *blocks*.

The negative thoughts and feelings of blocks take up attention and processing capacity, which sets limits to other potential actions. Thus blocks are dysfunctional emotional responses locking up resources of mind and body with a resulting downgrading of performance and learning (Evison 2001). Although blocks are individual, where people have similar experiences, as in an educational system, many will have similar blocks. Blocks frequently observed in adults include:

- **Performance anxiety blocks** – experiencing anxiety about performing in social situations e.g. working in groups, using a video recorder, being unable to pay attention to one's own performance in order to learn from it. Such blocks arise from shaming of poor performance by adults and/or peers (Dweck and Sorich 1999). They are labelled as 'evaluation apprehension' in group and team research, and as 'social anxiety' in psychology.
- **Putdown blocks** – aggressive, sarcastic, or judgmental remarks applied to others or to self. Scheff (1997) claims that socialization of shame expressiveness forms the basis of destructive anger and conflict. Evison (1990a) found that trainers' use of behaviours that were reminders of teacher putdowns was inversely correlated with ratings of learning facilitation.

- **Thinking blocks** – experiencing confusion, or mind going blank, or inability to recall a 'known' fact. They arise when teachers punish wrong answers more intensely than not knowing (Holt 1965).
- **Powerlessness blocks** – people believing they cannot do particular things or that it's not worth them trying. These arise from early experiences where particular actions have elicited positive or negative judgments about the person or their traits from 'significant others' (see Evison and Horobin 1988 for discussion of the genesis of self-concept blocks).

Although blocks are usually labelled by their most obvious characteristics, as above, they involve the whole organism. Like all emotional responses, they are gestalts of feeling, acting, thinking, and the supporting bodily processes (Evison 2001). The less obvious aspects of specific blocks emerge when they are explored.

Helpless or mastery thinking results from different learning cultures

Extensive research with school children provides data on how different learning cultures influence learning. Dweck and Sorich (1999) review experiments that explore *helpless-* and *mastery-oriented* thinking. Theorizing that overall learning success depends on persistence in the face of difficulties, they used concept development tasks, with initial success experiences followed by failures. Students were encouraged to talk aloud during these tasks, so their problem-solving strategies and feelings were part of the data. These constituted inner coach information. Some of the studies are summarized below.

Given tasks at which they could succeed, there were no differences between helpless-and mastery-oriented students. When difficulties arose, however, helpless-oriented students denigrated their intellectual competence, had negative feelings, ceased to make efforts and were pessimistic about their future performance. They expressed beliefs that their abilities were fixed and finding tasks hard meant their ability was inadequate, leading them to stop trying. They chose tasks they could perform well rather than hard tasks they could learn from.

In contrast, mastery-oriented students, when tasks became harder, sought to improve their performance by increasing effort and seeking better strategies. They were also realistically optimistic about their future performance. They preferred tasks they could learn from even when there was a high risk of failure. They believed that intellectual ability could be developed by one's own efforts. Overall the mastery-oriented students were able to focus their available resources on learning tasks, while the responses of the helpless-oriented students correspond to having performance anxiety and powerlessness blocks interfering with learning.

In further studies, Dweck and Sorich (1999) found that helpless-oriented pre-school children had similar blocks, except that their beliefs were about being bad and not being able to change that. In contrast, mastery-oriented pre-schoolers experienced themselves as good even when failing at tasks. Encouraged to use dolls to role-play adult reactions to their mistakes, helpless-oriented children role-played judgmental reactions from adults. Mastery-oriented children however role-played adults praising them for effort put in and for the strategies they tried.

The researchers followed up these findings with experiments that showed judgmental criticism that reflected on the child's traits, or on the child as a whole, fostered an intense helpless reaction in response to later setbacks. In contrast, criticism indicating that more effort or a different strategy was called for, set up a mastery-oriented reaction when children encountered later obstacles. They also showed that although children were happy receiving judgmental praise, it had the same negative outcome as judgmental criticism. This is not surprising as judgmental praise for a good performance implies punishment for a poor performance.

Dweck and her colleagues were not the first to note that rewards are ineffective motivators of learning. Kohn (1993) collected many studies of both children and adults, showing that when rewards are given for the achievement of tasks, those rewarded do less well in terms of real life change criteria than those working without rewards.

These experiments linked particular learning cultures to the development of facilitative or destructive inner coaches. They also showed that these inner coaches can be influenced by later learning cultures.

Relating learning cultures to learning outcomes

Learning cultures can be assessed for effectiveness in promoting learning by correlating typical behaviours of participants with learning outcomes. Aspy and Roebuck (1976) used the battery of instruments listed below to research classroom processes. Their extensive series of studies found pupils of teachers with higher scores on these instruments had more successful learning outcome measures.

Positive relationship-building

Behaviourally-anchored rating scales were developed from those used in counselling skills research. Five separately rated scales were applied to audiotapes, covering Meaning (Empathy), Genuineness, Success promotion, Respect, and Student involvement.

Cognitive functioning

A behaviour category set was developed from Metfessel et al.'s (1969) instrumentation of Bloom's educational objectives. Categories distinguishing 'Giving' or 'Asking for Facts' from 'Giving' or 'Asking for Thinking' were used. Higher learning achievements are associated with the thinking categories.

Indirect versus direct teacher influence

Using the Flanders Interaction Analysis Categories (1965), better learning achievements were found to be associated with teachers who used higher ratios of Indirect to Direct influence categories. *Indirect influence*: accepts feelings, praises or encourages, accepts or uses ideas of students, asks questions. *Direct influence*: lecturing, giving directions, criticizing or justifying authority.

This research provides objectives for learning facilitators wishing to increase their skills in facilitating effective learning cultures. However, the research instruments above are unsuitable for developing skills. A technology that can be used for both research and training is provided by Rackham and Morgan (1977). Interpersonal messages are categorized into natural mutually exclusive speech units using observable semantic and non-verbal characteristics of the messages, with an inter-observer reliability of 0.95 and above. For an example of using this technology to develop a behaviour category set that distinguishes between different counselling approaches see Evison and Ronaldson (1975) and for the subsequent use of this set to evaluate a counsellor training programme see Ronaldson and Evison (1975).

Using this technology in a research project with a multinational's IT trainers in five European countries, Evison developed a set of thirty behaviour categories that covered all trainer–trainee communications. Samples of trainer–trainee behaviour were recorded, categorized, and correlated with a variety of trainee ratings of learning facilitation (Evison 1990a). The three categories with the highest positive correlations with ratings of *learning-facilitation* were labelled *Respecting People* and the three categories with the highest negative correlations with ratings of learning-facilitation were labelled *Negating People*. Categories that encouraged thinking, also laughing, gave significant results. The following definitions are condensed from Evison (1990b).

Respecting People *behaviours*

- *Showing Respect*: acting respectfully and treating everyone as fully capable of managing their own learning.
- *Affirming Learning Capability*: expressing confidence in individuals' or groups' learning ability.
- *Appreciating Achievements*: appreciating achievements, strengths or skills, without using evaluative or judgmental words.

Negating People *behaviours*

- *Threat Reminders*: using language that acts as a reminder of painful experiences in learning situations when young.
- *Using Fouls*: making disparaging personal remarks: putdowns, sarcasm, blame, negative judgments.

- *Giving Approval*: using positive evaluation to describe performance, working practices, or personal qualities.

The Giving Approval behaviour category equates to Dweck and Sorich's 'judgmental praise', and to Kohn's 'positive rewards'. All such interpersonal messages foster helpless-oriented behaviour because they trigger negative self-concept blocks. Moreover, the other Negating People categories are ways of making negative judgments about an individual and hence triggering blocks. Similarly the Respecting People categories are ways of affirming the worthwhileness of the individual and will also work to interrupt the self-putdown blocks of the listeners.

The culture of a group is an emergent property of the behaviours within the group. When integrations of the trainer data were explored it was found that the ratio of Respecting People to Negating People behaviours formed the best measure of learning–facilitation culture. The higher the Learning–Facilitation Ratio (LFR), the more effective the culture in facilitating learning. In the research the most effective trainers had a LFR of 30:1 and the least effective trainers had an LFR around 1:1. In Evison's experience an LFR of over 10:1 is necessary for an effective group learning culture. Note also those learning cultures with LFRs around 1:1 leave participants dependent on their own internal learning cultures: the self-talk labelled *inner coaches*. The prevalence of learning blocks means many people have inner coaches with LFRs of less than one so their self-talk interferes with learning.

The conclusions drawn are that effective learning cultures offer all participants full respect, ways of reducing blocks, and activities that encourage thinking. Judgmental behaviours negate all of these components so need eliminating.

Theoretical underpinnings: learning cultures need to maximize positive emotions

The behaviours composing Respecting People and Negating People are associated with the social emotions of pride and shame. According to Scheff (1997) these emotions control social bonding: a term that corresponds to Evison's definition of culture. Scheff's theory links the development of secure bonds within the family with what he terms cultures of *solidarity* while insecure bonds lead to cultures of *alienation*. He says, 'the theory ... suggests that the *structure* of actual social relationships involves mixtures of alienation and solidarity, and that the exact proportion can be determined through the analysis of verbatim discourse' (Scheff 1997: 73). This parallels the behaviour category measurements of LFR. In addition, he has a concept of inner relationships paralleling the inner coach and inner learner, stating 'alienation can occur not only from others but from self' (Scheff 1997: 74).

According to Scheff (1997: 74) 'The *dynamics* of relationships are explained in terms of the emotion that accompanies solidarity, pride, and the one that accompanies alienation, shame. Pride signals and generates solidarity. Shame signals and generates alienation.' For Scheff's other papers and books concerning shame and its links to sociological phenomena see his website (2005). Thus cultures that support learning are ones in which pride is the dominant emotion, while cultures that support blocks are ones where shame predominates. Understanding how to change the latter into the former requires a sound theoretical base for managing emotions. The 'integrative theory of emotional responses' provides such a base (Evison 2002). Key points of this theory are as follows.

Emotions are envisaged as forming the basic operating system whereby humans survive, adapt and learn as individuals and groups. They provide the motivation and resources for whole organism interactions with environments: the physical and social environments and also the internal environment of the conscious mind. Basic positive and negative emotions have different and complementary functions inbuilt by evolution. This view is consonant with a growing body of research in fields varying from psychoneurophysiology to linguistics, with theorizing linking the nature of humans to the characteristic ways their bodies interact with their physical and social environments (see Varela *et al.* 1991 and Johnson 1987).

Functional positive emotions

Interest, joy, love and pride all motivate and organize body and mind resources for learning to enhance long-term survival: the *learning mode*. In the pleasurable emotions of learning mode, individuals are relaxed and alert with maximum choice over actions and able to call on their skills, knowledge and required energy as needed. This mode forms the ongoing base state to which homeostatic processes will seek to return the individual's mind and body after interruptions.

Functional negative emotions

Disgust, anger, fear, grief and shame all motivate and organize resources for dealing with physical and psychological threat, overriding learning mode to maximize short-term survival: the *emergency response mode*. In this mode individuals have their attention compulsorily focused on the threat and the appropriate muscles are aroused for action. The sympathetic nervous system organizes energy support for those muscles activated whilst the threat continues. Failure to act is painful.

When a threat ceases, inbuilt homeostatic processes utilize the parasympathetic nervous system to conserve resources, returning mind and body to learning mode. If a threat has been mastered the activated muscles start to relax, sending a signal to the parasympathetic nervous system which then operates the reset process: termed a *mastery-reset*. If a threat is survived without being mastered reset is needed to release aroused muscles and threat-focused attention to prevent interference with performing the next task and to minimize wear and tear to the body. In this case when the individual perceives the threat has gone away, non-purposive actions of the aroused muscles relax them and initiate reset to learning mode: *failure-reset*.

These *failure-reset* processes are emotionally expressive ones that are typically inhibited by socialization. They are specific to the aroused emotion: shaking from fear, storming from anger, retching from disgust, crying from grief and laughing from shame. Such inhibition leaves the individual in pain, which drives conditioning processes to produce the dysfunctional emotional responses called blocks: *blocked mode*. To reset from blocked mode to learning mode requires reproducing the conditions that govern failure-reset – namely an absence of current threat plus the restimulating of the original aroused emotion – resulting in *therapeutic-reset*.

The theory suggests that reset to the positive emotions of learning mode from emergency response mode or blocked mode can be initiated by: mastery experiences, removal of threats from awareness, muscular relaxation, physical exercise and the use of inbuilt failure-reset processes. Laughing as the reset process for shame is particularly relevant in learning cultures. These processes form the basis of a toolkit for change for individuals and groups. For a more complete account of this theory and supporting research see Evison (2001). Strikingly parallel theoretical concepts, based on extensive child development research, are summarized by Sroufe (1996).

Another thread of underpinning theory hypothesizes that we are social creatures before we are individuals; e.g. Dweck and Sorich (1999) demonstrate that the learning–facilitation abilities of inner coaches depend on the relationships with key adults during early development. There is a great deal of evidence from different research areas that all development follows the social to individual path e.g. the regulation of emotional arousal, the development of language, self-consciousness and thinking ability. For up-to-date reviews of this thread, including brain research pointing to inbuilt social awareness at birth, see Thompson (2001). This thread emphasizes that major strategies for developing lifelong learners need to focus on changing learning group cultures rather than on individual attributes.

Secure bonding cultures facilitate lifelong learners

Secure bonding cultures provide participants with the maximum time in positive emotions so that learning is maximized. They also promote the self-efficacy beliefs needed by lifelong learners. In learning contexts such cultures are called *supportive learning groups*. The processes exemplified below represent characteristics of secure bonding cultures whilst also being instrumental processes for bringing about the desired changes.

Structuring co-operative working relationships

Working relationships in learning situations can be structured by activities in which participants are asked to: listen respectfully, support others' learning, maintain confidentiality for personal information, avoid putdowns and negative judgments of others and self and use laughter to defuse any negative impacts of infringements of these guidelines. This can be done with varying degrees of formality. More formal activities suitable for older children and adults are *reciprocal role pairs* and a *supportive learning contract*.

Working in reciprocal-role pairs

Participants take the roles of active learner or listener and exchange these roles halfway through the activity time – typically three minutes for each participant. Learners are asked to use the time to explore the topic by talking out loud as thoughts occur to them, without seeking to make a presentation or impress the listener or even to fill all their time with talking. Listeners are asked to give supportive attention to learners without interrupting in any way i.e. no questions, comments or non-verbal judgments. Their role is to provide a non-threatening environment and it does not matter if they do not make sense of what the learner is saying. Confidentiality precludes the listener asking questions or bringing up any topics outside the timed sessions. Kirby (1993) argues that this activity enables participants to surface relevant past experience, to explore their ideas on a topic or to explore implications of presented information in a supportive non-judgmental culture.

Equal time activities enhance co-operative relationships by signalling that everyone is an equally worthwhile group member regardless of ability. They also maximize everyone's involvement in talking and listening so maximizing their learning opportunities.

Using a supportive learning contract

Group participants are asked to opt into behaviours that maximize everyone's ability to learn, agreeing to:

a   Set themselves challenging learning goals.
b   Support other people's learning by treating them respectfully.
c   Keep all personal information confidential.
d   Avoid putdowns or negative judgments of others or self.
e   Use laughter to defuse infringements of the contract, on the basis that no-one is expected to be perfect.

(Evison 2001: 261)

Encouraging self-efficacy and minimizing blocks

The strategies below are discussed in Evison (2001) with further supporting research cited.

Increasing emotional resilience

Persistence in the face of difficulties requires maintaining self-efficacy beliefs and pride – both increased by mastery experiences. Remembering unrelated mastery experiences increases self-efficacy for difficult tasks. Mastery experiences are stored as *affirmational resources* (Steele *et al.*1993) which may be increased by *celebrating achievements* and *appreciating strengths and skills* of self and others.

Using positive experiences

Activities that keep attention focused on pleasant experiences, including pleasant memories, will remove threats from awareness, resulting in automatic reset to learning mode.

Disinhibiting emotional controls

The active relaxation of tense muscles by physical loosening, shaking, stretching, or yawning disrupts block responses initiating reset to learning mode (Kirby 1993).

Using humorous reframing

There are simple techniques for facilitating laughter in, or about, distressing situations. These equate to the use of black humour.

Building trust

Herriot *et al.* (1998) argue that successful culture change depends upon key people relating with mutual trust. Although their book is focused on employment relationships, many points apply to facilitating–learning cultures. Trust is built through activities that encourage personal sharing in a safe non-judgmental context: sharing feelings, values, blocks, and working in reciprocal-role pairs. Evison (unpublished research, 1985), using a trust scale relating directly to other group members, found that supportive group structured activities used for two to three hours resulted in new groups significantly increasing their levels of group trust.

Laughing instead of getting stuck

Laughing is the reset process for shame emotions and shame-derived blocks which undermine secure bonding. We become vulnerable when laughing because the muscles aroused are antagonists to those required for fight or flight. This means we only laugh when we are safe, so laughter in a group signals a safe group, strengthens group cohesiveness and mediates social support (Fry 1994). Laughter acts as a readily accessible and acceptable mediator of culture change.

Strategies crucial for successful culture change

Organizational researchers and practitioners agree that achieving culture change is difficult. This is because it involves block reduction, skill development and changing social relationships i.e. intellectual, emotional and social development. The crucial strategies are:

Winning hearts and minds

Stepping into the unknown, particularly when it appears antagonistic to established ideas and methods, is typically threatening to everyone involved. All stakeholders in culture changes need to be provided with experiences – or reminded of relevant parts of their existing knowledge – that enable them to understand the benefits and motivate them to support change. Moreover, the wider the gap between participants' existing cultures and the new one, the more extensive the work to make the new culture desirable. An example in the learning situation context is having participants review positive life/work experiences separately from negative ones. The links between positive emotions, high performance and wellbeing emerge, as do the contrasting links between negative emotions, poor performance and stress. Suggesting everyone's learning will be greater in a supportive environment then makes sense, and participants are motivated to opt into a supportive group contract.

Enabling participants' ownership of their culture

For lasting change, participants need to be actively involved in maintaining their own supportive learning culture. Without this the new culture is being sustained by rewards and punishments – an ineffective process for long-term change. A supportive learning contract gives participants ownership. Less formally the idea that the group is a team co-operating to help everyone learn can be used to encourage participants to take on responsibilities.

Learning the new culture's language

Since culture could be regarded as consisting of the social behaviour that makes up relationships in a group, changing culture means the discourse of the group changes. New ways of relating, new ideas and working methods need new language in which to explore them. Our language is interactive with our experience, understanding something is finding a metaphor for it that connects the experience to our existing store of knowledge (Johnson 1987). Learning the language of respecting people is done by activities in which the behaviours are used and observed and talked about. Such learning also contributes to participants taking ownership of a new culture.

Treating violations non-judgmentally

Changing culture takes time and old culture behaviours will keep intruding, particularly judgmental ones. To sustain change such violations need treating by non-judgmental responses that defuse shame blocks by inducing laughter e.g. put-downs of others or self can be labelled 'foul' said in a delighted tone of voice, and mistakes or errors responded to with 'Yippee! A mistake'. To help with internalizing the new culture such block disrupters need socializing as 'games' for everyone.

Current cultures that are difficult to change

Winning hearts and minds may be particularly difficult when major stakeholders are committed to ideas or working methods that are antagonistic to the new culture methods, as participants will lack motivation or even be hostile. Even small proportions of such participants in a group may be disruptive and limiting. In Evison's experience the cultures listed below are antagonistic to supportive learning culture:

- Professionals associating supportive learning processes with featherbedding and demotivating participants. They fail to distinguish between *support* and *special service* (Martin 1980). Professionals thinking anything to do with laughing or acting emotionally is childish or alternatively it is dangerous and out of control. These are common blocks in our culture.
- Group dynamics-based approaches that postulate natural life cycles in group development such as the Forming, Storming, Norming and Performing model (Tuckman and Jensen 1977). Such approaches are antagonistic to the structured activities that can be used to rapidly set up supportive learning cultures.
- Professionals committed to dealing with negative feelings by *staying with them* and *processing them immediately* are antagonistic to switching out of negative thinking and feelings to get on with current tasks. Originally derived from gestalt therapy these ideas are widespread, particularly in learning facilitators who do group work.
- Cognitivists who are convinced that thoughts rule emotions so dismiss or exclude emotion-based activities. While the body of research and theory known as post-cognitivism shows this idea to be inadequate, it is still a dominant one in our society.

Conclusions

To foster lifelong learners, supportive learning cultures are needed, not only in learning groups but also inside the minds of participants. Such cultures actively maintain positive emotions and tackle blocks, enabling participants to develop emotional resilience. To change a culture is difficult as it involves intellectual, emotional and social development. The new culture means participants in learning situations need to act as a co-operative team rather than a collection of individuals. Participation in such cultures is a pre-requisite for participants to develop a corresponding inner coach culture. The strategies described in this chapter are reliable ones for setting up supportive learning cultures and they have theoretical backing. However, increasing the numbers of lifelong learners in our society requires embedding change within learning-facilitator training institutions. This task is beyond the scope of this chapter. However, the strategies discussed here point the way to tackling such changes. In addition, progress can be catalysed by using the Respecting People/Negating People language to make allies of key change agents. This behaviour category language also provides a highly reliable technology for doing the necessary evaluative research.

References

Aspy, D.N. and Roebuck, F.N. (1976) *A Lever Long Enough*, Washington, DC.: National Consortium for Humanizing Education.

Dweck, C.S. and Sorich, L.A. (1999) 'Mastery-oriented thinking', in C.R. Snyder (ed.) *Coping: the Psychology of What Works*, New York: Oxford University Press.

Evison, R. (1985) 'Setting up supportive groups rapidly in counselling and educational settings', paper presented at workshop of same name at the London Conference of the British Psychological Society, London, December.

Evison, R. (1990a) *Encouraging Excellence in Trainer Classroom Delivery*, Research report to the European Educational Services Division of Digital Equipment, Pitlochry, Scotland: Change Strategies.

Evison, R. (1990b) *Facilitating Learning: what helps and hinders*, Pitlochry, Scotland: Change Strategies.

Evison, R. (2001) 'Helping individuals manage emotional responses', in R.L Payne and C.L. Cooper (eds) *Emotions at Work: Theory, Research, and Applications for Management*, Chichester, UK: John Wiley and Sons.

Evison, R. (2002) 'Developing human potential by reclaiming the creative resources locked up in dysfunctional emotional responses', paper presented at workshop of same name at the British Psychological Society Scottish Branch Annual Conference in Perth, November.

Evison, R. and Horobin, R. (1988) 'Co-counselling', in W. Dryden and J. Rowan (eds) *Innovative Therapies in Britain*, Milton Keynes: Open University Press.

Evison, R. and Ronaldson, J.B. (1975) 'A behaviour category instrument for analysing counselling interactions', *British Journal of Guidance and Counselling*, 3: 82–92.

Fry, W. F. (1994) ' The biology of humour', *Humor: International Journal of Humor Research*, 7: 111–26.

Herriot, P., Hirsh, W. and Reilly, P. (1998) *Trust and Transition*, Chichester: John Wiley & Sons.

Holt, J. (1965) *How Children Fail*, London: Pitman.

Johnson, M. (1987) *The Body in the Mind: the Bodily Basis of Meaning, Imagination, and Reason*, Chicago: University of Chicago Press.

Kirby, A. (1993) *A Compendium of Icebreakers, Energizers and Introductions*, Aldershot: Gower Press.

Kohn, A. (1993) *Punished by Rewards: the Trouble with Gold Stars, Incentive Plans, As, Praise, and other Bribes*, Boston: Houghton Mifflin.

Martin, R.J. (1980) *Teaching through Encouragement*, Englewood Cliffs NJ.: Prentice Hall.

Metfessel, N.S., Michael, W.B. and Kirsner, D.A. (1969) 'Instrumentation of Bloom's and Krathwohl's taxonomies for the writing of educational objectives', *Psychology in the school*, 6: 227–31.

Porges, S.W. (2001) 'The polyvagal theory: phylogenetic substrates of a social nervous system', *International Journal of Psychophysiology*, 42: 123–46.

Rackham, N. and Morgan, T. (1977) *Behaviour Analysis in Training*, Maidenhead: McGraw-Hill.

Ronaldson, J.B. and Evison, R. (1975) 'Integrating theory and practice in counsellor training', *British Journal of Guidance and Counselling*, 3: 219–27.

Scheff, T.J. (1997) *Emotions, the Social Bond, and Human Reality: Part/whole analysis*, Cambridge, UK: Cambridge University Press.

Sroufe, L.A. (1996) *Emotional Development: The Organisation of Emotional Life in the Early Years*, Cambridge: Cambridge University Press.

Steele, C.M., Spencer, S.J. and Lynch, M. (1993) 'Self-image resilience and dissonance: the role of affirmational resources', *Journal of Personality and Social Psychology*, 64: 885–96.

Thompson, E. (2001) *Between Ourselves: Second-Person Issues in the Study of Consciousness*, Thorverton, UK: Imprint Academic.

Tuckman, B. and Jensen, M. (1977) 'Stages of small group development revisited', *Group and Organisational Studies*, 2: 419–27.

Varela, F.J., Thompson, E. and Rosch, E. (1991) *The Embodied Mind*, London, England: MIT Press.

Chapter 10

An analysis of the relations between learning and teaching approaches

Keith Trigwell

The purpose of this chapter is to contribute to our understanding of good teaching in higher education. The distinction between 'surface learning' approaches and 'deep learning' approaches is well established in the literature. However, we know surprisingly little about the relationship between these approaches and teaching. The author argues from a series of research studies that to produce 'deep learning' approaches in students, which achieves higher quality learning outcomes than a learner-focused teaching approach, that addresses conceptual change, is more effective. Furthermore, training teachers to adopt this approach seems to have an impact and this in turn contributes to enhancing lifelong learning.

Introduction

Lifelong learning (and the students engaged in that learning) has been investigated and analysed in a variety of ways and from many different perspectives. In this chapter, the focus is on the qualitative variation in the ways university students approach their learning, the relations between those approaches and the quality of learning, and the effects on learning of variation in teaching.

The student learning perspective taken in the chapter is no longer new, but since the ideas first appeared some 30 years ago, it has contributed to a significant change in the direction and application of student learning research. The key features of this perspective are that students' approaches to learning are seen to be relational rather than mainly characteristics of the student, and that variation in approaches to learning is related to variation in the quality of the outcomes of learning.

The study of university teaching from the same perspective is more recent, with the first substantive publications appearing from Australian studies conducted in the early 1990s. This chapter contains a summary of some of the research that has investigated the qualitative variation in students' approaches to learning and teachers' approaches to teaching, with an emphasis on the studies that have investigated the links between the two. While this work was conducted in an Australian context, its wider relevance has been demonstrated in replication studies in other contexts. The chapter ends with some results from recent research that has confirmed and extended the earlier studies.

Qualitatively different approaches to learning

In the early 1970s in Sweden, Marton and colleagues developed new ways of studying the way students approached reading tasks, initially in education (reported in Marton and Booth 1997). The origins of this approach derive from a desire by Marton to move beyond the study of artificial learning tasks to look at how students were actually learning. He focused his research on learning in the context in which learning would normally occur and described the variation in how the students learn, not from the point of view of the researcher, but from the student's own view of their approach. In considering these two elements, Marton developed a new research approach which took a relational perspective and differed from other approaches in two fundamental ways. First, it was argued that in studying a phenomenon, such as students' approaches to learning, there are a limited number of qualitatively different ways in which the phenomenon is experienced by a group. Commonalities across the group are ignored or set aside in the search for clusters of qualitative variation. The range of categories constitutes the variation in the meaning of that phenomenon as experienced by that group. And second, that these qualitatively different categories are hierarchal and are logically related, forming an outcome space. The research approach is known as phenomenography (Marton 1981; Marton and Booth 1997).

Using a relational approach, the Swedish group and others identified two qualitatively different student approaches to learning, labelled a 'deep' approach and a 'surface' approach. Students who adopt a deep approach to learning are more likely to engage in learning that lasts than students who adopt a surface approach to learning (for a summary, see Trigwell *et al.* 1999). An approach to learning is evoked by students' perceptions of their situation (a relationship between the context and the student) and so it is not fully a characteristic of either the student or the context. A student's approach to learning does change with changing perceptions of their learning situation (Entwistle and Ramsden 1983) and their perceptions of it can be changed by university teachers and administrators.

Definitions of approaches to learning also vary with the context of learning. The following are derived from several sources.

> The motivation associated with a deep approach to learning is to understand ideas and seek meanings. In adopting this approach students have an intrinsic interest in the task and an expectation of enjoyment in carrying it out. They adopt strategies that help satisfy their curiosity, such as making the task coherent with their own experience, relating and distinguishing evidence and argument, looking for patterns and underlying principles, integrating the task with existing awareness, seeing the parts of a task as making up the whole, theorizing about it, forming hypotheses, and relating understanding from other parts of the same subject, and from different subjects. Overall they have a focus on the meaning in the argument, the message, or the relationships but they are aware that the meanings are carried by the words, the text, the formulae.

In adopting a surface approach to learning, students see tasks as external impositions and they have the intention to cope with these requirements. They are instrumentally or pragmatically motivated and seek to meet the demands of the task with minimum effort. They adopt strategies which include: a focus on unrelated parts of the task, separate treatment of related parts (for example principles and examples), a focus on what are seen as essentials (factual data and their symbolic representations) the reproduction of the essentials as accurately as possible, and rote memorizing information for assessment purposes rather than for understanding. Overall they would appear to be involved in study without reflection on purpose or strategy, with the focus of that study being on the words, the text, or the formulae.

(Trigwell *et al.* 1999: 91)

The aim in taking this view of student learning is to describe the key aspects of how students vary in their approaches to learning rather than necessarily fully describing the way students go about learning. Some aspects of learning may not be included. For example, quantitative dimensions, such as how well a student is applying such an approach. Variations in approach do not include elements that are shared, such as an overriding vocational orientation. What they do include are those aspects thought to explain previously unexplained variation in the quality of the learning outcome.

The investigation of relations between learning approaches and outcomes requires large-scale quantitative studies:

For these studies to work, (a) there needs to be a means of identifying and quantifying the variation in the variables being related: if there is no variation there will be no correlation; and (b) the variation needs to be hierarchical. Relations between variables where one or more are not hierarchical are unlikely to be meaningful. The outcome space of a phenomenographic analysis contains a hierarchy of internally-related categories which, if not directly suited to relational studies, offer insight into how such studies might be conducted.

(Trigwell and Richardson 2003: 41)

While its origins are not phenomenographic, an inventory designed to measure qualitative variation in approaches to university learning of Australian students (Study Process Questionnaire, SPQ) has been developed by Biggs (Biggs *et al.* 2001). However, the SPQ does contain a Deep Approach to Learning scale, and a Surface Approach to Learning scale, each with intention and strategy sub-scales.

The implications of the variation in approaches to learning for lifelong learning are illustrated in the studies of relations between learning approach and outcomes of learning. Studies in the 1970s on approaches to student learning (Marton and Säljö 1976; Biggs 1978; Entwistle and Ramsden 1983) initially reported the differences between deep approaches and surface approaches to learning. Studies then and since have consistently shown that deeper approaches to learning are related to higher quality learning outcomes (Marton *et al.* 1997; van Rossum and Schenk 1984; Trigwell and Prosser 1991; Prosser and Millar 1989).

Until recently the association between the ways university teachers teach and these approaches and outcomes of learning were unknown. In the rest of this chapter, the studies designed to explore these relations are described.

Qualitatively different approaches to teaching

Studies of university teaching in Australia have articulated qualitative variation in approaches (Martin and Balla 1991; Samuelowicz and Bain 1992, 2001; Trigwell and Prosser 1996a). This variation is illustrated in the following two quotations taken from interviews with Australian university science teachers:

> Teacher A: So in preparing for an hour lecture I decide what I want the students to get out of this lecture, specifically what I want them to be able to do as a result of this lecture. So that is one of the first parts of planning my list if you like, planning my lecture. I also plan them in a way so that I know the notes that I want the students to get. I'll write my notes in such a way so that the students don't have to decide when to take notes, I tell them to. I'll dictate to them, I have handouts prepared, I have gaps in them that they fill in and I take that decision away from the students about when and how to take notes.

> Teacher E: I think, more explicitly what I want to achieve with, eh, buzz-sessions and the questions, and stuff [in lectures] is confronting students with their pre-conceived ideas about the subject which quite often conflict with what we're talking about, the official dogmas as it were. Um, so you've got to bring out that conflict and make the people aware that what they already know may not be what is the official line, as it were.
>
> (Trigwell *et al.* 1999: 139, 141)

The extracts illustrate the extremes of the qualitative variation found in approaches to teaching of science teachers. In the phenomenographic study from which they derive (Trigwell, *et al.* 1994), five qualitatively different approaches to teaching were constituted. The extract from Teacher E illustrates one approach, called a Conceptual Change/Student-focused (CCSF) approach, which is inclusive of the other four. In adopting this approach teachers have a student-focused strategy with the aim of changing students' conceptions of the subject matter. The least inclusive approach, called an Information Transmission/Teacher-focused (ITTF) approach (illustrated in the quote from Teacher A), involves a teacher-focused strategy aimed at transmitting information to students. Transmission elements of the ITTF approach are included in the CCSF approach, but the student-focused element of a CCSF approach is not a part of the ITTF approach. Because of this inclusivity, a CCSF approach is

Table 10.1 Examples of items from the approaches to teaching inventory (ATI)

Information transmission/Teacher-focused (ITTF) approach

Intention item: I feel it is important to present a lot of facts in the classes so that students know what they have to learn for this subject.

Strategy item: I structure this subject to help students to pass the formal assessment items.

Conceptual change/Student-focused (CCSF) approach

Intention item: I feel a lot of teaching time in this subject should be used to question students' ideas.

Strategy item: I make available opportunities for students in this subject to discuss their changing understanding of the subject.

considered to be a more sophisticated or complete approach than the more limiting ITTF approach.

Using the outcome space of the phenomenographic study referred to above, an inventory designed to measure qualitative variation in approaches to teaching of Australian teachers, the Approaches to Teaching Inventory (ATI), was developed (Trigwell and Prosser 2004). It includes items designed to capture the variation described above, and in the quotes from Teachers A and E. Like the SPQ it includes intention and strategy items, examples of which are given below. This questionnaire was used to study relations between learning and teaching approaches.

Relations between learning and teaching approaches

When asked to describe the type of approach to learning teachers prefer of their students, the response is almost always a deep approach. Given this preference among teachers, is there a teaching approach that is positively related to deep approaches to learning, and if so, is this also the approach to teaching adopted by these teachers? To explore this question, two surveys of students and their teachers were carried out in Australia in the mid 1990s. One study involved 48 first year science classes (46 teachers and 3956 students) while the second covered a broad range of disciplines, and involved 55 large first year subjects with feedback from 408 teachers and 8829 students in the classes of those teachers.

The data from both studies were subjected to correlation, cluster and factor analyses as reported elsewhere (Trigwell *et al.* 1999; Trigwell *et al.* 1998). In summary, the results, with classes as the unit of analysis, showed that an information transmission/teacher-focused approach to teaching is strongly and positively associated with surface and non-deep approaches to learning and that a conceptual change/student-focused approach to teaching is positively associated with deep and non-surface approaches to learning. The correlation results from the multi-disciplinary study are shown here (Table 10.2) as an example of the nature of the relations.

Table 10.2 Correlation between teachers' approach to teaching and students' approach to learning variables

Variable	Variable			
	Deep	Surface	CCSF	ITTF
Deep approach to learning	–	–0.22	0.38*	–0.15
Surface approach to learning		–	–0.48*	0.38*
CCSF approach to teaching			–	–0.30
ITTF approach to teaching				–

*p (probability) < 0.05, n (number in sample) = 55
CCSF   Conceptual Change/Student-focused
ITTF   Information Transmission/Teacher-focused

When teachers report that their focus is on what they do in their teaching, when they believe students have little or no prior knowledge of the subject they are teaching, when they do little more than transmit facts so that students will have a good set of notes (ITTF approach), then their students are more likely to adopt a surface approach to learning. Conversely, when teachers report that they have the student as the focus of their activities, where it matters more to them what the student is doing and learning than what the teacher is doing or covering, where the teacher is one who encourages self-directed learning, who makes time (in formal 'teaching' time) for students to interact and to discuss the problems they encounter, where the teacher assesses to reveal conceptual change, where the teacher provokes debate, uses a lot of time to question students' ideas and to develop a 'conversation' with students in lectures (CCSF approach), then their students are less likely to be adopting a surface approach and more likely to be adopting a deep approach.

Studies which show relations between what teachers do and what their students do are uncommon in higher education. Greeson (1988) reported research on activities in two classes: one student-centred and the other teacher-centred. Each class contained 16 students, and one lecturer who served as the instructor for both classes. The results showed that although the outcome of the two classes was not statistically different, the overall students' experience in the student-centred class was more favourable. The student-centred self-directed method of teaching was rated consistently higher by the students than the traditional teacher-centred approach. For example, higher values were recorded on variables such as organization and direction, interest and enthusiasm, and presentation and clarity. This study is tentatively suggesting that student-centred approaches are more desirable. Similar results were found in Hong Kong by Kember and Gow (1994). Using the university department as the unit of analysis, they found substantial relations between teachers' orientation to teaching (learning facilitation or knowledge transmission) and the approaches to learning of students (deep or surface) in the department.

The relations observed in the studies described in this chapter are significant because they show connections between teaching and outcomes of learning which point to ways to improve student learning through teaching, and therefore help to define good teaching. Numerous studies have contributed to the growing evidence that surface approaches to learning are related to lower quality outcomes of learning as noted earlier. In the new studies described above, a pathway connecting variation in approach to *teaching* and the quality of student learning outcomes has been established.

This connecting pathway assists in the development of programmes to improve student learning. Research (Entwistle and Ramsden 1983) that indicated that student perceptions of their learning environment are related to their approaches to learning was a source of information used in attempts to improve learning. By focusing on changing students' perceptions of those aspects of the learning environment described by students to be related to their approaches to learning, it is possible to improve the quality of learning. The results from the teaching/learning relations studies described above highlight the importance in these attempts of also working with academic staff to encourage the adoption of CCSF approaches to teaching. In order to change the way teachers approach their teaching (to focus more on their students rather than their own performance) it may be necessary to address conceptions of teaching and learning (Trigwell 1995; Trigwell and Prosser 1996b). Where teachers conceive of learning as information accumulation to meet external demands and conceive of teaching as transmitting information to students, they approach their teaching in terms of teacher-focused strategies. On the other hand, where teachers conceive of learning as developing and changing students' conceptions, they conceive of teaching in terms of helping students to develop and change their conceptions and approach their teaching in a student-focused way.

Teaching that is student-focused, that encourages self-directed learning, that includes time (in formal 'teaching' time) for students to interact and to discuss the problems they encounter, that assesses to reveal conceptual change, that provokes debate, uses a lot of time to question students' ideas and to develop a 'conversation' with students in lectures, is good teaching. While recognizing and rewarding good teaching in universities has been well researched (Ramsden *et al.* 1995) these CCSF approach elements are often not included.

The foundations of the research perspective adopted in this research are continuing to be explored in the teaching context. Data on teachers' approach to teaching collected in Helsinki and Oxford (Lindblom-Ylänne *et al.* 2004) show that the same teacher, in different contexts, reports adopting different approaches to teaching. This result is supportive of the relational bases of this perspective. Teachers can also change their approach to teaching over time. Academics at the University of Oxford who are participants in a Postgraduate Diploma in Learning and Teaching in Higher Education were asked to describe their teaching approach to a particular subject before and after completing the course using the ATI. The results of that study show statistically significant increases in CCSF scores and no significant change in ITTF scores over the year of the course. Gibbs and Coffey (2004) observe similar changes in approach to teaching. When compared with a control group, university teachers in a teacher 'training' programme show no change in ITTF scores and increases in CCSF scores over the life of the programme, and the latter are associated with changes in their students' approaches to learning. These studies suggest that changes in approaches to teaching are possible and may lead to changes in learning.

In conclusion, the major outcomes of this research, that teachers who themselves report adopting more of an ITTF approach to teaching have students who themselves report adopting a more surface approach to learning, and that teachers who report adopting more of a CCSF approach to teaching have students who report adopting a more deep approach to learning, are seen as a means through which lifelong learning might be enhanced. Without a result such as this, much of the previous research from the student learning perspective on teaching and learning in higher education would be for nought. However, there is still work to be done. No mention has been made until now of causality or the direction of causality in describing the relations observed in these studies. They were not designed to yield such information and in any event, the issue of causality is problematic. For example, the context established by a teacher using a conceptual change/student-focused approach may influence students to adopt a deep approach, but it may be equally likely that some teachers adapt their approach to teaching in response to the requests of students to, for example, go through problems in a transmission/teacher-focused manner. Such issues are the focus of continuing research.

Acknowedgements

Much of the original work described in this chapter was conducted by the author in collaboration with Michael Prosser, whose contribution is acknowledged.

References

Biggs, J.B. (1978) 'Individual and group differences in study processes', *British Journal of Educational Psychology*, 48: 266–79.

Biggs, J., Kember, D. and Leung, D.Y.P. (2001) 'The revised two-factor study process questionnaire: R-SPQ-2F', *British Journal of Educational Psychology*, 71:133–49.

Entwistle, N. and Ramsden, P. (1983) *Understanding Student Learning*, London: Croom Helm.

Greeson, L.E. (1988) 'College classroom interaction as a function of teacher- and student-centered instruction', *Teaching and Teacher Education* 4: 305–15.

Gibbs, G. and Coffey, M. (2004) 'The impact of training of university teachers on their skills, their approaches to teaching and the approach to learning of their students', *Active Learning*, 5: 87–100.

Kember, D. and Gow, L. (1994) 'Orientations to teaching and their effect on the quality of student learning', *Journal of Higher Education*, 65: 59–74.

Lindblom-Ylänne, S., Trigwell, K., Nevgi, A. and Ashwin, P. (2004) 'Variation in approaches to teaching: the role of discipline and teaching context', paper presented at *The Scandinavian Baltic Sea Conference*, June.

Martin, E. and Balla, M. (1991) 'Conceptions of teaching and implications for learning', *Research and Development in Higher Education*, 13: 298–304.

Marton, F. (1981) 'Phenomenography – describing conceptions of the world around us', *Instructional Science*, 10: 177–200.

Marton, F. and Booth, S. (1997) *Learning and Awareness*. New Jersey: Lawrence Erlbaum Associates.

Marton, F. and Säljö, R. (1976) 'On qualitative differences in learning. I. Outcome and process', *British Journal of Educational Psychology*, 46: 4–11.

Marton, F., Hounsell, D. and Entwistle, N.J. (eds) (1997) *The Experience of Learning: Implications for Teaching and Studying in Higher Education*, 2nd edn, Edinburgh: Scottish Academic Press.

Prosser, M. and Millar, R. (1989) 'The "how" and "what" of learning physics', *The European Journal of Psychology of Education*, 4: 513–28.

Ramsden, P., Margetson, D., Martin, E. and Clarke, S. (1995) *Recognising and Rewarding Good Teaching*, Australian Government Printing Services: Canberra.

Samuelowicz, K. and Bain, J.D. (1992) 'Conceptions of teaching held by teachers', *Higher Education*, 24: 93–112.

Samuelowicz, K. and Bain, J.D (2001) 'Revisiting academics' beliefs about teaching and learning', *Higher Education*, 41: 299–325.

Trigwell, K. (1995) 'Increasing faculty understanding of teaching', in W.A. Wright (ed.) *Teaching Improvement Practices: Successful Faculty Development Strategies*, Bolton, MA.: Anker Publishing Co.

Trigwell, K. and Prosser, M. (1991) 'Relating approaches to study and the quality of learning outcomes at the course level', *British Journal of Educational Psychology*, 61: 265–75.

Trigwell, K. and Prosser, M. (1996a) 'Congruence between intention and strategy in science teachers' approach to teaching', *Higher Education*, 32: 77–87.

Trigwell, K. and Prosser, M. (1996b) 'Changing approaches to teaching: a relational perspective', *Studies in Higher Education*, 21: 275–84.

Trigwell, K. and Prosser, M. (2004) 'Development and use of the approaches to teaching inventory', *Educational Psychology Review*, 16: 409–26.

Trigwell, K. and Richardson, J.T.E. (2003) 'Qualitative and quantitative: complementary approaches to research on student learning', in C. Rust (ed.) *Improving Student Learning Conference Proceedings*, 10: 37–49.

Trigwell, K., Prosser, M. and Taylor, P. (1994) 'Qualitative differences in approaches to teaching first year university science', *Higher Education*, 27: 75–84.

Trigwell, K., Prosser, M. and Waterhouse, F. (1999) 'Relations between teachers' approaches to teaching and students' approach to learning', *Higher Education*, 37: 57–70.

Trigwell, K., Prosser, M., Ramsden, P. and Martin, E. (1998) '*Improving student learning through a focus on the teaching context*', in C. Rust (ed.) *Improving Student Learning. Improving Students as Learners*, Oxford: Oxford Centre for Staff and Learning Development.

van Rossum, E.J. and Schenk, S.M. (1984) 'The relationship between learning conception, study strategy and learning outcome', *British Journal of Educational Psychology*, 54: 73–83.

Chapter 11

Lifelong learning

The role of emotional intelligence

Tina Goodwin and Susan Hallam

Since the 1990s there has been an increasing interest in emotional intelligence and its relationship to motivation. In this chapter the authors draw on empirical work involving a study of students undertaking a computer course. Several of the class struggled to complete their programme of study, due to problems of fitting it in with work and personal commitments, and many were dis-satisfied with the teaching approach. Half of the original class dropped out of the course. This account examines how these adults coped with their emotional difficulties and makes practical suggestions about how tutors might utilize emotional intelligence to improve teaching and learning.

Introduction

Research into motivation in adult learning has tended to focus on the individual's motives for attending courses and the obstacles that may prevent attendance (La Valle and Blake 2001; McGivney 2001). Intrinsic and extrinsic motives have been identified (McGivney 1995; Woodley *et al.* 1987), while studies of drop out have highlighted issues including inappropriate placement of students on courses, students' prior expectations and the poor quality of resources in colleges (McGivney 1996; Martinez and Munday 1998). Blaxter (1999) found that life crisis events and an unsafe and insecure social living environment kept students away from classes. Interpersonal relationships within the class were also important, a finding supported by Goodwin (1996) who identified unsatisfactory class organization as influencing drop out.

Adult motivation for learning

It is beyond the scope of this chapter to review the extensive literature on motivation but, briefly, research adopting a psychological perspective and undertaken with a range of populations has shown the importance of the individual's perception and interpretation of events in their subsequent influence on motivation. Expectancy-value models incorporate three elements: value components which include the value ascribed to the task, its intrinsic value, and utility; expectancy components which include beliefs about the ability to perform, self-efficacy, control and expectancy for success; and affective components which are related to anxiety regarding performance (e.g. Eccles 1983). The models suggest that learners are highly motivated when they value the task that they are to undertake, for its own sake or for its usefulness; when they feel that they can tackle the task, have control over their performance and are able to succeed; and when their performance is not disrupted by nervousness and anxiety.

Other approaches have stressed the extent to which learners have specific learning goals. These are particularly powerful motivators if they are linked to individuals' self-concepts through their perceptions of positive 'possible selves' – visions of themselves in the future that are realistic and attainable (Markus and Ruvolo 1989). Needs to achieve or to attain competence can also be powerful motivators (Murray 1938; Koestner and McClelland 1990). The attainment of personal goals is mediated by the extent to which the individual can regulate their behaviour and persist when tasks are difficult. Also important is the way that failure and success are attributed. If failure is attributed to what is perceived to be a stable characteristic, for instance, ability, the learner is likely to give up. If failure is attributed to a chance factor, perhaps a particularly difficult examination paper, motivation is likely to be sustained (Weiner 1986).

Emotional intelligence

Closely related to motivation, in particular in relation to persistence in learning, is the concept of emotional intelligence. This concept has its roots in the work of Thorndike (1920) who described what he called 'social' intelligence as the ability to understand others and act intelligently in human relationships. Gardner (1983), in his theory of multiple intelligences, further developed the idea referring to intra-personal and inter-personal intelligences, the former concerned with the extent to which the individual is self-aware, the latter with their skills in understanding and relating to others. 'Emotional intelligence' was first formally defined by Salovey and Mayer in 1990. They suggested that it consisted of five domains: knowing one's emotions; managing emotions; motivating oneself; recognizing emotions in others; and handling relationships. This conception was adopted by Goleman (1996) in his book *Emotional Intelligence: Why it can Matter More than IQ* which popularized the concept raising awareness of the importance of the emotions in the way that we manage our everyday lives. Later, in an attempt to align emotional intelligence more closely with other intelligences, Salovey and Mayer suggested four major skill areas: perception and expression of emotion, assimilation of emotion in thought, understanding and analysing emotions and the reflective regulation of emotion (Mayer and Salovey 1997). An early, similar, but slightly different construction was outlined by Bar-On (1997) who suggested that emotional intelligence included intra-personal skills, inter-personal skills, adaptability, stress management and general mood.

Currently, there is no agreed conception of the nature of emotional intelligence. Petrides and Furnham (2001), in an attempt to provide some kind of overarching conceptual framework, undertook a content analysis of existing definitions and identified 15 distinct components which were common to more than one model. These were adaptability, assertiveness, emotion expression, emotion management (of others), emotion perception (of self and others), emotion regulation, impulsiveness (low), relationship skills, self-esteem, self-motivation, social competence, stress management, trait empathy (taking someone else's perspective), trait happiness (being cheerful and satisfied with life), and trait optimism (looking on the bright side). Their work highlights the lack of clarity of the concept 'emotional intelligence' and the tensions between contrasting conceptions which view it either as a relatively stable personality trait, or as a meta-cognitive capacity related to the development of knowledge and understanding of one's own emotions and those of others and the skills to manage them to promote learning, well-being and success.

The neurological basis of emotional intelligence

Emotional responses to incoming stimuli are controlled by the amygdala which evaluates sensory input for its emotional meaning in a relatively primitive and automatic way, a function which has had evolutionary value, but is now less satisfactory for our functioning in the modern world. The amygdala receives input about sensory information directly and quickly from the thalamus, a relay station for incoming information, before the information has been processed by the conscious thinking part of the brain, the cortex (LeDoux 1993). Information is processed very rapidly and messages are sent to other parts of the brain which can, for instance, trigger flight or fight hormones which in turn prepare us for action. It is this process that can lead us to act without conscious cognitive thought. The prefrontal cortex provides a more complete cognitive assessment of emotional situations and operates to attempt to control our emotions but it takes longer to react to incoming information. As Goleman puts it, in some cases 'the amygdala's extensive web of neural connections allows it, during an emergency, to capture and drive much of the rest of the brain – including the rational mind' (Goleman 1996: 17). The amygdala also retains emotions that are linked with the knowledge derived from the interactions in our everyday lives and the high levels of arousal occurring in relation to emotional events seem to imprint these memories very strongly. These memories subconsciously influence our future reactions to similar events. Strong emotions can also diminish the capacity of working memory (the part that enables us to retain information that we need for undertaking a given task or problem), for instance, anxiety can inhibit examination performance, or disrupt learning over long periods of time when there is long-term emotional stress, for instance death of a family member. There is increasing evidence of the role of the emotions in determining levels of attainment, truancy and exclusion in school pupils (Petrides et al. 2004) and job performance and job satisfaction in adults (Wong and Law 2002).

The assessment of emotional intelligence

Since the recognition of the important role that emotional intelligence can play in our lives, there have been a number of attempts to assess it. Tests are often based on self-report questionnaires and assess the individual's perceptions of their own emotional self-efficacy (e.g. Schutte *et al.* 1998; Bar-On 1997). An alternative approach is to attempt to assess what has been called 'cognitive-emotional-ability' (Mayer *et al.* 2002). Here, participants might be given an abstract design and asked to indicate the extent to which they believe that a series of distinct emotions are depicted in it. Responses are assessed against those of the majority of respondents and consensus by experts.

Enhancing emotional intelligence

There have been a number of initiatives which have been designed to enhance emotional intelligence. In the USA, the Self-Science Curriculum teaches children about self-awareness, managing their emotions, taking responsibility, and how to develop empathy and skills of co-operation, conflict resolution and negotiating compromise. Other school based programmes have integrated emotional learning into the curriculum using stories as illustrations to generate discussion, while other programmes have focused specifically on reducing violence (see Goleman 1996 for details). Similar work with adults in the workplace has demonstrated that interventions can lead to an increase in measured emotional intelligence, although the impact on behaviour itself has been little researched (Slaski and Cartwright 2003).

Research with adult learners

A recent study, summarized below, explored the nature of the emotions expressed by adults engaged in a formal course of learning, and the kinds of strategies (problem- or emotion-focused) that they adopted in coping with difficulties experienced (Lazarus 1991). A multiple case study strategy was adopted to explore the learning experiences of 24 adult learners (14 females and ten males) in one adult community college and its satellite centres. All were attending an 'Introduction to Computers' course for two hours each week for either 12 or 15 weeks. A computing course was chosen as the focus of the study because of the need of many adults to develop computing skills and because interaction with computers can, of itself, give rise to emotional responses. The age range of the sample was 33–76. The participants were working full or part time, or were retired. The learners were allocated to research and comparator groups, the latter to account for the effects of the research process itself. All learners were interviewed face to face, individually before beginning and after completing their course. The learners in the research group were also interviewed by telephone after arriving home from their class for the first three weeks of the course and then for every other week until the course ended. Learners who dropped out of the course were interviewed at the point of their leaving.

The pre-course interviews focused on learners' reported motives for participation, their feelings and emotions in relation to computers and the course, anticipated challenges, and information regarding previous studying. The telephone interviews conducted with learners during the course explored their feelings and emotions in response to attendance at specific classes. Post-course interviews undertaken with students at the end of the course or when they dropped out explored retrospective feelings about the course, perceptions of their progress and achievement and the extent to which expectations had been met. A total of 149 interviews were conducted. The data were analysed using NVivo, a computer-assisted qualitative data analysis software package.

Learners' pre-course emotions and motivation

Most learners reported more than one reason for taking the course. More than half (58 per cent) indicated that they were studying to keep up with technological progress, 29 per cent expressing a particular desire to learn how to use a computer, 25 per cent indicating a vocational purpose. Specifically mentioned were broadening career opportunities, insurance for the future, and enhancing the management of a business. Seventy-one per cent indicated that they were studying for leisure or personal reasons, for example to help their children, for personal satisfaction, to broaden their life perspective or for church work. Eight per cent reported studying having received a recommendation from friends. Thirteen per cent indicated that the course would be a challenge.

Not all learners were highly motivated before beginning the course. Some who were highly motivated dropped out, while others, less motivated initially, went on to complete the course. For some students fear underpinned their motivation, specifically fear of losing their job. Others were hoping to gain promotion as a result of their increased skills, some wanted to demonstrate to themselves and others that they were able to complete a computing course, while for others the skills acquired would assist in overcoming health problems, in particular arthritis. Some had clearly articulated, specified goals – wanting to own and be able to use a computer and access the Internet. Barriers to participation were similar to those commonly reported: lack of time, fitting classes in with work and other commitments, difficulties with childcare, and inadequate public transport. Forty-two per cent raised the issue of fear of working with computers. Most expressed determination to overcome any difficulties.

A range of emotions was expressed at this stage. Twenty-four per cent of participants reported that they were looking forward to the course, 20 per cent were excited. In contrast, 18 per cent reported fear, of computers and being made to look foolish. Fifteen per cent indicated that they were nervous and 15 per cent reported apprehension. When asked about their expectations almost half did not know what to expect, while the remainder indicated that they expected to acquire a basic knowledge of computing. Only 13 per cent of the sample mentioned previous learning disappointments, although some were concerned about the impact of their age on their ability to learn.

Impact of the course on students

Five of the 24 students interviewed dropped out of the course. Six reported that they almost dropped out. The key underlying reason for drop out or for considering it was perception of a lack of progress. In only one case was drop out linked to practical obstacles, in this case difficulties with taking time away from a business. In some cases lack of progress was attributed to personal failings but in most cases deficiencies in the teaching were cited, along with poor facilities and resources. Those who almost dropped out continued because of personal determination not to give up, linked strongly to self-concept, strong peer support, fear of losing face with friends or wishing to make the most of the financial investment made in the course. For those in the research group, the research project itself was influential in the decision to continue. Those who completed the course without having considered dropping out reported that it had met their expectations and that they felt they had been successful. Overall, 42 per cent of learners indicated that their confidence had improved as a result of the development of their computing skills; 16 per cent made reference to their satisfaction with the course and 24 per cent reported high morale and feelings of optimism and self-confidence.

The negative impact of the course on some learners included low morale, loss of face, self-doubt, self-consciousness, inadequacy and self-blame. Some reported tiredness and stress in trying to attend the course while responding to other commitments. Seventeen per cent of the learners intended to progress to a higher level computing course on completion while 21 per cent felt that they wanted to take a similar course elsewhere with better facilities and teaching more suited to their needs.

Emotional responses to the course

There was considerable variability between learners in the extent and kinds of emotions reported. Some maintained consistent responses throughout the course while for others emotions fluctuated widely from week to week. Some consistently exhibited negative feelings about their learning, anxiety being their main emotional response. Some focused on their learning goals and reported positive feelings referring to their enjoyment, interest and pleasure. They felt that they were making progress and had gained confidence throughout the course even though prior to it some had expressed negative feelings. They had received positive reinforcement from tutors and had good relationships with them. The course satisfied their learning needs. One did drop out but this was through pressure of work and lack of time rather than factors related to the course itself.

In contrast, others, while initially feeling that they were making good progress and expressing positive emotions, gradually became disillusioned. For Jane, early nervousness diminished as she felt accepted by the group and made valued friendships. Over time, however, this was insufficient and her perceived lack of progress left her feeling frustrated. She felt let down and disappointed because teaching had not matched her needs. These feelings were shared by members of the group who subsequently supported each other's learning. For instance, Lucy indicated that she was made to feel inadequate: her emotions varying from depression to having some confidence back to hopelessness. She was concerned that she would be made to look stupid and attributed her difficulties to her lack of ability. She completed the course only because she felt supported by the other students.

Margaret, although reporting studying out of necessity, dropped out after an emotional outburst to the tutor in the class due to her frustration with her lack of progress which she attributed to the teaching methods. Early in the course she felt inadequate and impatient because of a lack of tutor direction which led to increasing annoyance. Initially, to cope with her powerful emotional reactions she adopted a withdrawal strategy, going outside to smoke and giving herself time to gain control, but over time her frustration increased and ultimately she voiced her discontent in front of the whole class and walked out. Her final interview indicated her disappointment with the structure of the class, the teaching methods and the pace. In contrast, Peter, also attending out of necessity, maintained a more detached approach speaking at various times of enjoyment, confusion, tedium, 'ploughing through it', and 'it having to be done'. This unemotional approach served him well and enabled him to complete the course.

Dawn, after initial fears and doubts because of previous negative learning experiences, became excited and happy as she felt that she was making progress. But later in the course she felt that the tutor did not have sufficient expertise to further her knowledge and she became angry at his insensitivity and his sexist remarks. Despite this she did not leave the course. Her experiences and reactions were not uncommon.

Coping strategies

Sixteen of the 24 students reported that they had adopted some kind of coping strategy (problem- or emotion-focused) to overcome the difficulties that they experienced in relation to their learning. Frustration with teaching methods was the most common emotion experienced (eight learners). Half of these dropped out and half nearly dropped out. Some learners expected tuition to be formal with the teacher standing at the front of the class explaining what they were to do. They were disappointed when this did not happen. One tutor expected students to work on their own from worksheets while he offered additional support to individuals. This approach did not suit all learners. Several students reported that their tutor wasted time.

Learners in one class expressed their dissatisfaction to the tutor and asked for more whole class explanation. Others who experienced such a formal approach were also dissatisfied. Frustration derived from the teaching approach and the repetition of what they already knew. In this case the students developed strategies to attempt to manage the tutor. They tried to distract him, were reluctant to move when asked to gather round for explanations and returned to their seats when they felt explanations were unproductive.

Crucial was whether there was a mismatch between preferred ways of learning and the teaching methods adopted by the tutor. Closely related to this was the issue of pace – too fast or too slow. Where the pace was too fast, initially learners attributed the problem to their lack of ability, often linked with their age. Where class members communicated with each other and there was a consensus that the pace was too fast for the majority, attributions changed and inadequacy in the tuition became the focus of attribution. Where the pace was too slow learners ignored the tutor, supporting each other in working at a quicker pace.

Learners adopted a range of practical strategies to resolve the problems that they were experiencing. Several practised at home. Where learners' perceptions about the quality of teaching were shared, some raised their concerns directly with the tutor. This had varied success. In other cases learners worked together looking to each other for support. Emotional coping strategies included developing friendships and the use of humour. Sometimes persistence was related to self-image. Some learners continued with the course because they did not want to lose face with friends. For others perceiving themselves as 'stickers' precluded dropping out. The frustrations experienced in classes were in some cases compounded by other problems. For instance, paying for expensive childcare to attend a course where progress was limited was not cost-effective and led to drop out.

Implications for practice

Taking the conceptions of emotional intelligence proposed by Bar-On (1997) and Salovey and Mayer (1990) there was evidence of the presence of each sub-skill and its application in at least some of the learners. All were aware of their emotions and were able to describe their feelings. They were able to communicate with each other and most developed appropriate support systems for their learning and managed their emotions, adapting to the learning situation that they found themselves in. Most overcame their disappointments and frustrations. They continued with the course and managed their emotions through interpersonal interactions and the use of humour. The emotions that they experienced related to their perceived progress or lack of it in learning how to use the computer. Where progress was good, they experienced positive emotions that enhanced their self-esteem and self-efficacy. Where progress was perceived as unsatisfactory, attributions were made as to why this was the case. Initially this attribution was often related to their own lack of ability, but – as the course progressed – the quality of the teaching became an issue. This attribution enabled the learners to maintain their self-esteem. In some cases self-conceptions of not dropping out, developed over time from previous learning experiences, played a part in ensuring that the course was completed. For those leaving the course decisions were made rationally on the basis of the relative costs and benefits. In only one case did an emotional response to the learning environment, culminating in a confrontation with the tutor, lead directly to a learner leaving the course. This student felt that she had nothing to gain by continuing.

Overall, the research demonstrated the extent to which adults respond with strong emotions when they are frustrated by less than optimal learning conditions which prevent them from making progress. In this, albeit limited, study the main cause of the frustration was the quality and style of the teaching, exacerbated by the kind of difficulties which often emerge in learning to use a computer. Teaching learners with different levels of prior knowledge who were progressing at different rates was clearly a problem as was their desire for different types of tuition. Tutors were not always sensitive to learners' needs and lacked strategies for dealing with the teaching environment appropriately.

Tutors need to:

- explain the teaching approach which is to be adopted and provide a rationale for its adoption;
- provide opportunities for learners to express their fears and aspirations;
- be aware that adult learners have a wide range of positive and negative prior learning experiences which will influence their emotional responses to particular learning situations;
- ensure that work is matched to learners' levels of prior knowledge;
- ensure that the pace of work is appropriate for each learner through differentiating work within the classroom possibly through group work;
- monitor learners' progress and discuss with them any arising issues;
- encourage learners to develop support networks which operate within and beyond the classroom;
- provide informal and formal opportunities for learners to provide feedback on the quality of teaching and whether it is meeting their needs.

Overall, tutors need to have a range of pedagogical and inter-personal skills at their disposal which they can utilize in response to learner needs. They need to develop not only a wide range of teaching strategies but also their own emotional intelligence to be able to recognize and respond appropriately to the changing needs of their students.

References

Bar-On, R. (1997) *The Emotional Intelligence Inventory, (EQ-i): Technical Manual,* Toronto: Multi-Health Systems.

Blaxter, L. (1999) 'Joining, staying or leaving', *Adults Learning*, 10, 6: 12–14.

Eccles, J. (1983) 'Expectancies, values and academic behaviours', in J.T. Spence (ed.) *Achievement and Achievement Motives*, San Francisco: Freeman.

Gardner, H. (1983) *Frames of Mind: The Theory of Multiple Intelligences*, New York: Basic Books.

Goleman, D. (1996) *Emotional Intelligence: Why It can Matter More than IQ,* London: Bloomsbury Publishing.

Goodwin, T. (1996) 'A Critical Examination of Adult Education Student Drop-out in a Community Education Programme', (Unpublished BA Degree Thesis), University of Greenwich.

Koestner, R. and McClelland, D.C. (1990) 'Perspectives on competence motivation', in L. Pervin (ed.) *Handbook of Personality: Theory and Research*, New York: Guilford Press.

La Valle, I. and Blake, M. (2001) *National Adult Learning Survey 2001*, Nottingham, DfES Publications.

Lazarus, R.S. (1991) *Emotion & Adaptation*, New York: Oxford University Press.

LeDoux, J. (1993) 'Emotional memory systems in the brain', *Behavioural and Brain Research*, 58, 1–2: 69–79.

Markus, H. and Ruvolo, A. (1989) 'Possible selves: personalised representations of goals' in L.A. Pervin (ed.) *Goal Concepts in Personality and Social Psychology*, Hillsdale, New Jersey: Lawrence Erlbaum Associates.

Martinez, P. and Munday, F. (1998) *9,000 Voices: Student Persistence and Drop-out in Further Education*, London: FEDA.

Mayer, J.D. and Salovey, P. (1997) 'What is emotional intelligence?' in P. Salovey and D. Sluyter (eds) *Emotional Development and Emotional Intelligence: Implications for Educators*, New York: Basic Books.

Mayer, J.D., Salovey, P. and Caruso, D.R. (2002) *The Mayer–Salovey–Caruso Emotional Intelligence Test*, Users Manual, Toronto: Multi-Health Systems.

McGivney, V. (1995) 'Skills, knowledge and economic outcomes, a pilot study of adult learners in Gloucestershire', *Adults Learning*, 6, 6: 172–75.

McGivney, V. (1996) *Staying or Leaving the Course*, Leicester: NIACE.

McGivney, V. (2001) *Fixing or Changing the Pattern? Reflections on Widening Adult Participation in Learning*, Leicester: NIACE.

Murray, H.A. (1938) *Explorations in Personality*, New York: Oxford University Press.

Petrides, K.V. and Furnham, A. (2001) 'Trait emotional intelligence: psychometric investigation with reference to established trait taxonomies', *European Journal of Personality*, 15: 425–48.

Petrides, K.V., Frederickson, N. and Furnham, A. (2004) 'The role of trait emotional intelligence in academic performance and deviant behaviour at school', *Personality and Individual Differences*, 36: 277–93.

Salovey, P. and Mayer, J.D. (1990) *Emotional Intelligence, Imagination, Cognition and Personality*, 9: 185–211.

Schutte, N.S., Malouff, J.M., Hall, L.E., Haggerty, D.J., Cooper, J.T., Golden, C.J. and Dornheim, L. (1998) 'Development and validation of a measure of emotional intelligence', *Personality and Individual Differences*, 25: 167–77.

Slaski, M. and Cartwright, S. (2003) 'Emotional intelligence training and its implications for stress, health and performance', *Stress and Health*, 19: 233–39.

Thorndike, E.L. (1920) 'Intelligence and its uses', *Harper's Magazine*, 140: 227–35.

Weiner, B. (1986) *An Attributional Theory of Motivation and Emotion*, New York: Springer-Verlag.

Wong, C.S. and Law, K.S. (2002) 'The effects of leader and follower emotional intelligence on performance and attitude', *Leadership Quarterly*, 13: 243–74.

Woodley, A., Wagner, L., Slowey, M., Hamilton, M. and Fulton, O. (1987) *Choosing to Learn: Adults in Education*, Milton Keynes: The Society for Research into Higher Education and the Open University.

Chapter 12

A comparison of Piaget's and Biggs's theories of cognitive development in adults and their implications for the teaching of adults

Peter Sutherland

The ideas of Piaget are contrasted with those of Biggs in this chapter. These two thinkers have had a major impact on the psychology of cognitive development. Whilst the main focus of their work has been with children their relevance to adult learning is also important. The author draws on previous work to point out that not all adults reach the cognitive stage Piaget expected of them. If adult learning is to have an impact on teaching practice then the implications of this need to be thought through. Biggs argues for a distinction between formal 1 learning (characteristic of undergraduates) and formal 2 learning (characteristic of postgraduates). The Piagetian tradition puts the emphasis on development between stages; the Biggsian tradition puts the emphasis on development within a particular mode. It is argued that in Sutherland's version of the Piagetian tradition the personal circumstances of the adult need to be taken into account by their teachers.

Introduction

This paper focuses on the cognitive developmental aspects of adult learning. It is argued that it is important for those involved in lifelong learning to be aware of the state of cognitive development (or non-development) of their students in order to teach them at a suitable and appropriate level and to try to raise them to a higher level.

The work of two eminent practitioners has been utilized to draw a comparison. One, the French Swiss Jean Piaget, died over 20 years ago. It is argued that his ideas are still relevant to lifelong learning even if criticisms can be made of his work. In particular, his lack of awareness of the social and cultural aspects of education is a serious weakness. The other, the Australian John Biggs, has recently retired after a long career of research into cognitive development and learning. Early in his career he focused on children, but in more recent years he has focused on adults. In contrast with Piaget, Biggs has a strong interest in teaching. His last book (2003) has been very influential in discussing strategies for the modern era of mass higher education.

The application of Piaget's stages of thinking and theory of knowledge to adults has already been carried out by Riegel (1973), Arlin (1975), Labouvie-Vief (1980), Pascual-Leone (1983) and Sutherland (1999). Simultaneously the application of Biggs's levels has been carried out by Boulton-Lewis (1999). This paper compares and contrasts the theories of Piaget and Biggs by a process of analytic enquiry. Is there a common theme, or themes, and therefore a common message for teachers of adults? Or are the differences so great that each is *sui generis* and to be regarded by practitioners as needing to be applied in its own unique way?

The developmental frameworks of Piaget and Biggs are compared and contrasted and the implications for the teaching of adults explored, including a critique of both. The implications of both sets of ideas will then be drawn for teaching and learning in lifelong learning.

Ideas based on Piaget's tradition

Piaget made two major contributions to our understanding of cognitive development: his stages and his theory of how knowledge is acquired. His stages are outlined in Table 12.1.

Babies function only at a *sensori-motor* stage, learning by touching and seeing, whereas toddlers function at a *pre-operational* stage. They acquire the home language and can grasp phenomena in a simple way. Lower primary school children are at a *concrete operational* stage. They realize that principles remain the same, even if the appearance or situation differs e.g. the number of sweets remains six whether the sweets are spread out on a tray or packed together in a bowl. At the onset of high school adolescents reach the *formal operational* stage. They can work with and understand abstract ideas without having to see them. This contrasts with concrete operations where people still require physical props which they need to be able to see and touch in order to be able to think successfully.

From Piaget's (1930) early work many adult educators had assumed that Piaget regarded all adults as formal operational thinkers. If this were so, the adults would be capable of abstract thinking in the domains in which they are most proficient. This, by definition, should apply to an able elite who used to be that sector of the age cohort who graduated from university with a first class or upper second degree.

According to empirical evidence on the cognitive development of adolescents obtained in England by Sutherland (1992) and Shayer and Wylan (1978), and in

Table 12.1 Piaget's stages of cognitive development

Ordinal number	Stage
1	sensori-motor activity
2	language-based pre-operational thinking e.g. intuitive thinking
3	concrete operational thinking
4	formal operational thinking

Australia by Biggs and Collis (1982), not all adolescents can be assumed to be at the formal operational stage at 18 years of age. Therefore a considerable proportion of adults at 18+ (the approximate percentage is yet to be ascertained) remain at the concrete operational stage. According to Sutherland (1999) the thinking of another considerable proportion is *transitional* between concrete and formal operations. There may well be a sector of the cohort at the concrete operational level in some or all domains.

If this evidence is accepted, teachers in post-16 education should assume that some of their students are at concrete operational or transitional stages of thinking. This poses problems for higher education in some countries. The tradition in many countries has been a hierarchical elitist system where highly academic universities, established centuries ago, cater for abstract thinkers. There is a need for these to be complemented by institutions offering less academic, more practical courses for concrete thinkers or for institutions to facilitate the transition.

Other post-formal operational stages have been developed such as Arlin's (1975) fifth problem solving stage and Pascual-Leone's (1983) metasubjective theory. Perry (1970) developed his stages of undergraduate development from thinking. At the start of undergraduate study there is only one right answer decided by the teacher, but by the end of four years students are capable of more independent, abstract thinking. Belenky *et al.* (1986) offered a feminist response to Piaget's stages in terms of a woman gradually building up the confidence to construct her own knowledge according to her circumstances. More recently Baxter-Magolda (1992) has outlined a series of stages of epistemological development across the undergraduate and postgraduate years. These will not be discussed in detail here since the purpose of this paper is to compare only Piaget's original ideas with those of Biggs.

However, Riegel's (1973) ideas need to be mentioned because they are relevant to the argument of this paper. He adopted Piaget's ideas into his concept of *dialectical thinking*. He argued that a different form of formal operational thinking is needed for adults as opposed to the one Piaget defined for adolescents: a definition that regards contradiction and ambiguity positively instead of negatively. Many adult experiences are riddled with contradiction e.g. a mature student who was a failure at school yet who now wishes to study for a degree. Riegel argued that adults can and need to apply specific examples of asbtract (formal operational) thinking back to concrete situations in their lives. He, like Sutherland (1999), argued against Piaget's view that abstract thinking is the sole goal of adult thinking in all contexts. Instead there should be mutually beneficial movement between formal and concrete thinking, according to the context which the adult is in. Riegel, like Labouvie-Vief (1980), believed that adults gain from applying abstract principles back into reality.

Many of those who do not accept the validity of Piaget's stages nevertheless find his theory of learning a very powerful contribution to our understanding of cognition. At any stage the learner learns by the complementary processes of accommodation and assimilation: accommodating to the outside situation and assimilating the outward forms of the situation inside her/his own mind into a form which is easily dealt with by her/himself. Accommodation is the general process:

how a situation is perceived 'objectively' by everyone e.g. an Oxford dictionary definition of 'lifelong learning'. The adult is adjusting to the outside world. Assimilation is the particular process: how each learner perceives that situation e.g. an adult's personal construction of the 'lifelong learning' schema. The adult is adjusting the material to match her/his schemata (mental constructs). The learner uses first one process and then the other; until an equilibrium is reached. The learner then has a stable grasp of that particular concept at that stage e.g. concrete operations.

In adults equilibration can be seen as the resolving of paradoxes and ambiguity. What was previously perceived to be paradoxical is now seen as complementary within a more encompassing whole. This lasts until the equilibrium is upset by some new change in the adult's life e.g. being promoted to a more demanding job or discovering that one has cancer. The equilibrium which she/he reached previously is no longer valid. The whole process has then to be repeated until a new equilibrium is reached. Using this tradition a new focus on the transformation of adults' lives has been developed by Merriam and Caffarella (1999), Labouvie-Vief (1980) and Sutherland (1999). It is discussed at the end of this chapter under a comparison of the theories of Piaget and Biggs together with their applications.

The ideas of Biggs and their application to adults

One of the original influences on Biggs was Piaget. However, there were other influences such as the psychometric tradition and the curriculum outcomes movement. In the years between babyhood and the start of school Biggs's levels drew on Bruner's ikonic rather than Piaget's pre-conceptual thinking.

Biggs's model was applied (1982) to school learning; then more recently to adults by himself (2003), Boulton-Lewis (1999) and others. The Structure of Observed Learning Outcomes (SOLO) taxonomy was developed by Biggs and Collis (1982). This utilizes Biggs's levels which are outlined in Table 12.2.

Table 12.2 Biggs's levels of observed learning outcomes

1	prestructural – the learning is irrelevant.
2	unistructural – the learning is relevant, but the learner only focuses on one aspect.
3	multistructural – the learner focuses on a number of relevant parts but fails to integrate them.
4	relational – the learner integrates the different parts with each other in order to arrive at a coherent whole structure and meaning. An example of relational thinking is quoted by Boulton-Lewis (1999):'learning involves the sharing of knowledge to facilitate personal growth and a greater understanding of the world around me'.
5	extended abstract – that coherent whole is generalized to a higher level of abstraction. The learner generalizes and extends the whole to take on new and more abstract features.

In *prestructural* learning the material is irrelevant to the question or topic. In adult learning this would probably be regarded by most teachers as unacceptable and given a fail mark. Adults at the beginning of their courses may demonstrate *unistructural* and *multistructural* learning outcomes. However, their teachers may try to facilitate their development towards relational learning. Later in their development *extended abstract* learning may involve adding new elements on to the level the adult is at.

Biggs (personal communication) defined his idea of a mode. These are ways in which data can be structured: visual images can be structured ikonically, symbolic language formally. It then follows that when people reach adulthood they can work in many different modes. According to Biggs the emphasis is very much on the hope and expectation that the learner will move on to a higher level or mode than the one they are at. It is hoped or expected that the teacher/pedagogue will have a major role in this in the process which Biggs (2003) terms 'constructive alignment', whereby objectives, teaching methods and assessment are aligned in order to produce desired outcomes.

An application of Biggs's SOLO taxonomy to adults was carried out by Boulton-Lewis (1999). She argued that the results of a university education should be higher order thinking involving, for instance, graduates being able to reflect critically on both academic material and their own experiences. She utilized Norris's (1989) definition of critical thinking: critical thinkers are those who seek reasons, attempt to be well informed, use and acknowledge credible sources, consider alternatives and other points of view, withhold judgement until they have sufficient evidence and seek to be as precise as possible.

According to Arter, a scholar in the field of adult education (personal communication), the transition from multistructural to relational thinking is the key to development at the undergraduate level. The students need to be able to tie

Table 12.3 Biggs's (1995) hierarchical forms of knowledge

Formal 1 (typical of 1st year undergraduates)

- *Declarative knowledge* – factual knowledge of a discipline, represented in symbols. It is knowing what.
- *Procedural knowledge* – allows for purposeful manipulation of declarative knowledge for whatever purpose is needed. It is knowing how.
- *Conditional knowledge* – knowing when to use certain procedures and to access appropriate content. It is knowing when.
- *Functional knowledge* – involves performance with understanding.

Formal 2/postformal (typical of postgraduates)

- *Theoretical knowledge* – invloves a student having an explixit or implicit theory to which the knowledge relates.
- *Metatheoretical knowledge* – implies a student being aware of the learning processes involved in how they acquire knowledge.

together the various strands they are exposed to in a meaningful way. The teacher can try to facilitate and scaffold this by appropriate questioning and by encouraging self-questioning in the undergraduates.

According to Biggs (1993) both declarative and procedural knowledge are necessary for adults to be able to synthesize strands together. Declarative knowledge consists of factual knowledge of a discipline, represented in symbols, and the way in which it is structured for retrieval. Procedural knowledge allows the purposeful manipulation of declarative knowledge for whatever purpose is needed. Conditional knowledge involves knowing when to use certain procedures and to access appropriate content.

Biggs makes a distinction between formal 1 and formal 2 levels. Formal 1 involves declarative and procedural knowledge. Formal 2 involves metatheoretical and theoretical knowledge. Formal 2 is similar to Sutherland's (1992) theoretical explainer thinking. Formal 1 is asserted to be typical of first year undergraduates and formal 2 of postgraduates. Ramsden (1988) found that most graduating students are only capable of surface declarative knowledge in their discipline and do not think like experts in that area. Arter (personal communication) argues that a thinker who is at the formal 1 level applies ideas within a particular theory whereas one who is at the formal 2 level compares theories.

As indicated in Table 12.3 Biggs argues that theoretical and metatheoretical knowledge are at higher levels of abstraction than all four formal 1 types of knowledge. Declarative knowledge is largely factual. Procedural knowledge on its own is skill-based. Conditional knowledge includes both procedural and higher order declarative knowledge at a theoretical level so the person knows under what conditions Plan A should be followed or alternatively under what conditions Plan B should be followed. As Biggs (2003: 40) writes, 'the combination turns procedural into functioning knowledge which is flexible and wide-ranging'.

Boulton-Lewis (1999) argues that essays are the best way to assess formal 1 and 2 thinking. This can be done by SOLO taxonomy techniques. The SOLO taxonomy concept provides a model to challenge students to engage in i.e. formal 2 thinking. However, teachers need to explain to students in advance that they will be assessed according to the level of structural organization which they achieve. This requires students to take charge of their own learning:

- reading
- summarizing
- presenting
- discussing material with peers
- taking the responsibility to search the literature themselves.

Boulton-Lewis (1999) argues that Biggs's SOLO model provides criteria against which to assess this. Higher order thinking should involve rational thinking. The successful products of higher education are those who are adept at formal 2 thinking. They should provide the leadership class in any society.

Table 12.4 Biggs's 3P's model of learning

Presage	Process	Product
Student factors:	Target examples	The SOLO Taxonomy criteria are rarely used for assessment. Multiple choice testing can often be used for this.
• prior knowledge		
• ability		
• ways of learning		
• values		
• expectations		
Teaching factors:		
• curriculum		
• models of desired outcome		
• teaching method		
• climate		
• assessment		

Biggs himself (2003) has proposed ways in which his ideas can be applied to higher education. He proposes that appropriate teaching be aligned to the learning objectives of the course and to the assessment in what he describes as constructive alignment. Biggs also (1993) developed his 3P's model of learning, as outlined in Table 12.4.

When applying his 3P's model to teaching, Biggs (2003) states that there should be a balanced system in which all the components (Presage, Process and Product) support each other or, in other words, are aligned with each other.

A comparison of the theories of Piaget and Biggs

The comparison between Piaget and Biggs is summarized in Table 12.5. In the original focus on children at school, Piaget put the emphasis on determining what stage a child was at, whereas Biggs put more emphasis on facilitating the cycles of development within a level and the learning outcomes. Biggs (2003) made it clear that changes within a level are both quantitative and qualitative. It is hoped that present day researchers on Biggs's ideas, such as Boulton-Lewis, will continue to develop research on the cycles of development in adult students.

Both Piaget and Biggs, in their different ways, stress cognitive growth. However, Biggs has a more pedagogical stance in that he encourages teachers to create the conditions during which learning will take place. On the other hand Piaget was perceived from his early work as being more of an objective assessor of whether or not a child was at a certain stage of cognitive development.

Piaget's unit of terminology is the stage; Biggs's is the level and the mode. Biggs synthesizes the two traditions with his concept of a mode. Adults can work in many different modes, instead of being (as Piaget implies) fixed at a particular

Table 12.5 Differences between Piaget's and Biggs's models

Piaget	Biggs
Emphasis on attaining 'higher' stage.	Emphasis on learning.
The focus is on how an adult develops from one stage to a 'higher' one rather than on development within a stage.	There is organic cyclical growth within a particular level.
There is a concept of transition between major stages.	Transition is de-emphasized.
There is a theory of learning.	There is no explicit theory of learning.
A model of process and product.	A process model which gives rise to a means of assessing product.
Assessment tool not yet developed for adults.	A powerful tool for the assessment of adults.
Great interest in the personal circumstances of an adult.	The personal life situation of the adult is not regarded as of interest.

stage. Biggs himself (personal communication) regards his focus as being on cognitive growth within the level an adult is at now, as opposed to the Piagetian emphasis on the importance of attaining the next 'higher' stage. The Piagetian tradition has been less interested in changes within a stage, except for Piaget's (1953) work on sensori-motor development in babies and Sutherland's (1992) extension of Peel's (1971) stages.

The Piagetian tradition puts a great deal of emphasis on the transition between stages, whereas Biggs's work places less emphasis on the concept of transitions between levels. Biggs stresses a strong visual element by reverting to Bruner's terminology (i.e. ikonic) at the second level. On the other hand Piaget's equivalent stage – pre-operational – stresses the language aspect.

The most obvious difference is that Piaget provides an explicit theory of learning to accompany his stages, whereas Biggs does not. However, Biggs implies in his recent (2003) work that he has a constructivist theory of learning. Therefore both Piaget and Biggs (in the latter part of his career) fundamentally regard learning in the same way.

Both Piaget's and Biggs's models belong to the *process* school in the sense of being interested in *how* adults learn, rather than in *what* they learn. However, Biggs also provides a powerful tool for the assessment of *product* or outcome with his SOLO taxonomy. The Piagetian school have yet to develop a tool for the assessment of adults.

Overall more development work seems to have been done on adults using Biggs's model. However the potential for doing the same with Piaget's model is enormous and this is a task that urgently requires doing.

Sutherland (1999) has been particularly interested in factors which cause an adult's Piagetian stage either (a) to 'develop' from concrete to formal operational or (b) to 'regress' back from formal to concrete operations. After many years of cognitive existence at a concrete level it may be that the challenge of studying for an academic degree may stimulate an adult into 'developing' from concrete to formal operations. Or negative circumstances, e.g. an adult opting out of formal education in favour of manual work, may cause the opposite to occur. There is, as yet, little firm empirical evidence, so the discussion remains speculative. In contrast with this, those working on Biggs's ideas do not seem to be particularly interested in the circumstances under which an adult's SOLO level changes.

Application of the two theories to lifelong learning

Both theories imply that different teaching should be provided for students according to their stage/level. However, this may necessitate differentiated teaching for abstract- and concrete-thinking students within the single institution i.e. mixed ability teaching and mixed ability outcomes/qualifications. This might then necessitate either allocating students into different courses according to their stage/level or having mixed stage/level classes. Teachers would then need to learn how to teach mixed stage/level classes by differentiation; just as their colleagues in secondary and primary school have had to do. Only the abstract thinkers would receive degrees; the concrete thinkers would receive certificates.

Teachers utilizing the Piagetian tradition should encourage students to think in an abstract way by setting questions which demand such thinking e.g. 'Critically discuss the concept of democracy'. On the other hand there are concrete operational and transitional students who cannot yet do this. They will require learning support in some form: from peers, subject teachers or general learning support teachers similar to those provided in schools.

The comparison being made in this paper is very similar to Sutherland's (1999) Piagetian analysis: formal operational thinking has been traditionally expected in higher education, but some new entrants may only be capable of concrete operational thinking or may be transitional between concrete and abstract thinking. An important implication for teachers arises out of this: the need to help such students through a transitional stage into full formal operational thinking. An implication for researchers then arises: how to find techniques which help teachers do this.

Potentially, Piaget's stages provide a powerful assessment tool: to measure reliably the stage of thinking (concrete operational, transitional or formal operational) of a particular student in a particular subject. However, this tool still awaits further development work. Perhaps an even finer system of gradation could be devised similar to that which Sutherland (1992) evolved for school children's cognitive level.

What are the implications for the assessment of writing techniques of the Piagetian and Biggsian traditions? In the key academic activity of essay writing, the SOLO criteria may provide a clear model of the structure required for a 'good' essay. Boulton-Lewis (1999) argued that the SOLO criteria provide a particularly suitable tool for the assessment of essays. The Piagetian tradition has not yet attempted to give such direct help to students. The SOLO taxonomy model can also be used to challenge students to organize and present their knowledge so as to demonstrate understanding and to become critical thinkers.

Boulton-Lewis (1994) also argued that the SOLO taxonomy can be used to develop students' thinking as well as to measure it. At the end of undergraduate education the Biggsian tradition would expect a person to be a formal 1 thinker; the Piagetian tradition a formal operational thinker. At the end of postgraduate education the Biggsian tradition would expect a person to be a formal 2 multi-modal thinker; the Piagetian tradition a post-formal operational thinker.

Many of these implications will also apply to teaching in adult and community education. The range of stages/levels of students will be even greater. However, many of those who left school at 16 at a concrete operational stage may – as a result of their experiential learning in adult life – have matured into formal operational thinkers in certain relevant subject areas. Those students who have remained at a concrete operational stage may require learning support from teachers (or others) in subjects which are not purely practical and which require some degree of abstract thinking.

Conclusions

Both Piaget's stages and Biggs's levels and modes have great relevance to all forms of post 16-education. Although the author's thinking for this paper started with an awareness of the differences between the two, he now recognizes that the similarities are much more important than the differences. Nevertheless there are important differences of emphasis. The late twentieth/early twenty-first century version of the Piagetian tradition is represented by Labouvie-Vief (1980) and Sutherland (1999). They put the emphasis on the personal circumstances of the adult learner as they attempt to adjust to the challenges of adult life. Whereas the emphases of the Biggsian tradition are quite different: first to provide insight into ways of structuring and delivering the curriculum and second to provide a power-ful tool for the assessment of the academic work done by adult students. The Piagetian tradition provides broad stages; whereas Biggs's work provides insight into what is happening within a particular level and the related learning outcomes.

It is being argued that the two traditions complement rather than compete with each other. Each has provided different, but compatible ideas on lifelong learning. It is hoped that, from a synthesis of the two traditions, researchers and teachers of lifelong learning will be able to found new, enriched pedagogies and andragogies for the twenty-first century.

References

Arlin, P. K. (1975) 'Cognitive development in adulthood: a fifth stage?' *Developmental Psychology*, 11: 502–606.

Baxter-Magolda, M. B. (1992) *Knowing and Reasoning in Students: Gender-Related Patterns in Students' Intellectual Development*, San Francisco: Jossey-Bass.

Belenky, M. F., Clinchy, B. M., Goldberger, N. R. and Tarufel, J. M. (1986) *Women's Ways of Knowing: The Development of Self, Voice and Mind*, New York: Basic Books

Biggs, J. B. (1993) 'Models of learning, forms of knowing and ways of schooling', in A. Demetriou, M. Shayer, and A. Efkiledes (eds) *Neo-Piagetian Theories of Cognitive Development*, London: Routledge.

Biggs, J. B. (2003) *Teaching for Quality Learning at University*, 2nd edn, Buckingham: Open University Press.

Biggs, J. B. and Collis, K. E. (1982) *Evaluating the Quality of Learning: the SOLO Taxonomy*, New York: Academic Press.

Boulton-Lewis, G. M. (1994) 'Tertiary students' knowledge of their own learning and a SOLO taxonomy', *Higher Education*, 28: 387–402.

Boulton-Lewis, G. M. (1999) 'Applying the SOLO taxonomy to learning in higher education', in B. Dart and G. Boulton-Lewis (eds) *Teaching and Learning in Higher Education*, Melbourne: ACER.

Labouvie-Vief, G. (1980) 'Beyond formal operations: uses of pure logic in lifespan development,' *Human Development*, 23: 141–61.

Merriam, S. B. and Caffarella, R. S. (eds) (1999) *Learning in Adulthood: A Comprehensive Guide*, 2nd edn, San Francisco: Jossey-Bass.

Norris, S. P. (1989) 'Can we test validly for critical thinking?', *Educational Researcher*, 18, 9: 21–6.

Pascual-Leone, J. (1983) 'Growing into maturity: towards a metasubjective theory of adulthood stages', in P. B. Baltes and O. G. Brim Jr. (eds) *Lifespan Development and Behavior 5*, London: Academic Press.

Perry, W. G. (1970) *Forms of Intellectual and Ethical Development in the College Years*, New York: Holt, Rinehart and Winston.

Piaget, J. (1930) *The Child's Conception of Physical Causality*, London: Routledge & Kegan Paul.

Piaget, J. (1953) *The Origins of Intelligence in Children*, London: Routledge & Kegan Paul.

Ramsden, P. (1988) 'Studying learning: improving teaching', in P. Ramsden (ed.) *Improving Learning: New Perspectives*, London: Kogan Page.

Riegel, K. (1973) 'Dialectical operations: the final period of cognitive development', *Human Development*, 16: 346–70.

Shayer, M. and Wylan, H. (1978) 'The distribution of Piagetian stages of thinking in British middle and secondary children 11–14 to 16-year-olds and sex differences', *British Journal of Educational Psychology*, 48: 62–70.

Sutherland, P. (1992) *Cognitive Development today: Piaget and his Critics*, London: Paul Chapman Publishing.

Sutherland, P. (1999) 'The application of Piagetian and neo-Piagetian ideas to further and higher education', *International Journal of Lifelong Education*, 18, 4: 286–94.

Chapter 13

Academic study as a social practice

Chrissie Boughey

If we are to provide effective study skills, particularly for non-traditional students, then the way we think about and respond to it needs to be radically rethought. Drawing on the contribution of New Literacy Studies the author criticizes decontextualized approaches to 'study skills' which treat students as inadequate in favour of one which constructs them as social practices with implications for people's roles and identities. If students are to acquire 'epistemological access' to academic discourses there is a need to go beyond identifying the problem as simply one of teaching and learning. Some implications of this approach for more helpful forms of practice are identified.

Introduction

It is early afternoon and I sit down at my desk glad to have an hour or two to devote to some writing. Half an hour or so later, I am interrupted by a hesitant knock at my door. 'Come in', I call, reluctant to be disturbed but aware of the fact that if I don't respond the knocking will continue in spite of the fact that a notice pinned to the door clearly states that I can be consulted Mondays, Wednesdays and Fridays from eleven to one o'clock. The door opens and Moses, one of the mature students in one of the first year classes I teach enters. I know Moses well as he has introduced himself and told me some of his story. As a black South African denied access to a quality education during the apartheid regime, he had worked for nearly ten years as a waiter in a hotel before finally scraping together the money to return to study. His entrance to university had been dependent on the fact that his 'mature age' had allowed him to use a set of procedures which gives access to the South African higher education system to students aged 23 or more regardless of the fact that they have not achieved the minimum entrance requirements. Moses is keen to do well and has been assiduous in attending all his classes and completing all his assignments, something his younger peers are not always keen to do. 'Hello Moses', I say. 'How can I help you?'

'The assignment . . . ', he begins. 'What do I have to do?'

'We talked about the assignment in class', I tell him. 'And there's a notice explaining what you have to do on the notice board.'

There is no response. Aware that I am not going to get away without an explanation, I capitulate knowing full well that Moses will not be the only individual who will come to my door asking for a personal explanation. 'Sit down', I tell him, trying my best not to sound weary. 'I'll explain again.'

Study skills or literacy practices?

In many respects, Moses' need to come and negotiate a personal explanation of an assessment task might seem unreasonable given the teaching he has received in his university courses so far. His enrolment in an English class, for example, not only aims to provide him with the 'English Language Skills' his status as a speaker of English as an additional language enrolled in a university which uses English as the medium of instruction requires him to use, but also with reading skills, writing skills, note-taking skills, listening skills, speaking skills and sundry other 'study skills' the course designers have seen fit to include. Having been taught these skills, surely Moses should be able to use them to read and understand a printed assessment rubric? Even if his listening skills were not up to the task of understanding what was explained to him orally, surely his speaking skills should have allowed him to ask questions of clarification when the assignment was explained in class? For that matter, shouldn't his reading skills have allowed him to process the notice regarding consultation hours pinned to my door? Is Moses being perverse or deliberately disruptive? Are his actions a failure to apply his skills or has he simply not acquired them in the first place? Many of my colleagues problematize (and pathologize) Moses in such terms. That he does not use the skills he has been taught is perceived as a failure, an incapacity or a lack of motivation on his part. Is this really the case, or is another explanation possible?

In recent years, work in many areas of academic study has taken what Gee (2000) calls a 'social turn', shifting away from a focus on individual behaviour, and an understanding of such behaviour as a result of factors inherent to the individual, to a focus on understanding individuals and what they do in context. In the context of 'study skills', taking a 'social turn' means drawing on the ideas of those working in the field of anthropology (Street 1993, 1995), in ethnography of communication (Heath 1983) and in what is termed 'social linguistics' (Gee 1990, 2000). More specifically, it involves turning to what Street (ibid.) has termed the 'ideological model' of literacy and the field of New Literacy Studies.

Dominant understandings of what it means to read and write construct literacy as a socially and culturally neutral activity involving the decoding or encoding of meanings from and into script. In contrast, the ideological model constructs literacy as a set of activities, or practices, related to print which arise from, and are deeply embedded in, social contexts or social groupings. It perceives those practices as arising from values assigned to print and understandings of the role printed text can play in human experience. These values might well result in the privileging of written communication over oral communication or, equally, in oral communication being preferred to the written and even in printed texts being set aside and replaced by oral events (Heath 1983).

This understanding of literacy as a set of practices arising from value-driven social contexts, rather than as a set of asocial, acultural, apolitical 'skills', means that literacy has to be understood as a multiple, rather than a unitary phenomenon, and in the positing of *literacies* rather than a single *literacy*. A literacy not only embodies the kinds of texts individuals are likely to relate to (whether, for example, they will be prepared to consult a telephone directory or the classified advertisements, read a novel or a cartoon book, write a note to a family member or a letter to a newspaper or, equally, read or write an academic article) but also the ways in which they are prepared to *relate* to those texts. Is reading a case of understanding and accepting what is said (in the sense of the text becoming the 'word' which then has to be repeated) or is an individual prepared to engage with a text at the level of questioning and critique? Is writing a case of providing information, recounting knowledge which has been explained elsewhere or building a case based on evidence? The positing of multiple literacies also involves accepting that an individual can be multi-literate with each literacy related to the roles that individual adopts in life. A woman can be mother, wife, neighbour, colleague and academic and in each of these roles will not only engage with a variety of different types of texts (the mother role, for example, will not require her to work with academic journal articles) but will also engage with each type of text differently (reading a shopping list is both quantitatively and qualitatively different to reading a novel).

Work within the field of New Literacy Studies has examined what it means to be 'academically literate' (see Lea and Street 1998) showing, for example, that the construct of *academic literacy* is better conceived as the multiple *academic literacies* since what it means to read and write acceptably is determined by disciplinary context. Although there are some practices which stretch across all disciplinary boundaries such as the requirement that a piece of academic writing should have an 'argument', Lea and Street show that the way an argument is structured, and the kind of evidence which is used to substantiate it, differs according to discipline. Using research amongst student writers, they show how in history, for example, content and factual information serve to both structure and substantiate an argument. In anthropology, however, arguments are structured and substantiated through the *analysis* of content areas. This difference means that a disciplinary specialist assessing a piece of writing submitted for a course credit in anthropology, but which adheres to the rules for structuring and substantiating argument in history, will not necessarily identify or follow the structure of the essay.

Other work (for example, Geisler 1994) has examined the difference between academic literacies and school-based literacies. School-based literacies are reliant on understandings of knowledge as factual information (Mehan cited in Geisler 1994) rather than as something which is constructed and, thus, which can be contested. As a number of studies show (Heap 1985; Baker and Freebody 1989), school-based reading practices focus on using only information which is contained in a text in order to arrive at a response to a question. Students are not encouraged to consider ways in which the text might be inadequate or insufficient and are discouraged from drawing on understandings derived from their own experience or from other texts and which are thus external to the text they are reading at the time. School-based literacies are thus in direct contrast to academic literacies where readers are required to use both other texts and other knowledge to critique and challenge meanings in a text.

The literacies available to most students as they enter higher education have been developed and honed over more than twelve years of schooling. Such literacies are not sets of 'skills' which can be abandoned in favour of other more 'critical' reading skills taught in language classes and study skills tutorials but are rather issues of identity and roles readers construct for themselves. For those working within the field of New Literacy Studies, learning to read 'critically', for example, is not a matter of adopting a new set of reading strategies but rather of understanding and acquiring a whole set of new ways of relating to text involving the self sanctioning of critique and the use of information which is contextual rather than textual. The development of 'critical' reading practices is thus more complex and more difficult than approaches which construct it as a set of skills would have us believe.

Becoming academically literate does not only involve the adoption of a more critical role for oneself as a reader but also an awareness of the need to do lots of reading and, in the case of students such as Moses, the setting aside of a preference for oral information in favour of a disposition to *read*. First generation undergraduates in particular may never have been exposed to reading practices in the home and may thus have little awareness of what it means to be 'academic' in the sense of studying at a university.

Academic literacy also involves the production of written text and not only engagement with texts written by others. Writing, like reading, is closely related to an identity or role a writer constructs for him/herself. School-based literacies involve producing texts which have the purpose of demonstrating knowledge for a teacher or examiner (Geisler 1994). Understanding writing as a process of constructing a position or argument by analysing and synthesizing the views of others is not merely a matter of skill, but rather of the acquisition of a new role as learner which itself is dependent on valuing one particular kind of learning (often following the work of researchers such as Entwistle's (1987) 'deep' learning) which differs from that developed at school. It is unsurprising therefore that my academic colleagues complain that students still cannot write academic assignments and essays in spite of the fact that they have attended (and passed) language and skills courses. When the idea that ways of constructing an argument differ according to disciplinary context (Lea and Street 1998) is added to that of the need for students to reconstruct their roles as writers, then the difficulty they face can be enormous.

Problems experienced by students like Moses in writing at tertiary level are compounded when one considers the sort of writing tuition which has previously been available to him. Teachers and lecturers are concerned with issues such as grammatical accuracy, punctuation or 'structure' and often act on the belief that describing an acceptable writing product will allow students to write well. This sort of approach takes no account of the fact that students like Moses have little or no understanding of the rules for making meaning in writing or of the practices which will allow them to make those meanings effectively. Reliant on what Gee (1990) terms 'primary literacies' acquired through interaction with family members and other intimates in face-to-face conversation, they are accustomed, for example, to receiving immediate feedback on any lapses in meaning making in the form of questions, challenges and attempts by other participants in the conversation to extend meaning. Similarly, they do not appreciate the need to create a context for what they write assuming, as in the case of face-to-face conversation, that the context in which they write will be automatically carried over onto the page. When the fact that Moses' primary experiences of meaning making involve face-to-face conversations, then a piece of writing which begins 'According to this theory' can be explained as a lack of familiarity with one of the (unwritten) 'rules' of writing, namely that each piece of writing has to begin with the creation of a context for what will be said. Similarly, writing which rambles on in a seemingly incoherent fashion can be explained as a failure to appreciate that meaning is not being made satisfactorily in the absence of feedback from other participants in a conversation. Against this sort of background, teaching students such as Moses to write academic text involves much more than providing a set of skills or descriptions of what academic text should look like since understandings of the way meaning is made in writing as opposed to face-to-face conversation have to be developed.

It should be clear, therefore, that the development of academic ways of knowing, speaking, reading and writing is far more complex and problematic than is often assumed since the literacies students bring with them are rooted in roles and identities developed over eighteen or more years of life and twelve or thirteen years of schooling. Developing new roles and identities and the practices associated with them is a complicated business which challenges the self and is often met with resistance or despair. It is certainly not something which is likely to be achieved in a short time or through the reduction of what is involved to the acquisition of a set of 'skills'. If this is the case, then, how can literacies be developed at university? It is to this question that this chapter now turns.

Developing literacies through mainstream teaching

The remainder of this chapter will focus on a description of just a few of the activities which lecturers teaching mainstream courses could incorporate into their work in order to contribute to the sort of shifts, and lifelong learning, required of their students.

It has already been noted that the context of the university differs from the context of the school most notably in the way each institution understands knowledge and its construction. Schools along with many other social institutions tend to support an understanding of knowledge as fact and of learning as reproduction.

Universities, on the other hand, understand knowledge as something which is constructed or discovered through research. Attempts to work with students' understandings of what constitutes knowledge therefore have the potential to make a significant contribution to the development of academic literacies. Ideally, a literacy enriched course would not only seek to make overt the 'rules and conventions' (Ballard and Clanchy 1988) for what can constitute knowledge but it will also seek to make clear ways in which knowledge is constructed within particular disciplinary contexts. Ideally this would mean exposing students to data gathering and analysis techniques early in their undergraduate careers. In my work in South Africa, for example, I have seen students enrolled in foundation modules in a Faculty of Humanities gather data on a range of issues related to the construct of identity, one of the core topics of study. In groups, students went out and interviewed women about their attitudes to a range of topics including smoking or their willingness to wear trousers. Other groups interviewed black male students about their preferences for social venues on campus or on their attitudes towards having a white girlfriend. Once the groups had collected data, they gathered together under the supervision of the lecturer to analyse and relate what they had learned to theories and positions explicated in the literature and prescribed as course reading. The written assignment for the course was data based in that it required students to use the data to exemplify, comment upon or challenge positions in the literature. This sort of experience provided a rich source of insight into the way knowledge is constructed in the university and, importantly, how it is nuanced and is open to critique and comment.

Whilst an activity such as that described above is itself conducive to getting students to engage with the literature critically, other more focused strategies can also be useful. An example of one such strategy would be the use of a reading journal. For many students, reading an academic text involves either making notes to summarize the most important points or highlighting those points within the text itself. This sort of reading focuses on remembering what the author has said and thus affirms a conception of knowledge and of learning as essentially reproductive rather than constructive. A reading journal requires students to respond to what they have read, by linking points made in one text to those in another, by exploring what the text says in relation to their own experiences or by using those experiences to affirm or contradict what it says. A journal response aims to develop the writer's own 'voice' in relation to those of others. Instructions for keeping a journal are simple. Students need to be told to buy a notebook or open a file on a computer. The reference for the text to be read is then written or typed at the top of the journal entry. Students then read the text focusing on understanding rather than remembering. A journal entry in relatively informal 'Dear Diary' mode is then written after the text has been read. Reading journals can be incorporated into the work of a course and can even constitute an assessed task. They can also form the basis for further discussion or other tasks since every student who has written a journal entry theoretically has something to say or something to draw on for further work.

The idea that many students are familiar only with the strategies for making meaning in primary speech-based literacies has already been discussed. One of the most productive things lecturers wishing to contribute to their students' academic literacies can do, therefore, is to guide them to an understanding of how those strategies need to be modified in order to produce academic text which satisfies their readers. This can be done through the provision of written comment on students' texts not in the form of an endnote (the paragraph of comment many academics expend considerable time in writing) but in the form of direct questions and comments in the body of the text which aim to show students where their writing is not meaningful.

A piece of writing which fails to contextualize sufficiently because the writer is assuming that context will 'carry over' from other classroom contexts can be challenged by questions at the point where more contextualization is required asking for more information. A question such as 'I need to know what exactly you are referring to here – can you explain more?' makes more sense to a student than an overall comment that the assignment required more contextualization. Similarly, direct questions about the structure of the text inserted at points where the structure falls down ('Haven't you already said this?' or 'I don't really see the link between this idea and what you were saying in the last paragraph, can you explain?') are more likely to guide students into producing a more coherent piece of writing than an overall comment that the text 'lacks structure'. Other comments challenging a position or claim made in writing ('What about …?' or 'How do you explain what X says in relation to this point?'), can help students to understand the need to anticipate and respond to other views in order to substantiate the claims they are making or the position they are adopting in the text overall. Finally, when writing is apparently incoherent, then a comment such as 'I really don't understand what you are saying here, can you explain again?' will direct the writer to the point in the text where meaning making is not successful much more effectively than an overall comment that the text is 'incoherent'. Responding in the body of the text in this way is successful because it corresponds to a strategy students are already familiar with – the need to rephrase, expand, elaborate or reconsider something in a face-to-face conversation in response to a comment or question from others involved in the speech situation. Clearly responding in this way is more effective if students are shown how to and then asked to redraft in the light of the responses. Allowing students to submit a draft of an assignment, responding to that draft and then assessing the finished piece of work which has been redrafted means more work for the lecturer and this is not always possible in large classes. When this sort of approach can be adopted, however, the effects on the development of writing can be substantial.

Conclusion

This chapter has argued against dominant understandings of poor academic performance as due to a lack of skills in favour of a more contextualized 'social' approach involving shifts in identity and understandings of what it means to learn and thus to speak, read and write at a university. While Moses was facing a particular set of difficulties in learning to 'be' at university given his own history as a black South African, the task facing the majority of students enrolling at universities across the world is not substantially different given the disjuncture between school-based and academic learning. As long as we continue to construct students' 'problems' in some of the ways identified in this chapter (see also Boughey 2002), however, we will not succeed in providing what Morrow (1993) has termed 'epistemological' access to the values and ways of knowledge production which underpin academic ways of reading, writing and speaking. The willingness of mainstream lecturers to contribute to the task of enliterating their students and of facilitating the acquisition of dominant academic discourses thus becomes an issue of equality and not just of teaching and learning. This chapter has described just a few of the practices which are available to mainstream lecturers in order to contribute to this process. There are undoubtedly others and the identification and development of them is something which can provide an enormously interesting challenge for those willing to take up the task.

References

Baker, C. and Freebody, P. (1989) 'Talk around text: construction of textual and teacher authority in classroom discourse', in S. de Castell, A. Luke and C. Luke (eds) *Language, Authority and Criticism: Reading on the School Textbook*, London: Falmer.

Ballard, B. and Clanchy, J. (1988). 'Literacy in the university: an "anthropological approach"', in G. Taylor, B. Ballard, V. Beasley, H.K. Bock, J. Clanchy and P. Nightingale, *Literacy by Degrees*, Milton Keynes: Open University Press and SRHE.

Boughey, C. (2002) 'Naming students' "problems": an analysis of language-related discourses at a South African university', *Teaching in Higher Education*, 7, 3: 295–307.

Entwistle, N. (1987) *Understanding Classroom Learning*, Sevenoaks: Hodder and Stoughton.

Gee, J.P. (1990) *Social Linguistics and Literacies: Ideology in Discourse*, Basingstoke: Falmer.

Gee, J.P. (2000) 'The new literacy studies: from: "socially situated" to the work of the social', in D. Barton and R. Ivanic (eds) *Writing in Community*, London: Sage.

Geisler, C. (1994) *Academic Literacy and the Nature of Expertise: Reading, Writing and Knowing in Academic Philosophy*, Hillsdale, NJ.: Lawrence Erlbaum.

Heap, J. (1985) 'Discourse in the production of classroom knowledge: reading lessons,' *Curriculum Inquiry*, 15: 245–79.

Heath, S.B. (1983) *Ways With Words: Language Life and Work in Communities and Classrooms*, Cambridge: Cambridge University Press.

Lea, M. and Street, B.V. (1998) 'Student writing in higher education: an academic literacies approach', *Studies in Higher Education*, 23, 2: 157–72.

Morrow, W. (1993) 'Epistemological access in the university', *AD Issues* 1: 3–4.

Street, B.V. (1993) *Cross-cultural Approaches to Literacy*, Cambridge: Cambridge University Press.

Street, B.V. (1995) *Social Literacies: Critical Approaches to Literacy in Development, Ethnography and Education*, London: Longman.

Chapter 14

Self-regulation
A multidimensional learning strategy

Martha Cassazza

In this chapter the focus is on the construct of self-regulation and the significant impact it can have on learning. Self-regulation implies learners are actively engaged in defining their learning and monitoring its progress. Effective self-regulation involves a repertoire of strategies that will help learners take charge of their own learning. Goals should be set in advance and should be attainable. The theoretical underpinning of this chapter is the TRPP (theory, research, principles and practice) cyclical model. A number of studies are cited to substantiate the argument that students who self-regulate achieve more than those who do not. Teachers can act as role models for the students until the process becomes automatic for the latter.

Introduction

In order to understand the construct comprehensively, self-regulation will be described through a four dimensional framework called TRPP (theory, research, principles and practice), a model designed by Cassazza and Silverman (1996). These four lenses will allow readers to integrate what is known about self-regulation and critically reflect upon that integration in order to apply it to their own practice. The lenses will help to create an awareness of recent research and how it supports the theoretical foundation. Through the integration of various theories and research, principles related to self-regulation will emerge that will help provide guidelines for effective practice.

Establishing the construct

Basically self-regulation is the process by which individuals both evaluate and regulate their learning. In order to effectively engage in this process, learners must consider themselves actively in control of the learning activity and, indeed, be at its very centre. It is generally related to goal setting because in order to evaluate one's progress, there must be a standard against which to measure achievement; goals can function as such a standard. Progress toward the goal, or the lack of it, is then regulated by the learner through the application of appropriate strategies. The learner must be adaptive and willing to try a new strategy when one doesn't seem to be working. These dual components, evaluation and regulation, are built upon the assumptions that the learner constructs goals and also has access to a repertoire, or toolbox, of 'fix up' strategies to apply when goals are not being met or the academic tasks change.

Theories that try to explain self-regulation have emerged from multiple schools of thought: contructivist, social cognitive, information processing, and behaviourist represent a few. There are, however, general components that provide an underlying foundation across all perspectives (Zimmerman and Schunk 2001). One common feature includes the idea that self-regulated learners are purposeful in their use of strategies and that they are striving to improve their academic achievement. They have most likely set goals for themselves and are actively engaged in moving toward them. A second general component is that of a feedback loop constructed by self-regulated learners. This loop enables them to monitor the effectiveness of their study strategies in order to make appropriate modifications when necessary. A third feature addressed by most theories includes a look at motivation and why some learners choose to self-regulate while others do not. This feature is often explored through research related to achievement, goal accomplishment, and/or self-efficacy. Lastly, most theories related to self-regulated learning address the issue of the additional time and effort required to regularly utilize it. Learners most likely need to consider the outcome worthwhile and consistent with their overall set of goals.

Reviewing the theoretical foundations

Let's take a look at some of the theoretical components that inform the construct of self-regulation. In this chapter, we will primarily explore the concept from a social cognitivist perspective. This view holds that self-regulation is situationally specific. Theorists of this school argue that learners adapt their strategies to specific domains and that self-regulation does not develop automatically; rather, it develops at first from social sources (an instructor for example) and then shifts to self-activation through four phases. Schunk (2001a) has proposed such a model of how self-regulatory competence develops. His levels do not necessarily represent hierarchical stages, but they do demonstrate one overall conceptualization of the process.

The first of these levels is *observation*. During this phase, learners take their cues from a model who includes instruction, task structuring and encouragement. This, naturally, requires practice with considerable feedback from the instructional model. The second level is *emulative* where the learner approximates the general performance patterns of the model. These first two levels are social in nature due to the significance of the modelling component. From here, the process of internalization begins, and the learner assumes more control. The third level of development is *self-control*. It is here where the learner independently uses study strategies although the strategies are still very similar to those suggested by the model. It is only during the fourth, or final, level of self-regulation where the learner actually adapts skills and strategies to the current learning situation.

No longer is the model the primary influence; rather, the learners are able to assess the learning task and construct appropriate strategies. During this time period, the learners are also motivated through personal goals, and self-efficacy becomes an important component. The learner comes to believe that their strategies make a difference and has a sense that the outcomes are a direct result of their individual efforts. In this model, the consequences of one's actions serve as information sources and motivators which, in turn, lead to the learner's selective application of strategies.

Zimmerman (2000) has proposed a three phase model that describes the key processes that come into play during self-regulation. These processes include forethought, performance and self-reflection. During the forethought phase, the learners analyse the task at hand in order to set goals and plan the application of strategies while simultaneously reviewing expected outcomes and examining their own personal belief in their ability to control the outcomes. The performance phase includes the actual implementation of strategies related to the task, focusing attention, and attributing failure or success to one's behaviour. The final phase, self-reflection, includes both self-judgment and self-reaction. It is here where the learner evaluates the performance and also the level of satisfaction related to the outcome. This includes thinking through how to adapt strategies for the next learning task underscoring the cyclical nature of self-regulation. This final phase will influence future forethought phases related to the next task.

For self-judgment to be effective, the learner must have set standards for performance. These standards take the form of goals created by the learner at the outset of the task. Locke and Latham (1990) discovered that when goals are self-constructed, learners have a greater commitment to the task, and performance is more likely to be affected. Self-set goals also lead to increased self-efficacy, the belief in one's ability to succeed at a given task. When a learner perceives a discrepancy between performance and goals, dissatisfaction occurs. This can lead to either an increased effort or a decision to stop trying. The learners will most likely continue if they have the belief that, through strategy adjustment, they can succeed. Once the goal is attained, the feeling of self-efficacy is reinforced, and the learner goes on to set new goals (Schunk 2001b).

Goals have many properties that are significant to this construct. They do not, however, automatically contribute to self-regulation; it is the activation of particular properties that facilitates achievement. Utilizing goals as standards both informs and motivates learners. It enhances and also sustains motivation (Schunk 2001b). Properties of goals that contribute to effective self-regulation include: specificity, proximity and difficulty level (Bandura 1988; Locke and Latham 1990). Goals with explicit standards (specificity) help to increase one's self-efficacy because they are easy to measure. More general goals are not easily measurable and consequently are not as motivational. As an example, it is more motivating for a learner to set a goal of reading ten pages during a specific time frame than it is to try to read as much as possible. Proximal goals, those that are tied to short-term outcomes, are also more motivating than long-term goals as it is easier to observe movement toward a task that can be completed in a time frame that is closer at hand. One way to apply this to long-term projects is for the learner to break longer tasks into a series of shorter, more frequently measurable components. The third property, difficulty, is also significant as learners are not motivated by goals that are perceived as either too hard or too easy. Goals that are challenging while attainable lead to increased self-efficacy. Bandura (1997) adds to this discussion about goals by articulating that one must value a goal before it becomes motivating. If individuals do not care about their performance, goals will be of little use. When goals are valued, learners tend to anticipate consequences and reward or punish themselves rather than wait for an external signal e.g. grades at the end of the term.

Goal orientation as it relates to self-regulated learning has been extensively studied by Pintrich (2000). He has proposed a general framework for classifying goals which includes two basic types: mastery and performance. When a learner applies a mastery approach, the individual is focusing on learning or understanding a particular task. When a performance standard is applied, the individual focuses instead on comparing his performance to that of others. Within these two overall classifications, there are two distinctive forms: approach and avoidance. Mastery goals with an approach focus help the learner work toward self-improvement while those with an avoidance focus look toward *not* failing or *not* misunderstanding the task. Approach performance goals are those which motivate the learner to achieve the highest scores while the avoidance form focuses on *not* being the lowest performer in class. In general, research seems to confirm that those who engage in an approach-mastery goal orientation are more apt to be self-regulated learners. Pintrich also points out that there is most likely a reciprocal relationship between mastery goals and the learner's level of interest with mastery goals leading to interest and interest leading to mastery goals.

Historically, the research has indicated a negative relationship between performance goals in general and outcomes. Performance goals, with their emphasis on outperforming others, have often tended to lead to the application of more superficial learning strategies. Learners utilizing this approach are frequently influenced by the belief that more effort is a signal to others of lesser ability, so they consequently tend to avoid strategies such as asking for assistance or seeming to spend more time on a task. With the recent distinction that adds the approach/avoidance forms, additional perspectives are emerging that suggest that an approach performance goal may be positive. Especially for those learners who are competitive, this approach may lead to the application of more learning strategies and also increased motivation as they place a high value on finishing first.

Describing the TRPP framework

So far we have looked briefly at a theoretical foundation related to self-regulated learning. It is not inclusive, but it includes several of the most common constructs found within the area of self-regulation. This foundation helps to inform us about the general concept, but it only represents one part of the overall picture. In order for the concept of self-regulation to have real meaning, we need to continue exploring it through additional lenses. As described earlier, the TRPP model provides us with a model for doing so (see Figure 14.1). Through this model, we can look at the interaction among four components: theory, research, principles and practice. It is a cyclical model of connections where the components are not viewed in isolation; rather, they are integrated to ultimately lead to maximizing student potential. One can begin the cycle with any of the components. For instance, in this case we have already begun to look at self-regulation by reviewing theory. We chose to begin here because theory is one way to organize information for further review and also to provide an informational base. An underlying assumption of TRPP is that no one theory explains all behaviour. A more eclectic approach is much more useful in developing instructional strategies.

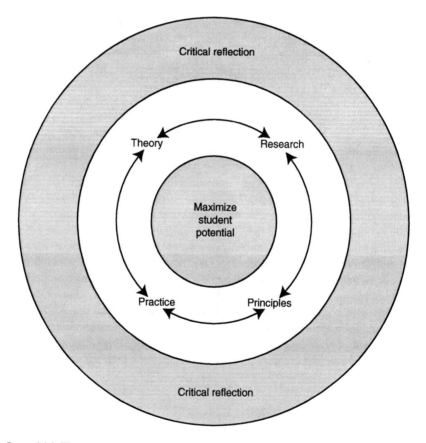

Figure 14.1 Theory, research, principles and practice model

Following our review of theory, a next step might be to look for research that either supports or refutes the theory that we have articulated. When Belenky *et al.* (1986) began their classic work related to women and their ways of knowing, they began with a review of Perry's work on learning stages based on his research conducted with males. This review led them to conduct their own research that led to distinctive principles and practice for female learners.

In addition to the four basic components of TRPP, the factor that engages the entire model and actively drives the connections is the process of critical reflection. This process enables us to really see the connections and to discover new meaning as various interactions are explored. It forces us to see inconsistencies and to question what we may have simply accepted without the advantage of the four lenses. These interactions lead us to new insights which will in turn help us to improve practice.

TRPP is intended to be a dynamic framework. It requires an attention to new research and new ways of thinking about theories related to learning. These, in turn, force us to examine long-standing principles and instructional practices. To apply the model to this chapter's organization, we now need to turn to the research to see how it relates to the theoretical constructs we identified earlier. Since the primary components of self-regulation that emerged in the theory section included goal setting, the role of instruction, adaptive behaviour and active engagement, those are the areas that we will concentrate on as we turn to the research. Following this, we will link the theory and research in order to construct principles that will guide our decision making as we consider how to best provide instruction.

Examining the recent research

There has been a great deal of research conducted related to the effects of constructing learning goals. In a study that looked at goals and motivation with college freshmen (Van Etten *et al.* 1998), students reported that experiencing success in setting grade goals for themselves subsequently led them to set higher goals. Receiving consistent feedback in relation to goal attainment increased motivation, and motivation was increased when self-set standards (mastery goals) were constructed as opposed to trying to compete against others (performance goals). The students also reported that distal (long term) goals rather than proximal goals were counterproductive. In addition, students in the study who had goals were more likely to have positive self-efficacy beliefs which led them to participate more frequently in the process of goal attainment. As they progressed toward goal attainment and received feedback, their self-efficacy also improved. Others have found that this increases motivation and the use of study strategies (Elliot and Dweck 1988; Schunk and Swartz 1993). The type of feedback is also significant. Locke and Latham (1990) found that when it includes information related to self-efficacy and emphasizes self-improvement, challenge and mastery, feedback influences goal commitment.

Locke and Latham also found that the higher the difficulty level of the goal, the more likely it is that performance outcomes will be better. The difficulty level, however, must be within the ability range of the learner. In addition to this finding, it seems as if goals that are difficult as well as specific also lead to increased performance.

Warkentin and Bol (1997) analysed the differences between high and low achieving students using an effort management hierarchy as it related to self-regulatory behaviour. They found that most students experienced difficulty in monitoring their efforts. They discovered more distinctions in the areas of planning (forethought) and evaluation. All students reported that regulation served a variety of functions for them including breaking their study sessions into smaller segments which helped them create intermediate goals and greater persistence. In the area of planning, the researchers found a difference between the high and low achievers in two categories. For instance, 91 per cent of the high achievers constructed selective study strategies; they looked at what was likely to be important and based their studying on that. On the other hand, only 44 per cent of the low achievers reported any pattern to their planning efforts. They also found differences in the nature of goals constructed by the students. Of the low achievers 55 per cent had 'remembering goals', where they were attempting to memorize information, whereas the high achievers set goals related more to understanding and remembering for future needs.

These same researchers looked at the evaluation component for these two categories of learners and found qualitative differences. The low achievers tended to utilize a more general reflective process where the high achievers looked more specifically at what may have worked. Additional research has demonstrated that highly self-regulated learners evaluate themselves more often, attribute poor performance to a deficiency in their strategy application rather than to a lack of ability, experience greater self-satisfaction and also adapt more effectively than poorly self-regulated learners (Kitsantas and Zimmerman 1998; Zimmerman and Kitsantas 1997, 1999). Self-regulators also replace strategies with more effective ones when their self-evaluative judgments indicate a need to do so (Zimmerman and Martinez-Pons 1990).

Winne (1995) suggested that self-regulated learning depends on environmental influences and that it develops incrementally through instruction. The research he reviewed demonstrated that effective interventions share four basic ingredients. First, they must provide the conditional knowledge that learners need to determine when a strategy has been successful. Second, they must provide the action knowledge including metacognitive, cognitive and behavioural skills related to self-regulation. Third, they must ensure that learners are motivated to apply the first two ingredients, and fourth, they assume a certain level of prerequisite knowledge in a particular domain. Pressley (1995) supports this finding as he contends that instruction must first be matched to the learner's zone of proximal development and then followed by teacher modelling, explanation and massed practice.

Winne also argues that monitoring one's learning 'levies charges' against a learner's working memory and may act as a barrier if a learner is still in the stage of acquiring new information. He contends that students who are less knowledgeable are 'charged more for monitoring' and that it can lead to increased errors as it has not become automated for them in a specific domain. He goes on to say that 'only after the declarative stage of skill learning, the point at which skills are ready to be proceduralized, can costs charged for monitoring fit into the learners' cognitive budgets' (Winne 1995: 178).

Simpson and Nist (1997) looked at one history course to determine how the behaviours of high achieving students differed from the low achievers. They found that those students who were successful shared two characteristics: they initially understood the instructor's academic tasks or they were flexible enough to modify their perceptions and strategies over time. The poor performers did not understand the tasks and their behaviours were inflexible. Simpson and Nist concluded that understanding the task is foundational to strategy selection; otherwise, students select strategies that do not match the expected outcomes.

Related to the effects of instruction on self-regulation, Talbot (1996) states that it cannot be taught. Instead, instructors have the role of mediator; they must elicit behaviour from the learners who must experience ownership of the process which then becomes meaningful due to their personal involvement. The instructor's primary role is to increase student awareness of the connections between their intentions and their actions. His research also discovered different results with learning oriented (mastery) versus goal oriented (performance) learners. Those learners who were learning oriented utilized a variety of resources versus the more goal oriented who were not interested in evaluation strategies and subsequent outcomes.

A different perspective is provided through the work of Doring et al. (1997). They argue that the university must view self-regulation as an inherent component of the transitional process experienced by entering students and that the university must take an active role in promoting those skills. They contend that the skills of self-regulation should be embedded in content courses and that learners do indeed need help in setting appropriate goals which will then lead to a foundation for self-regulatory learning. From their view, teaching must include purposeful instruction related to goal setting.

Constructing the principles

From the research findings and the theoretical foundations that have been summarized here, the following set of principles related to self-regulation emerges. The following three principles could be used as guides to construct instructional strategies.

- Self-regulated learning enables learners to actively control their learning through adaptive strategies.
- Self-regulated learning is enhanced when learners make a direct connection between their use of strategies and the outcomes of their learning.
- Self-regulated learning helps learners to set learning goals that enhance academic achievement.

Applying instructional strategies

Using these three principles as guides for instructional strategies, let us look at each one briefly and develop a few teaching techniques that would enable us to bring what we have learned from the research and theory into the classroom. These principles are not inclusive, rather, they represent one way of linking theory to practice.

Principle 1: Self-regulated learning enables learners to actively control their learning through adaptive strategies.

A good beginning for this principle is for the instructor to model behaviour that clearly demonstrates active control and the need to adapt based on the assigned task. It is imperative that the task and its demands are first clearly understood by the students. The instructor cannot make assumptions based on a set of written directions; rather, he or she must take time to analyse the task with the students and clarify the expectations. Following this could be a discussion on what type of study environment might be needed to fulfil the task. Perhaps a student is not able to get a paper written because he lives in a home with several other family members who would be insulted if he retreated to a separate room to do his schoolwork. Having the discussion allows the student to realize that he actually has some control over his study environment, something he may not have even considered without the discussion. Perhaps he could go to the library either at school or in his community when he needs quiet time. Another option may be to form a study group with classmates where they collaborate on how and where to study. Another adaptive strategy might include seeking assistance from a tutor or attending a writing workshop. Students often think this type of assistance indicates their own inability to perform a task, but when the instructor promotes it as a positive resource that will help them progress with a given task, they may be much more willing to access it.

Principle 2: Self-regulated learning is enhanced when learners make a direct connection between their use of strategies and the outcomes of their learning.

If students do not evaluate the outcomes of their strategies for effectiveness, we can assume that they will continue to use some inappropriate methods because they do not see the connection between strategies and outcomes. For instance, many students believe that simply spending a certain number of hours will prepare them for a test. When they perform poorly on the test, they attribute their low performance to either a test that was too difficult or a lack of ability on their part. Both of these attributions indicate no awareness of how their strategy choices made a difference in the learning situation.

To enhance their sense of control and awareness of the connections, the instructor could directly go through specifically relevant study techniques for a test. The instructor could talk through, for instance, how to graph the principles for the next biology exam and actually lead the entire class through a practice model. In addition, the class could review notes in small groups in class and highlight significant ideas together in order to underscore the importance of selectively reviewing notes. The instructor could also invite a learning specialist to go over how to critically read a text in preparation for the test. Before the actual test, either the students or the instructor could create a practice test which would demonstrate the usefulness of the strategies employed in preparation. Following this practice, the students could then review exactly which strategies were most helpful and why.

Principle 3: Self-regulated learning helps learners to set learning goals that enhance academic achievement.

One effective way to get students thinking about goal setting is to require all students to write out their expectations for the class at the beginning of the term. The instructor will need to review the goals, most of which will likely be very general and oriented to performance e.g. grades and provide feedback to the students. By handing them back with comments that enable the students to construct more of a mastery orientation as well as specificity, the instructor will be introducing the concept of creating a standard by which to measure progress. In a writing course, the students could review the syllabus and reflect carefully on the topics listed, compare them to areas in which the student needs strengthening and write them up as goals that can be measured. Then each week, the instructor could ask the students to write a commentary on how much progress they have made toward reaching at least one of the goals. These commentaries should be valued either through credit awarded or specific feedback from the instructor.

In terms of writing goals for specific assignments, the instructor can model how to break long-term projects into a series of short-term goals. If there is a term paper due at the end of the term, perhaps the entire class could engage in a discussion of the various components (identifying a topic, conducting research, citing references, and drafting a preliminary outline) and then break into small groups to actually brainstorm timelines and specific goals related to each part. By engaging in this activity, the students focus on the process of writing a paper and can measure their progress along the way rather than waiting until the end of the term. The instructor could ask the students to submit their intermediary steps and provide feedback along the way and perhaps even incorporate it into the overall grade.

Conclusion

It seems clear that the application of self-regulation strategies promotes active, engaged learners who see themselves at the centre of the learning process. Self-regulated learners set academic goals for themselves and then regularly monitor their progress toward achieving them. This monitoring provides them with information that allows them to adapt their strategies if they find they are not achieving the standard set by their own goals. This adaptive behaviour is what regulates their performance. It becomes a cyclical process as the learners are constantly evaluating and then regulating their progress based on the results of the evaluation. This assumes that the learners have access to a repertoire of strategies and are able to make appropriate adjustments when necessary.

This process does not usually occur intuitively, rather, there needs to be ongoing instruction that creates an awareness of how it connects to academic achievement. Teachers can serve as role models in the learning environment by describing the process, modelling study strategies and then ensuring that students have guided practice on specific academic tasks with regular feedback. The feedback needs to include information on goal setting and how the students' behaviour is directly linked to outcomes. Gradually, the responsibility for evaluation and feedback is released to the learner and self-regulation becomes automatic.

References

Bandura, A. (1988) *Social Foundations of Thought and Action: A Social Cognitive Theory*, Englewood Cliffs, NJ.: Prentice Hall.

Bandura, A. (1997) *Self-Efficacy: The Exercise of Control*, New York: Freeman.

Belenky, M.F., Clinchy, B.M., Goldberger, N.R. and Tarule, J.M. (1986) *Women's Ways of Knowing: The Development of Self, Voice, and Mind*, New York: Basic Books.

Cassazza, M.E. and Silverman, S.L. (1996) *Learning Assistance and Developmental Education*, San Francisco: Jossey-Bass.

Doring, A., Bingham, B. and Bramwell-Viol, A. (1997) 'Transition to university: a self-regulatory approach', paper presented at *The Annual Conference of The Australian Association for Research in Education*, Brisbane.

Elliot, E.S. and Dweck, C.S. (1988) 'Goals: an approach to motivation and achievement', *Journal of Personality and Social Psychology*, 54: 5–12.

Kitsantas, A. and Zimmerman, B.J. (1998) 'Self-regulation of motoric learning: a strategic cycle view', *Journal of Applied Sport Psychology*, 10: 220–39.

Locke, E.A. and Latham, G.P. (1990) *A Theory of Goal Setting and Task Performance*, Englewood Cliffs, NJ.: Prentice Hall.

Pintrich, P.R. (2000) 'The role of goal orientation in self-regulated learning', in M. Boekaerts, P. Pintrich and M. Zeidner (eds) *Handbook of Self-Regulation*, New York: Academic Press.

Pressley, M. (1995) 'More about the development of self-regulation: complex, long-term, and thoroughly social', *Educational Psychologist*, 30, 4: 207–12.

Schunk, D.H. (2001a) 'Social cognitive theory and self-regulated learning', in B.J. Zimmerman and D.H. Schunk (eds) *Self-Regulated Learning and Academic Achievement*, 2nd edn, Mahwah, NJ.: Lawrence Erlbaum Publishers.

Schunk, D.H. (2001b) *Self-Regulation through Goal Setting*, Washington, DC. (ERIC Document Service No. 462671).

Schunk, D.H. and Swartz, C.W. (1993) 'Goals and progress feedback: effects on self-efficacy and writing instruction', *Contemporary Educational Psychology*, 18: 337–54.

Simpson, M.L. and Nist, S.L. (1997) 'Perspectives on learning history: a case study', *Journal of Literacy Research*, 29: 363–95.

Talbot, G. (1996) *A Grounded Research Perspective for Motivating College Students' Self-Regulated Learning Behaviors: Preparing and Gaining the Cooperation, Commitment of Teacher*, Washington, D.C. (ERIC Document Service No. 414788).

Van Etten, S., Pressley, M., Freebern, G. and Eschevarria, M. (1998) 'An interview study of college freshmen's beliefs about their academic motivation', *European Journal of Psychology of Education*, 13: 105–30.

Warkentin, R.W. and Bol, L. (1997) 'Assessing college students' self-directed studying using self-reports of test preparation', paper presented at the annual meeting of *The American Educational Research Association*, Chicago.

Winne, P.H. (1995) 'Inherent details in self-regulated learning', *Educational Psychologist*, 30, 4: 173–87.

Zimmerman, B.J. (2000) 'Attaining self-regulation: a social cognitive perspective', in M. Boekaerts, P.R. Pintrich and M. Zeidner (eds) *Handbook of Self-Regulation*, San Diego, CA.: Academic Press.

Zimmerman, B.J. and Kitsantas, A. (1997) 'Developmental phases in self-regulation: shifting from process goals to outcome goals', *Journal of Educational Psychology*, 89: 29–36.

Zimmerman, B.J. and Kitsantas, A. (1999) 'Acquiring writing revision skill: shifting from process to outcome self-regulatory goals', *Journal of Educational Psychology*, 91: 1–10.

Zimmerman, B.J. and Martinez-Pons, M. (1990) 'Student differences in self-regulated learning: relating grade, sex, and giftedness to self-efficacy and strategy use', *Journal of Educational Psychology*, 82: 51–9.

Zimmerman, B.J. and Schunk, D.H. (2001) *Self-Regulated Learning and Academic Achievement: Theoretical Perspectives*, Mahwah, NJ.: Lawrence Erlbaum Publishers.

Part III

Informal and community contexts for learning

(Mis)recognizing lifelong learning in non-formal settings

John Preston

Mis-recognition is an aspect of social control that attaches different values to the activities of class fractions in non-formal settings. It can occur through ascribing social characteristics as natural properties of individuals. It can occur through devaluing class forms of active citizenship as 'abject'. It might also result from over-recognizing the outcomes of non-formal learning in individualized and moralized ways. In this critical analysis of policy the author draws on research conducted whilst employed at the Centre for Research on the Wider Benefits of Learning. He concludes that if lifelong learning is to be part of wider redistributive struggles it needs to reconnect with its radical traditions.

Bread and circus skills

Capital requires human labour power – 'muscle, nerve and brain' (Marx 1983: 167) – in order to create value and hence profit. Despite the priority attached to manual labour in the early stages of capitalism, all sorts of additional labour power are now sucked into the vortex of capitalist production. We are literally 'human capital' (Rikowski 1999). Through lifelong learning policy the formation of this human capital in its broadest sense is emphasized. Skills remain central to employability (DfES – Department for Education and Skills, 2003) although employers require labour power of diverse forms. Policy is increasingly aimed at creating 'soft skills' for employability – motivation, flexibility, communication and good health – although responsibility for these is increasingly transferred from the state to individuals and communities. Policy also seeks to support social cohesion through transferring public activities to the private domain. Parents are increasingly responsible for enhancing their children's conduct and skills. Communities are responsible for solving 'collective action problems', monitoring crime and raising funds for development. In all of these activities:

> Community Learning forms a vital part of the Government's drive to support social inclusion, to widen participation in learning, to build communities' self confidence and capacity and to promote good citizenship and personal development.
>
> (DfES 2002: 25)

Indeed, the DfES has funded a research centre where I have conducted much of my work (Centre for Research on the Wider Benefits of Learning) to identify and evidence the 'wider benefits' arising from lifelong learning. Increasingly, though, the non-formal and leisure courses and activities that might deliver 'soft skills' and 'wider benefits' are being compromised as policy emphasis shifts towards delivery of adult basic skills and level 2 (upper secondary school level) qualifications. To gain funding, providers are being asked to record and audit the 'employability' and 'wider benefits' arising from non-formal activities (DfES 2002) – a procedure which the Learning and Skills Council (who regulate and fund adult learning in the UK) and the National Institute of Adult Continuing Education (the key independent lobby group for adult education in the UK) refer to as Recognising and Recording Progress and Achievement in non-accredited Learning (RARPA) (Watters 2003; Nashashibi 2004).

The aim of RARPA is to bring the non-formal aspects and benefits of learning into the domain of auditing and inspection. Activities such as being involved in community committee work (Nashashibi 2004: 18), attending a gym (Nashashibi 2004: 22) and (sinisterly common in community outreach activities) forming a circus troupe (Nashashibi 2004: 28) are cited as activities where learning activities and their outcomes can be audited and utilized for funding purposes. Interestingly, in all of the RARPA documentation, the apparent desire of learners to have their non-formal activities assessed and accredited is explicit. Despite acknowledging learners' reservations concerning accrediting their non-formal learning (Watters 2003), the process will focus on the 'needs and interests of learners' (Watters 2003: 14), promote 'dialogue about learning and achievement between learners and tutors/trainers' (Watters 2003: 14) and will 'open up new possibilities for the learner (more impact)' (Nashashibi 2004: 7). All of this relies upon the identification of both learning and its benefits in various settings including the non-formal. This is not only a difficult technical problem (Plewis and Preston 2001) but also one in which mis-recognition might be expected to occur.

Mis-recognition

According to Bourdieu and Waquant (1992) mis-recognition is an activity whereby social position is seen to be natural and legitimate rather than strategic and arbitrary. For example, the awarding of grades to students is mis-recognized as reflecting effort and ability rather than their social position (Bourdieu 1988). In doing so, the awarding of grades 'allows the operation of a social classification while simultaneously masking it' (Bourdieu 1988: 201). However, mis-recognition is not only a particular categorization (an explanation which takes the arbitrary to be legitimate) but also a mode of differentiation (a way of fixing certain individuals or classes in abject social positions).

Skeggs (2004) argues that as well as fetishizing the achievements of the powerful, mis-recognition also 'occurs in reverse. That is, those at the opposite end of the social scale are also mis-recognized as having ascribed and essential characteristics'

(2004: 4). For example, the white working class have been frequently represented in policy discourse and the media as over-consuming, excessive and vulgar – 'as white trash' (Wray and Newitz 1997). White working class learners might face similar ascriptions (Preston 2003). This 'reading' of the white working class as waste or trash is '*a reading of the surface rather than a reading of the relationships that constitute the object ... a reading which displays the class-based investments of the reader*' (Skeggs 2004: 169 [her italics]). It is a purposive mis-recognition of the working class that serves as a class strategy of the middle and ruling classes. These two forms of mis-recognition (as category, as differentiation) are fundamental to a critique of attempts to identify learning, or the benefits of learning, in non-formal settings.

Mis-recognition I (categorization): 'individual benefits' of learning

From a feminist standpoint, Jackson (2004) argues that through emphasizing *individual* benefits of learning such as self-confidence for working class women we fail to recognize the nature of 'structural and institutional discrimination for working class women' (2004: 374). Increased confidence to participate in the community mis-recognizes the nature of individual 'benefit' – increased exploitation may be more apt as women are not paid for the value created through their work (care, informal policing, volunteering) in community settings (Delphy and Leonard 1992). Aside from mis-recognition of the gendered nature of non-formal learning there is also a danger of mis-recognition of the role of class as an *individual property*, rather than as a systematic process of oppression and conflict. Focusing on individual benefits of learning for individual members of a particular class (such as working class women) mis-recognizes the role of the members of other class factions (such as middle class men and women) in delimiting those benefits.

One way of examining learning in non-formal settings is to conceive of it as taking place within a greater set of social relations involving social class constituted as class factions. Class factions are not social classes in the orthodox Marxist sense. Rather than ownership of capital, wealth and access to wealth, creating and maintaining assets are important in the activities of class factions. These assets may be symbolic rather than economic although symbolic capitals (social, cultural, academic) are reducible to economic capital, and ultimately labour power (Bourdieu 1986). The maintenance of advantage requires purposive activities involving these symbolic capitals. These may be conscious or unconscious strategies aimed at consolidating class position by the exclusion of others or more subtle strategies of appropriation.

Class strategies have been applied to formal schooling (Ball 2003) but may also operate in non-formal learning contexts (Preston 2004). Examining non-formal learning in terms of class strategies moves us beyond examination of 'skill deficits' or 'cultural mis-matches' of the working class – a common mis-recognition. Rather, it involves an examination of how the activities of factions of the middle class preclude factions of the working class from securing learning or benefits of learning in non-formal settings. Drawing on previous work (see Preston 2004) I use brief portraits of two individuals from our biographical research – Susan and Francis – to explain how class strategies are central in interpreting how non-formal learning becomes (or does not become) beneficial.

Recently retired Susan, wealthy in terms of economic capital, followed a quite plausible path through the U3A (University of the Third Age: an informal learning organization for the retired) to start an investment club. This was perfectly in accordance with her habitus in terms of her stated desire to be with 'people like me' and her concerns for increasing wealth and self-sufficiency. Her desire to be with 'people like me' was both an internalization of class and a realization of class in terms of replicating homogenous, middle class, white associations. It was part of class formation, even into old age. Her economic capital and funds from the investment club enabled her to travel and engage in other non-formal learning opportunities. In the aggregate, actions such as hers were a class strategy. They both created and legitimized middle class exclusivity. On the other hand, Francis was notionally a member of artistic associations but was unable to fully valorize these memberships in terms of extending social networks. He perceived them as not being for 'people like him' – black, working class – and indeed, there were *no other* black, working class members. With only tenuous labour market status (he described himself as 'called up for training') and little economic capital (for travel to exhibitions and social events) he was unable to sustain membership of these associations. However, he was very much involved in black cultural groups. Whilst establishing a hierarchy of civic associations is not helpful, it is certainly true that the horizons for action for Francis were much narrower than those of Susan. This is not due to 'cultural deficit' or even that Francis was engaging in 'culturally appropriate' learning (common mis-recognitions of working class learners) but rather as a result of economic inequality and the colonization of even non-formal learning arenas by the middle classes.

There may be my own mis-recognitions in this account (perhaps in terms of the value of participation in various associations) and this analysis of non-formal learning in terms of class strategies has some weaknesses. In particular it assumes that class-factional interests within class factions might be common (but not between class factions) and that there is some form of social solidarity within the middle classes (although this may be true of educational and civic spheres rather than fields of employment). However, I would argue that using the relations between class factions to analyse non-formal learning enables us to recognize the processes of power and legitimation that would otherwise be overlooked.

Mis-recognition 2 (differentiation): 'abject' citizenship

The way in which 'active citizenship' has been defined in the current policy regime represents a case of mis-recognition as policy in which some forms of citizenship have been classed as abject whilst other 'active' forms of citizenship have been valorized. For example, the building of 'social capital' – local networks – to solve collective action problems is a target of government policy and part of active citizenship (Gamarnikow and Green 1999) whereas socialism and industrial action by militant trade unions clearly is not. Although 'active citizenship' and 'social capital' sound benign and value-free concepts, their ideology is communitarian and consensual rather than collectivist and conflict based (Fine and Green 2000). Therefore, the use of these terms de-legitimates certain forms of action. In terms of learning in non-formal settings, it is clear that the ALI (Adult Learning Inspectorate who inspect adult education in the UK) have a communitarian conception of active citizenship, defining it as:

> The process whereby people have to *improve the quality of life for others* and make a conscious effort to do so: the process whereby which people recognize the power of organizations and institutions to act in the *interests of the common good* and exercise their influence to do so. Adult learning contributes to active citizenship.
>
> (ALI 2002: 6 [my italics])

According to the ALI, the aim of learning should be to co-exist with others in 'self-managing sustainable communities' (ALI 2002: 6).

As can be seen in these quotes, there are a number of recognitions concerning the role of the 'active citizen'. For example, that individuals aim to increase the 'quality of life for others' or the 'common good' implies that there are shared, mutual goals in society which would not necessarily conflict. That 'the power of institutions' might be harnessed to act in the interests of all implies that existing structures and institutions are fit to serve democratic purposes. Finally, that the aim of active citizenship should be towards 'self-managing, sustainable communities' implies a communitarian orientation that might not accord with more collectivist and radical conceptions of citizenship. Although the ALI may assume that there are few students with a Marxist or Anarchist orientation in learning settings, their definition seeks to de-authorize the activities of many who might class themselves as 'community activists'.

This issue of what is recognized or mis-recognized as active citizenship in non-formal settings is not just a problem for the ALI. Indeed, mis-recognition in this area is common. For example, protests by (predominantly) working class women against paedophiles on their estates in the UK in the last five years have been described as 'witch hunts' in the media (Thompson 2000). However, in coverage of a campaign against child abusers on a working class estate in Portsmouth, the protestors were described differently from those campaigning in the middle class area of Balham, South London, drawing the distinction between 'recognized' (middle class) and 'mis-recognized' (working class) forms of protest:

> SCREAMING anti-paedophile demonstrators stepped up their protests on the streets of Portsmouth last night, despite pleas from police and local officials to stay at home. As events threatened to degenerate into mob rule, a

crowd of 300 protesters collected outside the homes of suspected paedophiles yelling: 'Hang him! Hang him!' During a seventh consecutive night of vigilante action, protesters – some of them mothers pushing prams – demanded the removal of 15 local men named on an unofficial list of alleged sex offenders.

> ('Innocent families driven out as paedophile protest continues':
> *Daily Telegraph*, 10 August 2000)

WHEN the Home Office decided to site a hostel for recently released high-risk offenders, including paedophiles, in an area known as 'Nappy Valley' it had not reckoned on the tenacity of its residents.

But unlike Paulsgrove, near Portsmouth, where mobs rioted last year after finding a sex offender living in their midst, the protest in Balham, south London, was a model of middle-class moderation. Now the Home Office has said that it no longer intends to house serious offenders at Bedford Hill and will consult residents about what to use it for.

> ('Residents see off plan for high-risk offenders' hostel':
> *Daily Telegraph*, 3 February 2001)

The ways in which various forms of protest are portrayed in these accounts highlights the distinction between 'recognized' and 'mis-recognized' citizenship. It particularly shows how social learning in non-formal settings might not be recognized in working class communities. 'The sorts of social capital that working-class families are more likely to activate are not those valorized by the New Labour project' (Gewirtz 2001: 375).

In Portsmouth, the residents are described as a 'screaming' 'mob', putting their own children at risk. The depiction accords with new-Right portrayals of the working class (or underclass) as out of control (Murray 1984). In Balham, however, the protestors are described as 'tenacious', contrasting with the 'mob rule' of Portsmouth. When the nature of these protests in Balham is described, the unlawful protest in terms of blocking the road is put in neutral terms, unlike the 'lawlessness' of the activity in Portsmouth:

> A website was set up, an action group was established, leaflets distributed, and candlelight vigils and marches were staged ... when a panel of those responsible tried to explain their proposals to a residents' meeting hundreds of people blocked Balham High Road for two hours.
>
> (*Daily Telegraph*, 3 February 2001)

In citing these examples, whether the protestors were correct or misguided in their action is a matter of opinion. There are, though, significant classed differences in the ways in which these actions were reported. Necessarily, this might mean that in assessing learning in non-formal settings we might mis-recognize the participation of some groups as invalid and abject, particularly if the ALI definition of active citizenship is used to guide this recognition. As Thompson (2000) argues, the action of the women in Paulsgrove *does* demonstrate active citizenship and participation, albeit mis-recognized : 'it is the kind of activism which is best understood as defiance and as resistance to traditional (and middle class) constructions of femininity, participation, respectability and subordination' (Thompson 2000: 23).

Over-recognition

As I have shown, attempting to recognize the benefits of learning potentially mis-recognizes the activities of some. However, in terms of non-formal learning it might not be the pernicious effects of mis-recognition that are of most current concern. In the effort to name and classify the outcomes of non-formal learning we are in danger of (what I term) over-recognizing, as well as mis-recognizing, learning. Over-recognition is a form of mis-recognition in which the *unidentified or mis-recognized becomes 'recognized'*. This might be seen positively in that it gives the opportunity to more properly hear the 'voices' of marginalized learners. Indeed, Rose (2002) usefully employs the autobiographies of working class learners and radical autodidacts to re-construct a history of adult learning which is frequently unspoken. However, giving voice should not be conflated with empowerment (Hadfield and Haw 2001). As discussed earlier, the 'technologies' designed to elicit learner voices (such as RARPA) are created to facilitate the auditing of individualized learning within a moral framework of (normatively) good citizenship and behaviour. This has consequences for learners in non-formal settings.

First, in using marginalized voices to explore the association between learning and outcomes we might become concerned with the latter (outcomes) rather than the former (learning). In other words, we might recognize particular benefits whilst neglecting the learning itself. This potentially de-authorizes the learning of some. Their learning is of use only in that it can deliver benefits and is not necessarily of intrinsic value. In addition, learning could (and should) be challenging and unsettling rather than therapeutic and conducive to social cohesion. The specification of positive outcomes of non-formal education in terms of mutuality and common purpose (ALI 2002) fails to recognize that conflict between the state and its subjects has been necessary in the pursuit of democracy (Skocpol and Fiorina 1999).

Second, the use of 'learner's voices' or the confessional mode regarding the benefits of learning may actually act against the interest of learners. The political purposes of 'biography' or 'voice' – *forced telling* (Skeggs 2004: 123) is not a recent development. The use of biography and 'voices' of the marginalized as a basis for provision of aid dates back to the philanthropic efforts of the COS (Charity Organisation Society) in the nineteenth century (Mooney 1998). The COS developed a casework approach in assessing the needs of the poor and in doing so both individualized and moralized the problems faced by clients (Mooney 1998: 75). In terms of research 'telling for welfare' has similarly become systematized as evidence-based policy with individual, redemptive stories providing part of the basis for government policy.

Moreover, once such benefits (as is now happening with soft skills and progression) become part of funding and inspection criteria for providers, this technique will move into non-formal settings. This may result in a 'naming and claiming culture' with learners desperately trying to positively identify aspects of their learning so that the harangued adult education tutor can enter them onto a form. Experience thereby becomes part of the property of providers in claims for funding, for inspection evidence and to enhance their reputation. This can be seen as further 'legislation for the materialization of the self' (Skeggs 2004: 125) in that current working class learners like the Victorian urban poor are required to document their (redemptive?) biographies. As has been pointed out to me by a practitioner, this would not necessarily apply to students who paid the full fees for their adult education courses and who would be spared the indignity of this process. One immediate consequence of such strategies might be the rejection by working class students of adult education and civic activity because of the supposed 'relevance' to their lives, the over-recognition. Being mis-recognized as in deficit, or pathologized, may make one sceptical of adult education as a 'cure' for this. Perhaps this, rather than under provision of 'relevant' or 'useful' adult education, may be one of the reasons why working class participation in formal adult education is so low.

Conclusion

In this chapter, I have considered some of the ways in which learning in non-formal settings may be mis-recognized. An emphasis on the individual, on the active citizen, mis-recognizes most working class people as deficient and abject with perhaps a few 'heroic' counter-examples. More recognition of this form is not the answer. Undoubtedly, recognition can be part of wider, re-distributive struggles (Fraser and Honneth 2003) but it is disingenuous to suppose that the types of recognition offered by RARPA, the ALI or the Wider Benefits Centre will further the emancipation of learners (or non-learners). I would suggest, as do others, that a question for community educators would be to consider whether they wish to collapse 'activism' into tick-box measures of 'active citizenship' or to recognize their radical traditions (Crowther 2004; Tobias 2000).

References

ALI, (2002) *Guidance for Providers on the Inspection of Adult and Community Learning: Interpreting the Common Inspection Framework*, Coventry: Adult Learning Inspectorate.

Ball, S. (2003) *Class Strategies and the Education Market. The Middle Classes and Social Advantage*, London: RoutledgeFalmer.

Bourdieu, P. (1986) 'The forms of capital', in J. Richardson (ed.) *Handbook of Theory and Research for the Sociology of Education*, Conneticut: Greenwood Press.

Bourdieu, P. (1988) *Homo Academicus*, Cambridge: Polity.

Bourdieu, P. and Waquant, L. (1992) *An Invitation to Reflexive Sociology*, Chicago: University of Chicago Press.

Crowther, J. (2004) '"In and against" lifelong learning: flexibility and the corrosion of character', *International Journal of Lifelong Education*, 23, 2: 125–36.

Delphy, C. and Leonard, D. (1992) *Familiar Exploitation: A New Analysis of Marriage in Contemporary Western Society*, Cambridge: Polity.

DfES (2002) *Success for All: Reforming Further Education and Training*, London: HMSO.

DfES (2003) *21st Century Skills: Realising Our Potential – Individuals, Employers, Nation*, London: HMSO.

Fine, B. and Green, F. (2000) 'Economics, social capital, and the colonization of the social sciences', in S. Baron, J. Field and T. Schuller (eds) *Social Capital: Critical Perspectives*, Oxford: Oxford University Press.

Fraser, N. and Honneth, A. (2003) *Redistribution or Recognition: A Political-Philosophical Exchange*, London: Verso.

Gamarnikow, E. and Green, A. (1999) 'The third way and social capital: education action zones and a new agenda for education, parents and community', *International Studies in Sociology of Education*, 9: 3–22.

Gewirtz, S. (2001) 'Cloning the Blairs: New Labour's programme for the re-socialization of working-class parents', *Journal of Education Policy*, 16: 365–78.

Hadfield, M. and Haw, K. (2001) '"Voice", young people and action research', *Educational Action Research*, 8, 3: 485–99.

Jackson, S. (2004) 'Lifelong earning: working-class women and lifelong learning', *Gender and Education*, 15: 365–76.

Marx, K. (1983) *Capital: A Critique of Political Economy: Volume 1*, London: Lawrence and Wishart.

Mooney, G. (1998) '"Remoralizing" the poor?: gender, class and philanthropy in Victorian Britain', in G. Lewis (ed.) *Forming Nation, Framing Welfare*, London: Routledge.

Murray, C. (1984) *Losing Ground: American Social Policy 1950–1980*, New York: Basic Books.

Nashashibi, P. (2004) *The Alchemy of Learning: Impact and Progression in Adult Learning*, London: LSDA.

Plewis, I. and Preston, J. (2001) *Evaluating the Benefits of Lifelong Learning: A Framework*, London: Institute of Education.

Preston, J. (2003) 'White trash vocationalism? Formations of class and race in an Essex Further Education College', *Journal of Widening Participation and Lifelong Learning*, 5: 6–17.

Preston, J. (2004) 'Lifelong learning and civic participation: inclusion, exclusion and community' in T. Schuller, J. Preston, C. Hammond, A. Brassett-Grundy and J. Bynner (eds) *The Benefits of Leaning: The Impact of Education on Health, Family Life and Social Capital*, London: RoutledgeFalmer.

Rikowski, G. (1999) 'Education, capital and the transhuman', in D. Hill, P. McClaren, M. Cole and G. Rikowski (eds) *Postmodernism in Educational Theory: Education and the Politics of Human Resistance*, London: Tufnell Press.

Rose, J. (2002) *The Intellectual Life of the British Working Classes*, London: Yale University Press.

Skeggs, B. (2004) *Class, Self, Culture*, London: RoutledgeFalmer.

Skocpol, T. and Fiorina, M. (1999) 'Making sense of the civic engagement debate', in T. Skocpol and M. Fiorina (eds) *Civic Engagement in American Democracy*, Washington DC.: Brookings Institution Press.

Thompson, J. (2000) 'When active citizenship becomes "mob rule"', *Adults Learning*, September: 23–24.

Tobias, R. (2000) 'The boundaries of adult education for active citizenship – institutional and community contexts', *International Journal of Lifelong Education*, 19: 419–29.

Watters, K. (2003) *Recognising and Recording Progress and Achievement in Non-Accredited Learning*, Leicester: NIACE.

Wray, M. and Newitz, A. (1997) *White Trash: Race and Class in America*, London: Routledge.

Chapter 16

Social movements, praxis and the profane side of lifelong learning

Jim Crowther

Lifelong learning in social movements is the focus of this chapter. Despite the fact that movements are potentially dynamic forces for social change their educative potential is largely ignored. The profanity of movements is that they create new knowledge, challenge established values and ultimately pose choices that threaten established social and cultural practices. What movements seek to achieve and how they go about it are important for learning and, potentially, for educational engagement. This varies, however, with the nature of the movement and its capacity for cognitive and political praxis. Moreover, educational intervention can co-exist with commitment and partisanship but it needs to thrive in the context of openness and the ability to question and doubt.

Introduction

Social movements open up dissonant spaces for learning and dissident sites of knowledge production which challenge the status quo. Welton (1993) claims 'new' movements are 'revolutionary sites of adult learning' and Foley (1999) sees struggles against oppression creating powerful learning experiences. According to Kane (2001) movements are 'schools of learning', which involve an educative process of politicization, through debate, explanations and justifications for action, song, music and poetry. Johnston (2003) suspects they have served to challenge and radicalize students far more than any number of courses on lifelong learning or community education. Also Martin (1999) points out they pose the big questions about the nature of life in ways that systematically subvert dominant ways of thinking based on 'the cultural politics of communities' that are systematically neglected by 'the political culture of the state'.

Understandably the interest in social movements is often associated with radical and 'left wing' politics. However, there is no reason to assume movements are always on the ideological 'left' or progressive (Holford 1995). They may, nevertheless, provide an unsanitized and critical version of lifelong learning through the knowledge they generate, the identities they foster, the learning processes and educational spaces they open up and their potential to mobilize and influence a wide range of people for collective action and/or personal transformation. Whether this is for good or bad – assuming we could agree these terms – is another matter! What also matters is that we are clear about what we mean by movements and in what sense we can understand them as vehicles of learning and sites for educational engagement. This is the purpose of this chapter.

The argument is that whilst movements involve processes of social learning, they significantly differ in terms of the educational space they create. There are two pivotal issues which influence this: the first is their 'cognitive praxis' (i.e. the knowledge they create, see Eyerman and Jamieson 1991) and the second is their 'political praxis' (i.e. the ideology of the movement and the action they pursue, see Holst 2002). The openness of movements to learn from their cognitive and political praxis is at the root of the issue.

The cognitive and political praxis of a movement needs some explanation. The distinction refers to the dichotomy between 'thought' and 'action'. The ideas relevant to a movement depends on its vision and its relation to modernity. Premodern movements are theocratic (secular and religious) and closed educationally. The fundamental premise of the movement is not up for discussion or debate. Post-modern ones are primarily interested in individualized learning and education for personal transformation and/or lifestyle 'politics'. Whilst they may be open ideologically the focus of their change effort is limited and the type of knowledge and experience valued will reflect this. Modernist movements reiterate Enlightenment values of progress and reason and therefore seek education that aids this task. However, the action they pursue is shaped by their ideological vision. Authoritarian ideologies (of 'left' or 'right') which are 'top down' create very different experiences from more open and democratic movements which allow 'bottom up' experiences to shape their goals and approach. The more top down the movements become, the less likely they are to learn from participants' experience of social action. In contrast, those that are open offer opportunities for educational intervention in terms of the role of movement intellectuals, organizers and supporters. A starting point for the analysis is to see movements as spaces for social learning.

Social learning processes

According to Wenger (1998) social learning involves participation in 'communities of practice' through which people acquire identities by coming together in a variety of enterprises sustained over a period of time. In this view learning is more than an intellectual activity because it involves the negotiation of competence and identities amongst participants in a community of practice. Kilgore (1999) argues social movements are contexts for social learning in which individual and collective identities are dialectically related and shaped by a vision and struggle for social justice. However, there is no real justification for assuming that this is necessarily a progressive vision or progressive struggle.

The movement itself is a collective actor and its ability to develop social learning processes will have an impact on its capacity to sustain different types of social action. The focus on social learning in movements, therefore, can be argued to contribute towards their broader goals. Wildemeersch and Jansen (1997) suggest that:

Social learning is action-and-experience oriented, it is critically reflective; it is based on the questioning of assumptions and taken-for-granted problem definitions; it is interactive and communicative, which means that the dialogue between the people involved is of foremost importance; it is also characterized by multiactorship, as the solution of relatively complex issues presupposes the collaboration of a diversity of actors. Social learning also contributes to the exploration and redefinition of the social responsibility of the actors involved.

(1997: 465)

This view emphasizes that learning occurs in various locations and relationships outside of formal educational contexts. It involves understanding means and ends and the ethics of both. The group is in control of the learning, its purpose and processes and is potentially able to maximize this by collaborative and co-operative patterns of interaction and communication. It involves internal processes of dialogue as well as public debate outside of the movement. In addition, Wildemeersch and Jansen identify 'aesthetic reflexivity' as a further dimension of social learning. By this they mean learning that is sensitive to bonds of affiliation and identification – as distinct from merely cognitive and rational processes of learning.

However, social movements are distinct 'communities of practice' in which people learn to enhance their collective agency, so we need to qualify the above account. For example, movements involve people acquiring new identities and social practices through struggle against the established order. Social learning theory underplays, therefore, the messy dimension of conflict, action and reaction amongst groups in struggle with differential resources of power. This impacts on what is learnt. The material context of the struggle is a key dimension in the framework adopted by Foley (1999) whereas for Finger (1989) it is primarily a cultural one. Unlearning in both perspectives is a starting point of a process of change. Conflicting and competing discourses of power and ideological differences are a central element of the field in which movements operate. Power can be exercised crudely of course and may precipitate different types of legal and illegal social action (Newman 2005). In addition, people learn selectively but not randomly in that learning is always filtered through meaning schemes and perspectives that are never neutral (see Mezirow this volume).

The issue of power is important for processes of social learning. Reflection on conflicts with 'enemies' and the space for this to occur is obviously significant (Newman 2000). External forces may, however, curtail such activity. For example, clandestine movements are unlikely to operate through open dialogue and debate in a context where they may be repressed. Also internal structures may limit this space. An authoritarian movement, for example, may not encourage collaborative and co-operative patterns of interaction as described above. Furthermore, if the experience of fundamentalist movements is anything to go by, dialogue and debate may be less effective in generating individual and collective identities than we would like to believe! So the processes of social learning may vary significantly in different movements. Ultimately, what matters more for the educator is, however, the 'curriculum' of the movement and the spaces it offers for educational intervention.

Characterizing social movements

Touraine's definition of social movements suggests three principles of categorization: the movement's identity (its self-definition), the adversary it seeks to challenge (that is, its principal enemy) and the vision of the movement (what goals it seeks) (cited in Castells 1997). Some 'old' social movements (such as the labour movement or women's liberation movement) as well as 'new' movements (for example, the environmental movement) and 'contemporary' movements (such as anti-capitalist groups) would fit this definition. It also implicitly views movements as educative in that identity formation, defining what a movement stands for and what it stands against, are clearly educational activities as well as political objectives. To achieve its vision a social movement needs to be organized because without this it is unlikely to make a difference. Organization also implies the accumulation of resources which can help sustain and extend the cognitive and political praxis of the movement.

Eyerman and Jamieson (1991) argue it is the 'cognitive praxis' of a movement which is essential to understanding it. By this they mean movements generate new knowledge, alternative world-views and technologies as well as new institutions and organizations. Movements are therefore educative *and* epistemological communities. The environmental movement, for example, has stimulated the search for new knowledge about the effects of pollution on the environment, it has fostered a more holistic world-view and the weighing up of values and priorities in living, it has generated alternative technologies to fit with the vision of a greener world and it has spawned new organizations to further its cause. Not all movements fit this definition, however.

Urban movements in Castells' (1997) terms mobilize around goals related to state provision such as housing and education, issues of cultural identity within a particular territory, and self-management in terms of autonomy from local state control over their environment. They can be resourceful communities for generating identities, defining the enemy and, if not exactly having an alternative world-view, at least possessing an agenda for more limited change. We should not ignore them because they may generate a 'political praxis' that is educative. For example, Martin and McCormack's (1999) experience of struggle for improved housing is a powerful example of the links between a local struggle and wider systems of inequality and control with implications for popular education practice.

Castells (1997) makes the distinction between urban movements interested in controlling time and those interested in controlling space. The former might make connections with a wider world-view, about the preservation of nature, for example, the latter are generally more reactive 'not in my backyard' movements which seek to hold onto a territory they control. 'When people find themselves unable to control the world, they simply shrink the world to the size of their community' (Castells cited in Gilroy 1987: 230–2). However, the potential of urban movements to influence the spaces they occupy is increasingly the focus of regulatory governance practices. In the UK context, for example, they are being cajoled and squeezed into the structure and practice of 'partnership' projects and processes of community development that are linked to the state's agenda rather than their own. Partnerships may facilitate participation but we should not conflate this with democracy. Asymmetrical relations of power between 'partners' and the role of the state in resourcing – and influencing them – are crucial. Therefore the space for grassroots-led change is diminishing through corporate practices that are decentralizing responsibility and at the same time reaffirming centralized structures of power (Meade and O'Donovan 2002). In addition, increasing material inequalities and poverty may be leading to degenerated urban movements in the form of gangs, which appeal to the disaffected urban poor (Castells 1997).

Dekeyser (1999) argues the functions of social movements are different from action groups particularly in relation to their 'political praxis'. Action groups focus on publicity stunts to embarrass and highlight 'the enemy' rather than mobilizing a mass of active participants to support the cause. They rely on 'chequebook activists' who make subscriptions to the action group but this might be as far as their involvement goes. These groups have a strong professional bias and show little interest in democratic decision-making processes or ideological debate. They focus on a narrow range of issues usually in relation to the activities of international organizations.

Movements and modernity

The distinction between modernity, post-modernity and pre-modern helps to clarify the purpose of intellectual work and its link to action for change. As Bauman (1987) points out, modernity refers to the period of the Enlightenment which was characterized by the idea of progress and reason as a way of controlling and acting on the world in order to change it. Pre-modern refers to theocratic authority claims as the basis for truth and action. Post-modernists reject 'grand narratives' of being able to control and shape the world for the better. Action is therefore provisional, tentative and localized.

Modernist movements

The commitment to Enlightenment values of reason as a guide for bettering society and sustaining social progress has been an important influence on various social movements. For example, the labour movement in the nineteenth century used education and learning through social action to further their vision. The activities of the Women's Guilds and the Women's Trade Union League did the same for women in their own struggles (Thompson 1983). This involved 'really useful knowledge' gained through reflection on experience, sustained study, and a clear social and political purpose as a guide for action (Johnson 1993). However, it is doubtful whether these movements have the same impetus today. The women's movement is in a cul-de-sac of feminist theorizing which dissipates and dilutes it from active engagement in women's struggles. The labour movement, on the other hand, is concerned with managing capitalism rather than replacing it. 'Merely useful knowledge' has replaced the demand for 'really useful knowledge'.

In the current context, education for 'really useful knowledge' is found in an array of contemporary anti-capitalist groups, environmental networks and organizations with no one single ideological focus. Street protest, reading leaflets, marches and demonstrations, theatre, song and music and all the paraphernalia of contemporary oppositional movements has been characterized as the 'andragogy of the street' whereby people engage in a form of self-directed learning which is spontaneous, uncontrolled and informal (Rudnicki 2004). Moreover, the growth of the 'informational society' has led to a wide variety of oppositional movements and the widening of resistance to exploitation and oppression by the careful use of new systems of communication. The *Zapatista* movement is a good example because it has successfully placed its struggle for the liberation of peasant communities in Chiapas and Oaxaca in Mexico on an international stage (see Castells 1997). In this process it has acquired some unlikely supporters. For example, the wealthy A.C. Milan football club in Italy is supporting them through donating signed football shirts for fundraising! These movements rely on ICTs, particularly the Internet and email, to create a virtual and embodied community of activists and alternative sources of counter-information independent from mainstream media. The generation of international support for localized social action can be particularly effective for achieving movement goals as Moore's (2003) account of eco-feminist action in Canada demonstrates. The social learning process can, in addition, be highly organized and developed systematically. The activities of the World Social Forum and European Social Forum show a commitment to sustained open and intellectual study as a resource for making social change. As Klein (2000) points out, popular education activity is having an important influence on the work of the anti-capitalist movement by creating space for reflection and critical discussion.

Similar points can be made about some of the new social movements which are selectively radicalizing social values (Welton 1993). They are involved in protecting the life world from its enemy the system world manifested in the dominance of the market and the ambivalent role of the state. Welton proposes these movements have a vision of a more holistic view of what it means to be human and a relational understanding of the connections between people and between people and their environment. The systematic distortion of communication generated by system priorities and interests over those of the life world motivate the need for critical learning processes and social action to address these.

Post-modern movements

Post-modern movements can be difficult to characterize because what is meant by the term post-modern is by no means clear or uncontested. In contrast to modernist movements, they generally subscribe to more limited aspirations and affirm the importance of a plurality of identities, local rather than grand narratives. Finger (1989) argues what is central to these movements is that social change is entirely linked with personal transformation, which he suggests is more authentically educational. These movements do not have an interest in the collective emancipation of society and are, instead, more attuned to personal and spiritual development as well as lifestyles and consumerism. The focus for learning is about reflecting on personal experience and the search for personal identities. Some environmental movements would fit this type of approach (Kovan and Dirkx 2003). The curriculum relevant to these aspirations involves separating the personal from the political.

Usher *et al.* (1997), from a different post-modern perspective, reject old movements as part of a well-intended but misguided totalizing project for transformation based on modernist aspirations and beliefs. Instead, they point to the significance of post-modern social movements as a means of creating diverse social and cultural identities and lifestyles. Adult learning can contribute, from their perspective, to the efficacy of people's performativity in ways that are participative and which enable subjugated knowledge and voices to be heard. This might occur through more arts-based cultural pedagogy rather than the sustained intellectual study implied in the search for 'really useful knowledge'. These may be radical movements, according to the authors, but not in the same terms as the radical movements that characterize modernist projects.

Pre-modern movements

It seems contradictory that it is the pre-modern rather than post-modern (or indeed modern) movements that are setting the agenda for change today. In the US, fundamentalist movements have had a significant impact on institutionalized politics in relation to election results (the re-election of Bush in 2004), foreign policy (the war in Iraq) and science (opposition to stem cell research) as well as in education. Creationism, for example, is being taught in some US state schools with the same status as evolution theory – a trend beginning to occur in the UK too (Wheen 2004). These developments are a powerful reminder of the influence and impact of pre-modern movements on a wide range of people.

Although the political praxis of al Qaeda is different from Christian fundamentalist groups its cognitive praxis is similar. The movement has its intellectuals (religious/political leaders), cosmology (based on an interpretation of the Koran), technologies (weapons) and organization (underground cells) that sustain it as a distinct epistemological community amongst other things. Its cognitive praxis is pre-modern in that it is a theocracy based on unchallengeable readings of religious texts and a world-view based on faith rather than reason. In educational terms the logical implication of fundamentalism is a pedagogy of rote learning and unquestioning acceptance of authorities who can interpret the meaning of sacred texts. Whilst its political praxis may be rejected, al Qaeda's action has had a powerful effect in its own terms of illuminating its 'enemy' and in solidifying the identity of the movement and its vision of a 'better' world. It is very difficult to locate this type of movement in terms of a social model of learning – at least not as identified earlier – although it seems a powerful movement in terms of generating a distinct identity which appeals to some people.

Discussion

The space for social learning and the space for educational activity in social movements are not equal. Movements may foster new identities, for example, but without creating the educational space to interrogate their appropriateness and value. In other words, education is a distinctively different process from social learning that requires openness to question and doubt – even where it is committed and partisan.

The case of pre-modern movements highlights the tension between movements that may be effective in generating learning processes through their political praxis; at the same time, they are distinctly hostile to educational activity which implies some degree of questioning and open exploration of problems. On the other hand, the cognitive and political praxis of post-modern movements is quite different from modernist ones. The focus on personal change, or a 'cultural politics' of style and performativity substitutes the political with the personal. This leads to activity that eschews the need for sustained organization and action in favour of loose networks which rise and subside in changing contexts. In modernist movements education is central to the development of different movement activities. Three different roles can be identified which create opportunities for educational activity: intellectuals, organizers and supporters.

'Movement intellectuals', to use Eyerman and Jamieson's (1991) term, are central to the organization of a movement. They play a key role in articulating the identity of a movement and propagating the knowledge, arguments and values that underpin it. They disseminate the movement's aims to its supporters as well as to the wider public and therefore have to be skilled communicators. The problem for movement intellectuals, as Gramsci (1980) identified, is in their relationship with their social base. The traditional intellectual, in his view, claims to stand above social groups and is detached from their social activity. Therefore movements need to generate their own leaders from out of their social group. For this to occur successfully there has to be a dialectical and complementary relationship between 'organic intellectuals' (in Gramsci's term) and the masses in order for 'thought' and 'feelings' to be mutually supportive and productive. Or to put it another way, as Marx stressed, 'the educator also has to be educated' – sustained opportunities for this two-way process of learning and educating is therefore a key resource for social change.

To maintain large movements resources, organizers and administrators are required. They, in turn, require technical skills which include knowledge and skills in management, strategic planning, fundraising, administrative work, research and communication. In other words, instrumental and communicative competencies are also important for a movement to function effectively (Crowther 2001). Where movements differ from many other organizations is that they often run on commitment and enthusiasm rather than professionally trained and salaried staff – although some may have both. In addition, few movements are adequately resourced and invariably they never have enough people for all the tasks that have to be done. The result is the concentration of experience in few hands, many activists with little in the way of relevant skills, heavy workloads and 'burnt out' activists who are periodically in need of 'recharging their batteries'. Reflective spaces for sharing knowledge and skills are important educational contributions to a movement's life (Whelan 2002).

Supporters learn in and through movement activity but there are different degrees of involvement so the extent of immersion and opportunities to reflect are important variables in the process of social learning. Those who take part in debates, demonstrations, meetings and related activities are also taking part in a process of critical reflection. How sophisticated this is, in educational terms, is an important issue. All too often the networks, knowledge and skills that movements create can be lost unless there is some deliberate and systematic attempt to make explicit what is learnt and to maintain some record of its activity (Dickie 1999). In terms of support, movements attract and repel different groups of people and this too might generate very different educational needs. Whilst it may be true that 'new' social movements find support among the well educated and middle class this is not always the case. For example, the disability movement is likely to attract a wide cross section of social classes. Educational processes that are inclusive may, therefore, have something to offer and to learn from such movements (Oliver 1997).

In defining their 'enemy' movements need also to identify allies if they are to have a better chance of realizing their vision. Building alliances is a strategic political goal but it is also an educational task. The potential to attract a broad constituency of diverse interests is substantial in some cases. The Iraq anti-war movement is a good example where the official knowledge and claims of the government were challenged and a broad alliance between different interests was formed. The biggest demonstrations in the UK since Chartism of the nineteenth century took place in 2003. A wide range of people and organizations were mobilized and this had an impact on politicizing young people too often castigated for their apathy. Whilst this alliance did not stop the war it has had an impact on the political climate whose long-term results are still unfolding.

Conclusions

Social movements generate dissidence and dissent from the dominant social and cultural values that inform our common sense and daily life. However, precisely because they are profane, adult learning in social movements is ignored in the official discourse of lifelong learning and its preoccupation with an individualized view of learning and its obsession with economistic concerns and social cohesion. While social movements challenge and broaden our understanding of lifelong learning we need to take into account their complexity, diversity and limitations in terms of spaces for educational intervention. In these terms movements are difficult to generalize about because their potential as spaces for educational activity is shaped by their cognitive and political praxis. However, movements shape the world we live in – for good or bad. Can lifelong learning afford to ignore them? If it does, what type of lifelong learning is it?

References

Bauman, Z. (1987) *Legislators and Interpreters*, Cambridge: Blackwell.

Castells, M. (1997) *The Power of Identity*, London: Blackwell.

Crowther, J. (2001) 'Learning in popular struggles: their educative potential and the role of the worker', in Cadernos Cieca 1 *Wider Benefits of Learning*, ESREA 2001 Conference.

Dekeyser, L. (1999) 'Adult education and social movements: the significance and workings of social movements as a part of civil society, an approach from the angle of adult and continuing education', in B. Merrill (ed.) *The Final Frontier: Exploring Spaces in the Education of Adults*, proceedings of the 29th SCUTREA Annual Conference: University of Warwick.

Dickie, J. (1999) 'Neighbourhood as classroom: reflections of an activist', in J. Crowther, I. Martin and M. Shaw (eds) *Popular Education in Scotland Today*, Leicester: NIACE.

Eyerman, R. and Jamieson, A. (1991) *Social Movements: A Cognitive Approach*, Cambridge: Polity Press.

Finger, M. (1989) 'New social movements and their implications for adult education', *Adult Education Quarterly*, 40, 1: 15–22.

Foley, G. (1999) *Learning in Social Action*, London: Zed Books.

Gilroy, P. (1987) *There Ain't No Black in the Union Jack*, London: Hutchinson.

Gramsci, A. (1980) *Prison Notebooks*, London: Lawrence and Wishart.

Holford, J. (1995) 'Why social movements matter: adult education theory, cognitive praxis, and the creation of knowledge', *Adult Education Quarterly*, 45, 2: 95–111.

Holst, J. (2002) *Social Movements, Civil Society and Radical Adult Education*, London: Bergin & Gavey.

Johnson, R. (1993) '"Really useful knowledge", 1790–1850', in M. Thorpe, R. Edwards and A. Hanson (eds) *Culture and Processes of Adult Learning*, Milton Keynes: Open University and Routledge.

Johnston, R. (2003) 'Adult educators and social movements: rhetoric, theory and practice', in I. Davidson, D. Murphy and B. Piette (eds) *Speaking in Tongues: Languages of Lifelong Learning*, Proceedings of the 33rd Annual SCUTREA Conference: University of Wales, Bangor.

Kane, L. (2001) *Popular Education and Social Change in Latin America*, London: Latin America Bureau.

Kilgore, D. (1999) 'Understanding learning in social movements: a theory of collective learning', *International Journal of Lifelong Education*, 18, 3: 191–202.

Klein, N. (2000) *No Logo*, London: Flamingo.

Kovan, J. and Dirkx, J. (2003) '"Being called awake": the role of transformative learning in the lives of environmental activists', *Adult Education Quarterly*, 53, 2: 99–118.

Martin, I. (1999) 'Popular education in Scotland today: introductory essay', in J. Crowther, I. Martin and M. Shaw (eds) *Popular Education in Scotland Today*, Leicester: NIACE.

Martin, H. and McCormack, C. (1999) 'Making connections: learning through struggle', in J. Crowther, I. Martin and M. Shaw (eds) *Popular Education in Scotland Today*, Leicester: NIACE.

Meade. R. and O'Donovan, O. (2002) 'Editorial introduction: corporatism and the ongoing debate about the relationship between the state and community development', *Community Development Journal*, Special Issue, 37: 1, 1–10.

Moore, N. (2003) 'Ecological citizens or ecoterrorists? Learning through environmental activism in Clayoquort Sound', in P. Coare and R. Johnston (eds) *Adult Learning, Citizenship and Community Voices*, Leicester: NIACE.

Newman, M. (2000) 'Learning, education and social action', in G. Foley (ed.) *Understanding Adult Education and Training*, Australia: Allen and Unwin.

Newman, M. (2005) 'Popular teaching, popular learning and popular action', in J. Crowther, V. Galloway and I. Martin (eds) *Popular Education: Engaging the Academy*, Leicester: NIACE.

Oliver, M. (1997) 'The disability movement is a new social movement', in K. Popple and M. Shaw (eds) *Community Development Journal*, 32, 3: 244–51.

Rudnicki, P. (2004) 'Antiglobalism – andagogy of the street', in *Between 'Old' and 'New' Worlds of Adult Learning*, ESREA Conference Proceedings (3–4).

Thompson, J. (1983) *Learning Liberation*, London: Croom Helm.

Usher, R., Bryant, I. and Johnston, R. (1997) *Adult Education and the Postmodern Challenge*, London: Routledge.

Welton, M. (1993) 'Social revolutionary learning: the new social movements as learning sites', *Adult Education Quarterly*, 43, 3: 152–64.

Wenger, E. (1998) *Communities of Practice*, Cambridge: Cambridge University Press.

Wheen, F. (2004) *How Mumbo-Jumbo Conquered the World*, London: Fourth Estate.

Whelan, J. (2002) 'Education and Training for Effective Environmental Advocacy', Unpublished doctoral thesis, Australia: Griffith University.

Wildemeersch, D. and Jansen, T. (1997) 'Strengths and limitations of social learning as a key concept for adult and continuing education in reflexive modernity', in P. Armstrong, N. Miller and M. Zukas (eds) *Crossing Borders, Breaking Boundaries*, Proceedings of the 27th Annual SCUTREA Conference, London: Birkbeck College.

Chapter 17

Learning cities, learning regions, lifelong learning implementers

Norman Longworth

If lifelong learning is to become a reality it will involve transformations across a variety of environments and organizations which are driven by social, environmental and cultural values and concerns rather than narrow economistic ones. In this chapter the author, who has been heavily involved in European initiatives in this area, documents and highlights some of the significant changes which have been taking place, and which need to happen, in relation to developments in learning cities and regions in order to develop the spatial dimension of lifelong learning.

Introduction

Learning cities, learning towns, learning regions, learning communities are terms now in common use as a result of the emphasis on the application of lifelong learning concepts into everyday life. Definitions tend to differ according to the provenance of the research and development activity and the interpretation of lifelong learning. Where it is based in the urban development departments of universities and cities a learning city or region will emphasize the physical and technological infrastructural elements of city regeneration. Where the focus is on employment, employability, organizational management and training for industry, the development of human and social capital for economic gain and competitive edge tends to predominate. Where the motivation is based on education methodology, curriculum and assessment, it will concentrate on e-learning, classroom management and the psychology of how people learn. The focus of this chapter is oriented towards a more social, environmental and cultural rationale. Lifelong learning is itself creating a paradigm shift – the age of education and training, which has served us well in the late twentieth century in satisfying the needs of a growing, upwardly mobile proportion of the population, is now giving way to the era of lifelong learning, in which the means, the tools and techniques are employed to target and motivate everyone in a city, town or region. Those cities that achieve this will be the winners in the paradox where intelligent local action leads to success in a globalized world.

Common denominators of lifelong learning

In the ebb and flow of philosophies about learning, we are not short of educational advice from the great thinkers of the day. The present age is no exception. It is an age of deep and persistent flood. Several thousand reports and papers, books and compendiums have been published by international and governmental organizations, by learned committees, by experts, universities and individuals over the past few years on the urgent need for, and the vast benefits to be gained from, implementing lifelong learning concepts. Not all of them agree on what these concepts are and many put a particular spin on them to fit their own perceptions and desired outcomes. But there are some constants and, from one of the seminal European documents, the European Memorandum on Lifelong Learning published in 2000, one can identify perhaps two major trend-setting common denominators.

The first is the need to implement change from the top-down, educator-led educational systems we now have, to procedures and processes that are more bottom-up, and based on the real needs of the learners – a 180 degree transfer of power and ownership of learning from teacher to learner. It is not fully accepted in cultures with a tradition of centralized direction of education, and nor has it penetrated much into the schools, but there are a number of implications based on concepts of who actually has ownership of learning, the sophistication of the available support systems that will arrest the haemorrhage of people away from learning at a young age, and the transformation of examination and assessment methods into 'learning opportunities' rather than instruments to reinforce failure. The list of other desirable changes is long, well known to lifelong learning practitioners and not always well understood by legislators and politicians.

The second common denominator transforms the function of the local authorities from passive implementers of national government policy into regional innovators of learning change. In order to become world-class learning locations, as they must if they are to maintain prosperity and social stability in a globalizing world, they must increase their commitment to introducing lifelong learning concepts into all parts of their empires. They must become 'learning cities', 'learning towns' and 'learning regions', progressing from the era of 'education and training' in which education was provided to those who required it when they required it, to a world in which lifelong learning is provided for all citizens wherever, whenever, however and from whoever it is required. The European policy document on the *Local and Regional Dimension of Lifelong Learning* is quite firm on this.

> Cities and towns in a globalized world cannot afford *not* to become learning cities and towns. It is a matter of prosperity, stability and the personal development of *all* citizens. Lifelong Learning covers all aspects of city life, including what happens in schools, universities, business and industry and local government offices.
>
> (Commision of the European Union 2001: 10)

We might then profitably look at the rise of the concept of the learning city and examine how it differs from what was there in the past.

The growth of the learning city and region

In antiquity, Plato's concept of *Dia Viou Paedaea* was built around the city itself. It encapsulates the idea that the primary rationale for encouraging citizens to learn was so that they could contribute to the life and growth of the city and the community at large, perhaps one of the first recorded examples of active citizenship and the learning city. Thus though learning was an individual pursuit, the rationale for taking part had its source in community, in living together harmoniously and in growing in understanding together. Many Islamic cities such as Damascus and Jerusalem were, between 900 and 1300 years ago, real 'learning cities', centres of culture and learning, participated in by most of their citizens, and probably truer learning cities than anywhere that exists in our modern world.

The concept has been in vogue over a number of recent years. In the 1970s, the Organisation for Economic Cooperation and Development (OECD) funded a project to create 'Educating Cities'. It invited seven cities from among its member states – Edmonton in Canada, Gothenburg, Vienna and Edinburgh in Europe, Kakegawa in Japan, Adelaide in Australia and Pittsburgh in the United States – to put education at the forefront of their strategies in order to justify the term 'Educating City'. More recently the term 'Learning City' has become more popular. Liverpool in the UK declared itself to be a 'City of Learning' in 1996, and was quickly followed by Southampton, Norwich, Edinburgh, Birmingham and others. The UK Learning Cities Network now numbers some eighty members. European cities such as Espoo, Gothenburg and Dublin followed their own learning city pathways. In Australia each state has its own Learning Cities Association and Victoria, in particular, justifiably prides itself on having persuaded the vast majority of its cities and towns to put principles into practice. Meanwhile, at another level, the city of Barcelona has, since 1992, led an Association of 'Educating Cities' now reaching some 250 members worldwide and OECD has carried out a major 'Learning Regions' exercise in Europe. The cities included in these initiatives are the leaders in the learning regions movement because they recognize that to prosper economically, socially and culturally, their citizens will need to come to terms with rapid and accelerating change.

Initiating the debate

Amidst all this plethora of activity in the 1990s, the European Lifelong Learning Initiative (ELLI), now unfortunately defunct, initiated a debate on what a learning city was, how it would define itself and how it might be distinguished from a city that was not yet 'on message'. Successive presidents of the association in the mid-1990s published a number of articles in its house magazine *Comment* to clarify the issues. In 1996, the European Year of Lifelong Learning, the book *Lifelong Learning* (Longworth and Davies 1996) was published describing the role and implications of lifelong learning for stakeholders in the city. In this the consequences of implementing lifelong learning principles in schools, universities, business and industry and local government were discussed, as was their potential contribution to working with each other to help the growth of community and city. This book was followed three years later by a more targeted book, subtitled *Learning Cities for a Learning Century* (Longworth 1999), containing examples from a wide variety of cities that were ahead of the rest in thinking and action, including the learning region of Kent in the UK.

The TELS Learning Cities project

The European Commission has not been idle in supporting research and development of the concept. In 1998 it initiated the pioneering TELS (Towards a European Learning Society) project which surveyed 80 European municipalities from 14 countries by measuring their progress towards becoming learning cities, towns and, in some cases, regions in ten domains and 28 sub-domains of their learning activities. This project is interesting in that it is one of the first to identify indicators by which municipalities can measure their own performance and progress. In order to do this, the project developed a 'learning cities audit tool' – in effect an interactive questionnaire with an educational purpose to help those completing it to understand more about the concept and its implications. The domains and sub-domains of city activity contained in this tool are shown in Table 17.1.

Some of these categories also provide indicators for new projects, each of which needs development. The way in which information is presented (item b) is indeed important if the reluctant learner is to be attracted back into the fold; leaders (item d) do need to be developed to help this process; and, contribution, celebration and family involvement (items j and h) are significant keys to success. Wealth creation (item h) through more and better learning is a powerful motivator for cities beset by problems of unemployment and deprivation, the corollary being that better learning leads to the first of the three OECD rationales for lifelong learning – greater prosperity, social stability and personal fulfilment.

Although not a formal research project with well-defined geographical or methodological parameters, TELS produced many insights into the state of knowledge about the state of lifelong learning awareness in a variety of European cities, towns and regions. It used ELLI's earlier work to provide the following two definitions:

> A learning city, town or region recognizes and understands the key role of learning in the development of basic prosperity, social stability and personal fulfilment, and mobilizes all its human, physical and financial resources creatively and sensitively to develop the full human potential of all its citizens. It

Table 17.1 The TELS Learning Cities indicators

Category	Explanation
a Commitment to a 'Learning City'	The extent to which the city or town has already started to implement plans and strategies which set it out on the path to becoming a learning community, and the thinking it has done to date.
b Information and communication	Ways in which lifelong learning ideas and plans are communicated to a) those responsible for implementing them and b) citizens at large. Including new curriculum development, teacher training, learning centres, use of the media, collection of information on learning requirements, etc.
c Partnerships and resources	The extent to which links between different sectors of the city have been encouraged and enabled, and their effectiveness enhanced. Includes links between schools, colleges, business and industry, universities, professional associations, local government and other organizations. Includes physical and human resource sharing, knowledge generation, mobilization, etc.
d Leadership development	The extent to which lifelong learning leaders have been developed and how. Including community leadership courses, project management, city management, organizational mix.
e Social inclusion	Projects and strategies to include those at present excluded – the mentally and physically disabled, the unemployed, minorities, women returners, people with learning difficulties, etc.
f Environment and citizenship	Projects to inform and involve citizens in city environmental matters. How the city is informing its citizens of all ages about citizenship and involving them in its practical expression in the city.
g Technology and networks	Innovative ways in which information and communications technology is used to link organizations and people internally, and with people and organizations in other communities. Includes use of open and distance learning, effective use of networks between all ages for learning and understanding of the internet.
h Wealth creation, employment and employability	Schemes and projects to improve the creation of both wealth and employment and to give citizens lifetime skills, knowledge and competencies to improve their employment prospects. Includes financial incentives, studies, links with industry, industry links with other communities, etc.
i Active citizenship and the personal development of citizens	The extent to which contribution is encouraged and enabled. Includes projects to gather and use the knowledge, skills and talents of people and to encourage their use for the common development of the city.
j Learning events and family involvement	Projects, plans and events to increase the credibility, attractiveness, visibility and incidence of learning among citizens individually and in families. Includes learning festivals, booklet generation, celebrations of learning, learning competitions, recognition events, etc.

(Longworth 2000)

provides both a structural and a mental framework which allows its citizens to understand and react positively to change.

(Commission of the European Union 2003: 5)

A learning community is a city, town or region which goes beyond its statutory duty to provide education and training for those who require it and instead creates a vibrant, participative, culturally aware and economically buoyant human environment through the provision, justification and active promotion of learning opportunities to enhance the potential of all its citizens.

(Commission of the European Union 2002: 111)

The latter definition suggests, perhaps for the first time, in European thinking at least, that there is the beginning of a movement away from the age of education and training into a much more inclusive and all-encompassing era of lifelong learning characterized by the fulfilment of everyone's human potential. From this, the notion of the development of human capital as a resource for the growth of social capital, so prevalent in today's national educational debates, can be much more profitably enacted through public policy.

Developing a policy for learning cities and regions

The results obtained by TELS confirmed a sorry lack of basic knowledge about the effects of lifelong learning in the majority of European municipalities. But they also uncovered the existence of some cities where much progress has been made, and more excitingly, a wish among most of the participating cities to know more. Indeed a good number of the participating cities admitted to becoming interested in the concept as a result of completing the audit, an interesting by-product of the survey.

Further, TELS became the European Commission's major source of information on the local and regional dimension of lifelong learning. Seminars were held in Brussels for interested regional organizations and papers were produced. This in turn resulted in the production of a European policy paper on the *Local and Regional Dimension of Lifelong Learning* (Longworth 2001) distributed to all member states for comments. From the experience of managing the TELS project I wrote in the European policy paper that:

At this embryo stage in learning city development there can be no other conclusion than that there is a long way to go. The majority of the municipalities coming into the project were unaware of the term 'learning city', much less what it signified. In that respect the project has itself initiated a learning process ...

(Longworth 2000: 9)

Some European Commission agencies, for example its vocational training arm, CEDEFOP, take a predominantly narrow economic and adult education rationale for the growth of the learning region, a view duplicated in some of the less perceptive member states. The European Commission itself, however, propelled by the memorandum and policy paper, adopts a wider view of the issues in its choice of projects to support. It recognizes the whole-of-life, 'cradle to grave' inspiration, exhibited in its 1996 'Year of Lifelong Learning'. Thus the full range of local lifelong learning applications is at the core of many of its Grundtvig projects for adult education and an increasing number of its Comenius projects for schools and teacher training. The Leadership in Lifelong Learning for Inspiring People Undergoing Transition (LILLIPUT) project, for example, has, from its base in Napier University in Scotland, developed more than 300 hours of web-delivered learning materials in 14 different domains of learning city operation, and its Promoting Active Lifelong Learning between cities and regions in Australasia, Canada, China and Europe (PALLACE) project has linked schools, museums, councillors and adult education institutions in learning cities and regions world-wide in order to stimulate a debate on how these stakeholders can creatively contribute to the growth of their learning municipalities.

Stakeholder audits – measuring lifelong learning progress in the learning city and region

It is perhaps the INDICATORS project, one of the major projects in the R3L programme, that has contributed most to the synthesis of new knowledge. R3L is a European Commission programme supporting 17 projects from all parts of the European Union. Its purpose has been to develop inter-regional networks that will themselves each develop a set of project outcomes and exchange information, experiences and ideas through the R3L website. INDICATORS was one of these.

The project outcomes provide one of the vehicles by which a whole city or region might also become a 'learning organization'. Managed from the University of Stirling in Scotland, the project has put together a series of tools which they call 'Stakeholder Audits'. These are carefully worded, interactive documents that enable respondees to understand the many basic elements of lifelong learning as it affects their organization, and to convert this new knowledge into actions that will implement its concepts both internally within the organization (i.e. turn it into a learning organization) and externally (i.e. work with other organizations to help build a learning society, a learning city or a learning region within the geographical area where the organization resides).

Stakeholder Audits are much more than questionnaires. The objective is as much to give insights and knowledge and provoke reflection as to gather data (though this is a desirable spin-off). In establishing a 'dialogue' between the designer and the respondee, it aims to pass over essential new knowledge and ideas that will provoke reflection and stimulate insight. Further, it allows the opinions, experiences and ideas of the respondee to be freely expressed and meshed with the requirements for change within the organization. In that sense it acts as a driver for change – emphasizing the dynamic nature of stakeholder organizations

– and can be used as a staff training stimulator, encouraging them to provide ideas for the development of innovative internal policies and strategies to accommodate learning organization principles. In all of this it tries to energize stakeholders to contribute to learning region development according to their role and ability.

Five audits have initially been developed and tested in situ – for local and regional authority administrations, for schools, for adult vocational education establishments, for universities and for small and medium-sized enterprises. They cover the whole gamut of lifelong learning indicators from the organization as a learning organization to quality and standards within the institution; from continuous improvement programmes for staff (and students) to the organization's role in the building of a learning city/region; from wider access to learning to the partnerships and the use of technology in distance learning, networking and multi-media development that will improve the organization's ability to develop, deliver and support learning wherever in the institution or city it occurs.

But it is the approach that is important. These are audits rather than questionnaires. Tools to be used rather than surveys to gather information. They contain quotations from reports and books to stimulate reflection and give authority, they invite opinion, experiences, feedback and the addition of city initiatives, and they proffer ideas and knowledge to energize a movement towards establishing a need and then developing or modifying a strategy to satisfy it. They can be used collectively under the leadership of a local or regional authority to establish the whole region as a learning organization.

According to Osborne *et al.* (2004) initial results are promising – local authorities in particular pronounce the tools to be useful and informative, they appear to promote reflection in schools and adult educational organizations and small businesses confess to being interested. However, the authors of the report also point out that the size of the sample is too small to provide conclusive evidence of success, and a much larger trial needs to be implemented.

From education and training to lifelong learning in the learning city and region

So what can we learn from this short round-up of learning city and region characteristics? First, there is so much happening in this area that much has, unfortunately but inevitably, been omitted. Second, we can accept that the learning city and region concept is a peculiar mix of the political, economic, social, financial, environmental, cultural, educational and technological, and that to omit any one of these is to render the result the poorer. Its dynamic comes from a whole variety of interlocking initiatives – new productive partnerships, leadership development, proper information and communication methods, celebration, focused surveys and studies, decent educational support structures, continuous improvement strategies for all, motivation and ownership of learning and all those contained in the left hand column of Table 17.2 below. This is why the indicators contained in the Stakeholder Audits of the INDICATORS project are so comprehensive. They may produce long documents but that is inevitable when the transformation from an education and training to a lifelong learning society involves such a rich mixture of complex factors.

Third, we can perhaps detect the paradigm shift that lifelong learning is initiating, particularly in the cities. Table 17.2 also acts as a summary. The aim is to isolate each factor, to examine it for its implications and then to continuously develop the strategy, initiate and re-initiate the action, energize and re-energize the people and innovate incessantly. As in a learning organization, the learning region is an endlessly developing entity, re-inventing and re-invigorating itself in never-ending progression. When learning stops, development stops. Table 17.2 therefore has been compiled from the list of learning region requirements, some of them in this paper, some in other documents and tools. It is most certainly incomplete. But it gives the city manager an idea of the magnitude of the task ahead. And it provides work for those people and organizations who are prepared to accept the challenge of change, to think outside the box and to participate in the development of their own learning cities and regions.

Table 17.2 From education and training to lifelong learning

	Topic	Education and training	Lifelong learning	Action
1	The city as a 'Learning Organization'	Education and training supplied to existing and committed learners by Learning Providers incities and regions as a statutory duty.	Everyone is empowered to learn according to their own needs, demands and learning styles. Focus on the development of *all* their human and organizational potential. Providers become *Learning Organizations*.	Carry out frequent surveys and studies. Find and satisfy customer needs for learning. Develop a city-wide lifelong learning strategy based on real need and good information. Develop Indicators to enable Learning Providers to become true Learning Organizations.
2	Decision-making, breaking barriers to learning	Educational decision-making in city rooted in a twentieth century mass education and training paradigm.	Decisions made on individual learning needs, demands and styles of all citizens of all ages and aptitudes.	Find the barriers to learning and dismantle them. Develop and market a strategy based on lifelong and lifewide learning for all.
3	Joined up local government	Cities, towns and regions foster empire-building within separate and discrete departments.	Cities etc. encourage cooperation between departments.	Invite all departments to submit plans for the development of lifelong learning in the local community, cf Japan.
4	Support for learning	Sparse mass educational support and back-up structures brought into service when problems arise.	Sophisticated on-going support structures concentrating on needs and demands of each learner in the city no matter what age.	Provide individual support including personal learning counsellors, community mentors, psychologists and early back-up.
5	Finding and using all resources	Educators as providers – sole distributors of information, knowledge and resource to learners.	Educators as managers – of all the resources and expertise available in a city, town or region.	Discover and use the talents, skills, expertise and knowledge within the community from all sources. In-service training to empower educators to use this.
6	Giving ownership to the learner	Ownership of the need to learn and its content is with the educator.	Learner, as customer, rules. As far as possible ownership of the need to learn and its content is given to individuals.	Develop and use techniques and tools to help individuals of all ages understand their own learning needs and styles e.g. audits.

continued

	Topic	Education and training	Lifelong learning	Action
7	Examinations as learning opportunities	Examinations used to separate successes from failures at specific times.	Examinations as failure-free learning opportunities confirming progress and encouraging further learning.	Influence development of innovative assessment tools embedded into personal learning programmes, and examined when the student feels ready.
8	Skills-based curriculum	Education in city institutions is knowledge and information based – *what* to think.	Learning in city institutions and the community is understanding, skills and values based – *how* to think.	Redevelop content dominated curricula into personal skills-based learning programmes that expand the capacity of people to engage in learning.
9	Joined-up learning	Education is compartmentalized according to age, aptitude and purpose.	Learning is lifelong in concept and content, providing links vertically and horizontally between age groups in buildings open to the whole community.	Open up learning to the whole community. Provide community-based facilities which encourage links between learning providers and people of all ages. Community schools, Lifelong Learning Centres, etc.
10	Access to learning	Courses developed and delivered by city learning providers on their own premises top-down.	Learning made available where, when, how and from whom the learner wants it with the learner's consent bottom-up.	Encourage providers to provide learning where people are – homes, schools, workplaces, pubs, stadia, church halls, etc.
11	Partnerships in the learning city	Each sector of the city, town and region determines and bids for its own needs.	Holistic – increases resources through cooperation between each sector of the community.	Facilitate partnerships between sectors as an investment in new resources and knowledge.
12	Active learning	City education providers deliver passive classroom-based education based on tested memory development.	Learning is an active, creative, exciting journey into the future involving learners in new experiences and developing positive values and attitudes.	Encourage active learning methods – brainstorms, data collection and analysis, creative discussion, case studies and simulations, visits, etc. to make learning fun, pleasurable and an expression of the most natural human instinct.

continued

Topic	Education and training	Lifelong learning	Action
13 Technology and networks	Cities, towns and regions provide inward-looking educational systems – to satisfy specified needs.	Outward-looking systems – to open minds, encourage broader horizons, promote understanding of others and develop trading links.	Twin with other learning cities. Use technology and networks to link people of all ages nationally and internationally to enhance understanding of other creeds, cultures and customs.
14 Focus on the learner	Education content is based on the needs of organizations and nations to provide evidence of progress.	Learning is based on the need to develop human potential, creativity and response to change and uncertainty in an unknown future.	Influence curricula etc. to develop education for competence, flexibility, adaptability and versatility. Keep options and minds open. Develop more sophisticated indicators of progress.
15 Promoting employability	Educates and trains for employment and short-term need.	Promotes learning for employability in the long term.	Carry out regular skills surveys leading well into the future. Cooperate with industry to determine needs.
16 Developing indicators	Learning providers resistant to new ideas, approaches and procedures.	Learning providers are flexible with a clear view of the ways in which new approaches can benefit them and their students.	Develop indicators allowing learning providers to measure and monitor their own progress and performance in becoming learning organizations.
17 Continuous improvement	Professionals and administrators attend educational courses according to need or desire. Occasional seminars in workplace.	Every professional, administrator and student in the city has a continuous improvement plan for personal skill and knowledge development embedded into the management system.	Encourage the development of written continuous improvement plans for all city staff and for all students. Extend these others in the community as desired.
18 Celebrating learning	Citizens see learning as a difficult chore and as received wisdom.	Citizens see learning as fun, participative and involving, and as perceived wisdom.	Celebrate, reward and recognize learning frequently at all ages and stages of learning.

continued

Topic	Education and training	Lifelong learning	Action
19 Learning and culture	Cultural life of city kept separate from education life and facilities.	Education and culture synonymous in a glorious mixture of learning opportunities from all parts of the community.	Turn all community buildings – libraries, museums, theatres, galleries, shopping malls, etc. – into new-look educational adventure playgrounds for everyone.
20 Active citizenship	Education as a top-down exercise by city institutions staffed by professionals with little community involvement.	The city as a hive of voluntary activity involving citizens in a large variety of supportive and interactive programmes which contribute to the growth of a learning city.	Encourage active citizenship by individuals, families, organizations and communities through volunteering and commitment. Organize and channel all the available good-will.
21 Marketing value of learning	Education and training as a financial investment for cities, organizations and nations.	Learning as a social, personal and financial investment in and by people for the benefit of nations, organizations, society in general and themselves.	Market learning strongly as an investment – by a city in its citizens, by a workplace in its workforce, by learning providers in their students' future, by people in their own future worth and happiness.

(Longworth 2005)

References

Commission of the European Union (2002) *Realising a European Area of Lifelong Learning*, Brussels: EC Publications Office.

Commission of the European Union (2001) *Creating Learning Cities, Towns and Regions, A European Policy Paper from the TELS project*, (N. Longworth ed.) European Commission, Brussels: DG EaC.

Commission of the European Union (2003) *The R3L Programme*, details on europa.eu.int/comm/education/ policies/lll/life/regio/index_en.html.

Longworth, N. (1999) *Lifelong Learning at Work – Learning Cities for a Learning Century*, London: Taylor and Francis.

Longworth, N. (2000) *Towards a European Learning Society (TELS)*, *Project Report* presented to the European Commission Nov. 2000, also available on www.tels.euproject.org.

Longworth, N. (2001) *The Local and Regional Dimension of Lifelong Learning – Creating Learning Cities, Towns and Regions* – A Policy paper, Commission of the European Unities, Brussels: DG EaC.

Longworth, N. (2005) *Learning Cities, Learning Regions – Powerhouses of Learning in the 21st Century*, London: Taylor and Francis.

Longworth, N. and Davies, W. K. (1996) *Lifelong Learning: New Visions, New Implications, New Roles – for Industry, Government, Education and the Community for the 21st Century*, London: Kogan Page.

Osborne, M. Longworth, N. Sankey, K. and Gray, P. (2004) *Report to the Commission on the INDICATORS Project*, University of Stirling, also on www.stirling.indicators.ac.uk.

Chapter 18

Literacy as social practice

Travelling between the everyday and other forms of learning

Yvon Appleby and Mary Hamilton

The framework of literacy as social practice is used in this chapter to analyse recent examples of everyday and community-based learning from two current research projects. Examples of how literacy and language practices can travel between everyday practices and systematic learning show that learning and teaching can be fluid, crossing boundaries and identities. The authors argue that identifying the 'crossover' learning strategies between formal and informal learning contexts is an important resource for developing effective community-based adult literacy programmes.

Literacy as social practice

What does literacy learning look like in everyday practice? In this chapter we take the perspective offered by the theory of literacy as social practice as a starting point and use case study data to develop the theory. We draw on two on-going research projects to explore how learning takes place in informal everyday settings and what the possible connections might be between these and the organized settings of systematic learning programmes, particularly community-based language and literacy ones.

We start from an anthropologically grounded view of literacy as part of social practices that are observable in literacy 'events' and are patterned by social institutions and power relationships. This encourages us to look beyond texts themselves to what people *do* with literacy, with whom, where, and how. The practical research focus is on what people do with texts in specific literacy 'events'. Descriptions of literacy events include: the *participants* – who is involved in an interaction with a written text and what parts they play; *activities* – what they do with the text; *settings* – where they do it physically – in the kitchen, in bed, on the bus; *domains* – the institutional spaces that organize particular areas of social life and the literacy associated with it such as work, religion, within the family or health; *resources* – these might be cognitive skills and knowledge; they might also be material tools such as paper, a wall, a computer, a can of spray paint, or a hammer and chisel.

This theory of literacy as social practice has been developed as an alternative position to the cognitive model of reading and writing that characterizes them purely as a set of skills and which led to perceptions of a great divide between orality and literacy. Brian Street (1995) has described this as a shift from seeing literacy as an autonomous gift to be given to people, to an ideological understanding of literacy, placing it in its wider context of institutional purposes and power relationships.

This approach focuses attention on the cultural practices within which the written word is embedded, how texts are socially regulated and used, and the historical contexts from which these practices have developed. It leads us to consider the uses of literacy in varying cultural and language contexts and how these fit with the range of available communication media. The focus shifts from literacy problems and deficits, to the many different ways that people engage with literacy, recognizing difference and diversity and challenging how these differences are valued within our society.

In their ethnographic study of reading and writing in one local community, Barton and Hamilton (1998) summarize the social practice view of literacy in six propositions:

1   Literacy is best understood as a set of social practices that can be inferred from events and are mediated by written texts. The focus is on action and process and on the material aspects of literacy.
2   There are different literacies associated with different domains of life.
3   Literacy practices are patterned by social institutions and power relationships, resulting in some being more dominant than others.
4   Literacy practices are purposeful and embedded in broader social goals and cultural practices.
5   Literacy is historically situated.
6   Literacy practices change and new ones are frequently acquired through informal learning and sense making.

(1998: 7)

In this chapter we focus on the last of these propositions. In terms of theories of learning, there is a strong link between a social practice account of literacy and recent approaches to theorizing informal, situated learning. A social practice account would claim, as Chaiklin and Lave do, that 'learning is an integral aspect of activity ... at all times' (1993: 8). We cannot help but learn, but *what* we learn, and *how far we are aware* of this activity as learning are complicated issues. Formal education is seen as just one, specialized, domain among many where learning will occur.

There is a growing body of empirical research studies using this approach (see Hull and Schultz 2002 for a recent review of these) that emphasize the diverse detail of literacies situated in different local settings. However, there is a need to develop more nuanced and theoretically grounded descriptions of the communalities and patterning of literacies across contexts, without resorting to traditional universalizing claims. Exploring such trans-contextual patterning is one of the main challenges for current research and we hope that the data presented in this paper can make a contribution to such explorations. Hamilton (2001), Brandt and Clinton (2002) and Clarke (2002) have begun to link ideas from actor network theory (Latour 1987; Law 1994) with literacy studies. George Marcus's (1995) notion of multi-sited ethnography makes similar points. These perspectives invite us to trace the threads of literacy practices, especially looking at how texts, people and activities (and therefore learning) travel across contexts, to detail how local, situated interactions are orchestrated into bigger patterns. These perspectives offer a number of concepts useful for understanding the nature of such trans-contextual links when considering learning in everyday lives. We will return to these ideas at the end of this chapter.

Data from two research projects

The Changing Faces project

The first set of data comes from a project called the 'Changing Faces of Adult Literacy, Numeracy and ESOL' (English for Speakers of Other Languages). We drew a sample of 100 adults from a longitudinal UK cohort study known as the National Child Development Survey (NCDS) to explore the relevance of adult basic education to the lives of people identified as having basic skills needs. There are over 17,000 people in this cohort, all of whom were born in one week in 1985 (see Bynner and Parsons 1997). The adults we interviewed have been identified (either through self-assessment or external testing) as having basic skills difficulties but have not necessarily participated in courses. We had a great deal of background information about each person; from their childhood family circumstances, educational experiences, tests and self-perceptions of literacy and numeracy needs in adulthood, employment experiences, aspirations and practices. The data discussed in the paper are from people who all live in the North West of England. This and the fact of their participation in the NCDS survey is the only shared context for the group – they are in effect a set of unrelated individuals, each telling a selective story about their literacy life.

The interviews centred on topic areas linked to the social practice theory of literacy: we asked about basic skills needs and aspirations in relation to life-course events and demands; awareness of policy, publicity and provision to help with literacy and numeracy; participation in formal education and training; informal resources and support networks people draw on in relation to literacy and numeracy and practical engagement with literacy tasks; the informal and collective acquisition of literacy/numeracy skills and the events which prompt such learning; the ways in which print literacy interacts with other media use, especially the new communications technologies, and how choices are made between them.

Changing Faces project: case study 1

Sue is in her mid-forties. She is divorced and disabled with very low scores on both literacy and numeracy tests. Sue lost both parents when she was a child. Although she attended school regularly, these deaths occurred at significant moments in her educational life (six and 15 years) and affected her performance in formal assessments of her achievement. Her own assessment of her abilities and her teachers' assessments are aligned and suggest better skills than the tests show. She does say she has lost some writing skills through lack of practice over the last few years, however. She presents herself as a reader of books and supports the children around her in their literacy.

From her background information we expected to meet a rather isolated and unsupported woman. However, Sue has siblings, in particular two brothers who have been important in supporting her throughout her life. They have children of their own which means that she has contact with an extended family network that includes nieces and nephews, as well as her own two children. Despite her poor health and high rating on the 'depression' index, she comes over in the interview as very positive and sympathetic to others: 'I'm the sort of person people tell their life story to'.

Since her health has deteriorated (she has recently been diagnosed with epilepsy), her options for taking part in formal educational courses are ever more limited even though her preference would be to learn in a group setting as she enjoys the social side of learning.

The Adult Learners' Lives (ALL) project

The second set of data is part of the ALL project, which is researching links between people's everyday uses of reading, writing, communication and basic skills provision. The ALL project is working in the North West of England and in the second year we worked at a bi-lingual family literacy centre in Liverpool. The area has a large well-established immigrant population, speaking many languages, recently extended by new arrivals and refugee and asylum seekers. From March to June 2004 bi-lingual interviews were conducted with women students from Oman, Yemen and Somalia with the help of two tutors who spoke Arabic and Somali. To acknowledge the women's diverse previous and current experiences (see Sato 2004) the interviews asked about early experience of literacy learning in their home country, experience of learning English at the centre and everyday uses of reading, writing, speaking and numbers. They were also asked about the use of learning materials used by the centre, specifically a learners' notebook, bi-lingual reading books, stories and games. Researching the everyday lives of some of the students provides information about how and where these materials are used and can add to a critical understanding of family literacy (Pitt 2002).

The centre developed a range of methods and materials for working with bi-lingual family literacy using dual language texts, games, storybooks, notebooks and cultural materials, including a Somali house. In researching and building the

Somali house people contributed their experiences, stories and knowledge of construction methods and materials. This was added to by a research trip to Somalia by one of the students, now a tutor, bringing back cultural knowledge and photographs to enable learners to make the house. Its construction enabled literacy learning (translating and writing from an oral tradition) to be embedded in cultural and literacy learning. The Somali house is used by people within this network and is taken into schools to support the learning of others, particularly bi-lingual children.

The women students made individual notebooks by sticking in prepared pages with everyday words, which, with the help of a tutor, were filled in with personal and family details. The pages were grouped around words and phrases like 'the doctors', or address, telephone and date of birth which were indexed for easy everyday use. Useful information like names of garments, days of the week and colours were learned and added. The notebooks went everywhere, in bags and pockets, with one having to be replaced as it had been literally worn out.

ALL project: case study 2

Faiza, like many other girls, didn't attend school in her village in Yemen. As a result she can't read or write Arabic script. Faiza married at fifteen and came to live in Liverpool ten years ago with her husband, who had lived in England since childhood. She has learned some English now, before this she stayed at home cooking, cleaning, looking after her children and taking them to school. She wants to become more independent, to be able to travel on buses and to read letters herself. With five boys and one girl she described travelling to hospital several times and having to memorize the bus number in order to get there.

Faiza wants to be able to read bills and appointments that come to the house and to know how her children are doing at school. She is learning Arabic to help with learning English; at the moment she forgets new words in English as she is unable to write them down in either language to help her remember. She says she finds numbers difficult and often confuses sixty for sixteen. She uses her notebook to record things like the children's ages, dates of birth, days of the week, months and her address and telephone number.

Everyday practices, informal learning and change: what our data tells us

Our data show how informal learning and sense making in everyday life occurs and how it can be 'carried' across contexts, including educational ones. These examples elaborate on the proposition from the theory of literacy as social practice that emphasizes the dynamic and changing nature of everyday practice and identifies the significance of informal learning.

We have many examples of literacy embedded in work, in organizing everyday life and in learning and using new technologies. Everyday learning takes place everywhere, including the 'dead time' between other activities – for example when travelling. Interviewees explain how they use a mixture of phone, print and face-to-face communication in finding out about local information. From this data we have identified a range of strategies through which informal learning and change is accomplished in everyday life and we discuss three of these below: (1) the use of narratives and stories; (2) 'trial and error' strategies that allow skills to develop in a flexible way; (3) skill sharing that scaffolds change through networks of support, whether in the home and family, at work or in the community. We have particularly strong evidence of exchanges and mutual support between children and adults, among siblings and friends.

These strategies occur in relation both to traditional print literacy and to new technologies and are, as we would expect, embedded in wider purposes, practical and communicative activities. Because of the embedded nature of literacy, people are not always aware that what they are doing is 'literacy' or 'numeracy'. This was very evident in the transcripts of the Changing Faces interviews where it sometimes took several attempts by the interviewer to get people to identify the 'mundane' reading and writing that they take for granted in their daily routines.

Stories/narrative

Faiza, like many of the women in the bi-lingual centre, is teaching her daughter to speak Arabic and tells her children stories from her Yemeni background. She uses stories to support her children's literacy and language learning whilst teaching them their wider family identity. Faiza wants her children to know about their grandfather and great-grandfather: 'I tell them from my old family'. Mediatore (2003) calls this 'cultural remembrance', fostering a sense of history within a displaced community: a bridge with heritage and maintenance of identity, particularly for migrant women (see also Buijs 1996). Stories are used as a learning tool between home and the centre, where many of the women improvised around texts to accommodate very young children and being less confident readers.

In the more settled lives of the interviewees in the Changing Faces study, cultural remembrance did not emerge explicitly as a theme. People do keep family records, including photo albums, but they did not mention oral, inter-generational story telling about family events. Most of the adults we spoke to were read to by their own parents and in turn read storybooks to children (as in the example of Sue). Story reading and book buying are seen as high status cultural activities. They are seen to be educationally important but were not specifically talked of as a reminder of history and culture. People also told us that they regularly watch DVDs or videos together as a family and this could be seen as a form of collective story telling.

Trial and error

The opportunity to experiment without being judged or penalized by others for making mistakes is a common feature of experiential learning (see Niks et al. 2003;

Coffield 2000). The Changing Faces data offer many examples of this, especially in relation to learning about new technologies and appliances in the home. Willingness to tackle new technologies is a subtle combination of confidence about handling technical things, strong motivation to find out about something, for yourself or for others, and the availability or perceived difficulty of investing time to do so. Dealing with new appliances in the home sometimes involves reading the instruction manuals but people described a whole range of methods of learning how to use these and people frequently commented: 'I'll try it out first, then when it doesn't work, I'll look at the manual.'

In both data sets home provides many opportunities for informal 'trial and error' learning and sense making through watching television, reading letters, looking at newspapers and the Internet, and talking to neighbours. Faiza used the television to help her learn English at home, in turn, when watching Arabic television she explains and corrects her children's spoken Arabic. Children and husbands enabled the women to practise their English by correcting mistakes within the home. Trial and error outside the home meant getting some things wrong like buying wrong packets of food or buying the wrong amount of dress material. Whilst home enabled practice of new skills this was sometimes constrained by other aspects of identity, particularly gender. One student's husband turned off the bedroom light, preventing her practising after the children had gone to bed, and another described her children not helping her with the housework so she had no time to learn. Sue describing using a mobile phone with her daughter echoed generational assumptions found in learning at home:

> We went to Huddersfield on Bank Holiday Monday and on the way back I got a text and I was trying to send one back and she said, 'mother are you writing a four page letter?' [laugh] Because it was taking me that long she said, 'give it to me – what do you want to say?' [laugh] Oh dear!

Building skills

Our data shows that scaffolding takes place in many settings. Taking the easiest route to learning something new often relies on someone else, at least at the beginning. People make use of funds of knowledge (Moll 1992) about teaching or supporting others to learn from their own experience. One man from the Changing Faces project described how he helped induct a younger man in the workplace, and how his own lack of confidence in using the written word enabled him to handle this sensitively. People also have work-related knowledge that they pass on to others. Sometimes people identified past habits and skills as interfering with their use of the new technology – one person complained that her expertise in using typewriters led her to bang on the computer keys too hard, producing unpredictable results so she has to 'have her daughter around' to sort these out for her. On the computer, where it is easy to look at the same screen together, people actually share the operations of surfing the Internet depending on their expertise:

for example 'He gets me onto the site and I scroll though it to find what I need' or 'I speak it and he writes it in'.

In the ALL project data, both children and parents were simultaneously teachers, translators and learners with no separate and fixed identities. Faiza, through the interpreter, explained that her two eldest sons were learning at Arabic school, helping her and each other:

> The two [second] eldest one he can read and write a bit more than the other one in Arabic, he's very good. Sometimes they help [me] if there is an Arabic word [I] can't understand, they help [me] read in Arabic too.

She helps her younger daughter with learning Arabic practising everyday words and reads in English to her pre-school son to prepare him for nursery school, as she talks to him mainly in Arabic at home. She uses colouring, story telling and assembling everyday images to help him learn – methods she has experienced herself as a learner. She does not do this for her older children, as they are more fluent in English than she is – showing how role relationships between parents and children change over time, along with the kinds of support they need and give. The women's support networks include family, friends and members of their community. Faiza's husband and her children support her literacy and language when going shopping, and on visits to the doctors or the chemist. Other students at the centre describe support from family members in reading and writing letters to the school, in doing their homework or completing learning tasks from the centre.

Sue supports her own and other people's children in reading and writing, by supplying resources like books, sitting with them listening to them read, reading to them, playing with them on computer games, identifying and acknowledging their learning. As a disabled person, she feels she has limitations, but one thing she does have is a lot of time on her hands. She is available for childcare – she can give 'quality time' without distractions. In turn, she is supported, especially by her brothers, but also by her own grown-up children who encourage her, facilitate her going to education by passing on information, giving her reading matter, offering lifts, and reminding her about events.

Some people described others who had acted as 'guiding lights' to them over a sustained period of time (Padmore 1994). For example one man had a business friend who had advised him about setting up his own company and helped with the paperwork. One interviewee describes a 'literacy broker' at work who helped her apply for a nursing training course.

Discussion and conclusions

Our data offer a rich and suggestive picture of the range and variety of literacy-mediated learning that may occur in everyday life in homes, communities and workplaces. Support and exchange of skills is ubiquitous and prompted by practical need: the bilingual women use support in and out of the learning centre to acquire everyday language and cultural familiarity. In the Changing Faces project, language learning was mentioned only in the context of holiday travel, but people offer and use support in relation to the literacies involved with new technologies, disability and health and to make the most of the specialized expertise that is distributed around their local community. We can see some of the links between what Faiza and the other women are learning at the bi-lingual family literacy centre and their everyday life at home. In addition, the data from the Changing Faces project shows us that literacies can cross between the workplace and everyday practices in home and community.

The data suggest some common features of informal learning in everyday settings that can help 'carry' literacy and language learning from one context to another:

- Overlapping networks of people who act at different times as literacy brokers, mediators, translators, scaffolding learning and moving fluidly between the roles of 'expert' and 'novice'.
- Material artifacts that can be used in more than one domain, creating equivalences between one context and another, such as the learner's notebook created in the bilingual centre for use in everyday settings, or the stories that can easily travel across domains and physical settings.
- A range of learning strategies (including trial and error, story-telling) that enable people to learn in their own way, without penalties attached, and help them situate and make sense of their experience, remember their history and imagine possible alternatives (see also Holland and Lave 2001).
- Making use of expertise with different communication strategies and media for learning that people have gained in other settings.
- Strong motivations and 'ruling passions' to get things done in their lives that prompt people to learn even in difficult circumstances.
- Building on learning *where people are* (as with holiday language classes) implying the need for access to a range of physical resources and learning opportunities not always structured as formal 'courses', as suggested in Hamilton (2000).

We can see how the bilingual learning centre validated many of these features of informal learning using a complex weaving between learning and teaching across different written and spoken languages occurring in different locations: at home, at school, in the community and as ESOL learners. These literacy and communicative social practices could be described as bi/multi-literacy (Saxena 1994) where the women used a range of literacies, associated with different domains of life, with much interconnection and crossing between them.

The notebook and stories created in the bi-lingual classroom travelled, quite literally, between the centre and home enabling translation between different sets of social practices. The notebook carried information that the students needed in their everyday lives: they were developed within a learning context and, as a text, supported the social practices of the women in their everyday lives. Similarly, stories as well as supporting intergenerational practices of reading, writing and speaking English (where the women are the learners) also support active cultural remembrance (where the women are the teachers). The Somali house shows how cultural knowledge can travel from the home into the learning environment.

Hull and Schultz (2002) also identify the importance of movement, travel and interconnectedness in literacy practices and learning between home and education. Brandt and Clinton (2002) suggest that literacy artifacts have a particularly important role to play in creating bridges because they are enduring and thus can stabilize meanings, yet they are easily portable across contexts. Literacy serves to build and sustain long, stable connections and networks across time and space. Literacy artifacts, in other words, can be particularly effective social agents in trans-contextualizing work (see also Jones 2000; Tusting 2000; Barton and Hamilton forthcoming, for suggestions about specific ways in which this can happen).

In summary, what emerges from our data is that situated literacy and communication practices are complex, intergenerational and multidirectional. Learning is visibly integrated and supported through everyday practice. Domain borders are crossed and re-crossed using many levels of literacy and communicative translation. Rigid boundaries between teacher and learner are challenged. Recognizing this prevents any simple dichotomy, or fixed boundaries, between public and private domains or between formal and informal learning. Some travel and crossing between contexts is purposely and actively sought (Faiza and the stories) whilst in other cases it happens in a more incidental way (the stories of expertise crossing between home and workplace in the Changing Faces project). By using the understandings from these studies, we can see the possibilities for building stronger bridges across the variety of contexts for learning, including formal education.

Acknowledgements

Thanks to Kath Gilbert of Smithdown Road, Bi-lingual Family Literacy Centre.

References

Barton, D. and Hamilton, M. (1998) *Local Literacies – Reading and Writing in One Community*, London: Routledge.

Barton, D. and Hamilton, M. (in press) 'Literacy, reification and the dynamics of social interaction', in D. Barton and K. Tustin (eds) *Beyond Communities of Practice*, Cambridge: Cambridge University Press.

Brandt, T. and Clinton, K. (2002) 'Limits of the local: expanding perspectives on literacy as a social practice', *Journal of Literacy Research*, 34, 3: 337–56.

Buijs, J. (ed.) (1996) *Migrant Women: Crossing Boundaries and Changing Identities*, Oxford: Berg.

Bynner, J. and Parsons, S. (1997) *It Doesn't Get any Better: The Impact of Poor Basic Skills on the Lives of 37 year olds*, London: Basic Skills Agency.

Chaiklin, S. and Lave, J. (eds) (1993) *Understanding Practice: Perspectives on Activity and Context*, New York: Cambridge University Press.

Clarke, J. (2002) 'A new kind of symmetry: actor-network theories and the new literacy studies', *Studies in the Education of Adults* 34, 2: 107–22.

Coffield, F. (2000) *The Necessity of Informal Learning*, Bristol: Policy Press.

Hamilton, M. (2000) 'Exploring literacy as social practice through media photographs', in D. Barton, M. Hamilton and R. Ivanic (eds) *Situated Literacies*, London: Routledge.

Hamilton, M. (2001) 'Privileged literacies: policy, institutional process and the life of the International Adult Literacy Survey', *Language and Education*, 15, 2–3: 178–96.

Holland, D. and Lave, J. (2001) *History in Person: Enduring Struggles, Contentious Practice, Intimate Identities*, Santa Fe: School of American Research Press.

Hull, G. and Schultz, K. (2002) *School's Out! Bridging Out-of-School Literacies with Classroom Practice*, New York: Teachers' College Press.

Jones, K. (2000) 'Becoming just another alphanumeric code: farmers' encounters with the literacy and discourse practices of agricultural bureaucracy at the livestock auction', in D. Barton, M. Hamilton and R. Ivanic (eds) *Situated Literacies*, London: Routledge.

Latour, B. (1987) *Science in Action*, Cambridge, MA.: Harvard University Press.

Law, J. (1994) *Organizing Modernity*, Oxford: Blackwell.

Marcus, G. E. (1995) 'Ethnography in/of the world system: the emergence of multi-sited ethnography', *Annual Review of Anthropology* 24: 95–117.

Mediatore, S. S. (2003) *Reading Across Borders: Storytelling and Knowledges of Resistance*, Hampshire: Palgrave Macmillan.

Moll, L. (1992) 'Funds of knowledge for teaching: using a qualitative approach to connect homes and classrooms', *Theory into Practice*, 31, 2: 132–41.

Niks, M., Allen, D., Davies, P., McRae, D. and Nonesuch, K. (2003) *Dancing in the Dark: How do Adults with Little Formal Education Learn?* National Literacy Secretariat, and Ministry of Advanced Education, British Columbia: Canada.

Padmore, S. (1994) 'Guiding Lights', in M. Hamilton, D. Barton and R. Ivanic (eds) *Worlds of Literacy*, Clevedon, UK: Multilingual Matters.

Pitt, K. (2002) 'Being a new capitalist mother', *Discourse and Society*, 13, 2: 251–67.

Sato, C. (2004) 'Rethinking adult literacy training: an analysis through a third world feminist perspective', *Women's Studies Quarterly*, 1, 2: 73–89.

Saxena, M. (1994) 'Literacies among Panjabis in Southall', in M. Hamilton, D. Barton and R. Ivanic (eds) *Worlds of Literacy*, Clevedon: Multilingual Matters.

Street, B. (1995) *Social Literacies: Critical Approaches to Literacy in Development, Ethnography and Education*, London: Longman.

Tusting, K. (2000) 'The new literacy studies and time: an exploration', in D. Barton, M. Hamilton and R. Ivanic (eds) *Situated Literacies*, London: Routledge.

Chapter 19

Lifelong learning in the community

Social action

Rod Purcell

This chapter focuses on transformatory learning for individuals and collectivities in the context of social action in communities. In a world where technical reason is dominant and politics is separated from ideology educational processes need to develop 'organized intelligence' and to challenge the way institutions currently operate. Social action programmes are intrinsically spaces for learning. Drawing on the work of Dewey, Illich, Gramsci and Freire the author argues that critical learning involves a process of 'Reflection-Vision-Planning-Action', which to be successful requires some degree of critical space to occur. There is no simple way to achieve this and the author provides different examples of successful popular education occurring in practice.

Contexts of learning in the community

Lifelong learning takes place in the community through a variety of locations and processes. It can be through formal learning programmes delivered on an outreach basis covering academic, vocational or recreational courses. It can be through the knowledge and skills developed from voluntary service, community, sporting and leisure activities. In particular it can be through participation in local partnerships activities with the local state. In the UK this activity mostly takes place under the social inclusion policy agenda, which includes such initiatives as community regeneration, active citizenship, new deal for communities, civil renewal and social capital formation (for a discussion of the relationship between these policies and the community see Taylor 2003). These programmes are an extension of the UK New Labour Government's communitarian approach that stresses both the rights of individuals to have a say in how their community functions, as well as the personal responsibility to be actively involved. In addition to the above, community-based lifelong learning can also take place through reflection on everyday tasks; for example parenting, caring for relatives or personal hobbies.

This chapter narrows down the focus and concentrates upon a growing area of learning and community activity, that of social action. This can be distinguished from the more mainstream community development/social inclusion activities through its independence from, and critical perspective on, the activities of the state. Social action is a broad and ill-defined term that has links to emancipatory and transformative learning. As Susan Imel (1999) argues, emancipatory education is difficult to achieve in a classroom setting due to overlapping complexities around power differentials amongst the student group, between students and teachers, and across racial, class and sexual divides. She also points out that there is a difference between simply empowering learners to develop self and socio/political awareness and transformative learning that implies an action dimension.

Social action learning therefore takes place in the community with the expressed purpose of promoting change. Advocates of social action would probably agree with Griff Foley (1999) who argues that involvement in local struggles, whether they are related to issues of community, environment, work, feminism, sexuality or ethnicity, can lead to people both unlearning dominant and oppressive cultural norms and developing more critical awareness of themselves, their community and wider social structures of inequality. Alvarez (1990) sees this process as exploring the interconnection between macro-economic and micro political factors. She argues that learning in struggle links educational interventions, learning, discursive practices, ideologies, micro politics and political economy with the process of emancipation at the centre. The key point is that the social action is defined and led by members of the local community and that the learning is derived from what is necessary to know in order to transform one's own quality of life.

Social action as a concept

The concept of social action comes originally from the sociologist Max Weber (1948) who was concerned to explore the subjective meaning human beings attach to their social interactions. Weber identified four types of social action:

1 *Zweckrational* – that is rational action to achieve a specific goal. For example attending evening classes to obtain job related qualifications.
2 *Wertrational* – is a value orientated activity that is pursued through an ethical or religious context.
3 *Affective action* – is derived from the emotional state of the person concerned rather than a independent rational weighing up of the pros and cons of an activity.
4 *Traditional action* – is based upon the continued application of established cultural norms and habits.

Our modernist cultural legacy, increasingly driven by technological imperatives and globalized economy, has embraced the *zweckrational* mode of social organization. This has led to the creation of the bureaucratization of work and much of social life. Henri Lefebvre (1995) argues that bureaucracy and patterns of consumption control the modern world and an effect of this process is that life has ceased to be a *subject* rich in experience, instead it is now an *object* of social organization. As a result the individual has few spaces in a modernist environment to find him or her. Individual needs and identity are submerged for the greater good of the company, institution or political party. Habermas (1974) has explored how citizens have been depoliticized as decisions, economic and political, are supposedly taken on rational and technical grounds rather than on ideology.

In contrast, people committed to social action in the community talk about helping people to enjoy a rich and transformatory life, through assisting their empowerment as subjects in their own right. As such this can be seen as a *wertra-tional* value-based activity. In this context Dewey (1935) explored the possibility of using education for both individual and social emancipation. He recognized that the educational process could be used to develop, what he termed, co-operative intelligence to provide a process for mediating competing social claims. Dewey also argued for the development of organized intelligence, to bring social conflicts into the open. However, he recognized that although education was a precondition for improving society, a radical change in how our institutions operated was also required if the emancipation of citizens and communities was to take place.

Institutions, however, can be seen as the cause of the problem rather than the solution. Ivan Illich (1973) argues that institutions inevitably become more concerned with their own self-serving interests and the creation of a monopoly, at the expense of their stated social purpose. They reinforce the dominant interest in society and select both those who will succeed socially and economically and those who will not. In doing so, traditional education commodifies the process of learning and objectifies learners to meet predetermined ends.

In the same vein, conventional notions of development are linked to increasing consumer prosperity without the need for any fundamental social change. Illich argues that increasing consumer prosperity cannot be achieved for all. In any case for true development 'we must learn a new language, a language that speaks not of development and underdevelopment but of true and false ideas about man, his needs, and his potential' (1971: 149). Furthermore, we live in a globalized environment where Peters suggests that there will be 'education wars, a struggle not only over the meaning and value of knowledge both internationally and locally, but also over the public means of knowledge production' (2003: 376). On this theme Burton-Jones (1999) makes the point that at the micro level the distinction between managers and workers, learning and working, are becoming increasingly blurred. In effect we are all becoming knowledge capitalists. Peters prefers the term knowledge cultures. Either way the creation and control of knowledge is becoming a critical area for the development of society.

In *Deschooling Society*, Illich argues that

> a desirable future depends on our deliberately choosing a life of action over a life of consumption, on our engendering a lifestyle which will enable us to be spontaneous, independent, yet related to each other, rather than maintaining a lifestyle which only allows us to make and unmake, produce and consume.
>
> (1973: 57)

through the creation of learning webs, skills exchanges, peer
ning and genuinely open access to resources for learning. On
tes a more vibrant socially useful educational environment.
h's term for such a process. At another level it promotes the
social capital and the potential for locally driven social action. In
ng learning could move from its UK incarnation as a strategy to
-skill the workforce, and becomes a central and continuing aspect of
life u.   y individual and community needs and interests.

The idea of developing new ideas about community needs and individual
potential takes us to the ideas of Paulo Freire and popular education. Based initially on his work on literacy programmes in Brazil, Freire (1972) identified several
concepts that are central to critical learning processes. He argued that people create and police their own personal boundaries that limit their potential for action
(boundary situations). These boundaries are learnt from messages contained
within the dominant culture (cultural invasion). The route to challenging this limitation and working for personal and collective change is based in moving from
what Freire termed 'naïve' to a 'critical consciousness' and the resulting reinter-
pretation of the world (*conscientization*). This can be achieved through a process of
education where the educator poses questions and facilitates collective learning.
Pre-determined knowledge is largely rejected as it is seen as an instrument of
social control. The objective is to develop new, local knowledge, to inform and
enable change at the personal, community and societal level.

In a similar vein, Gramsci (Hoare and Smith 1971) developed a number of
ideas that revised the basic Marxist interpretation of how society worked. For the
purposes of social action there are two critical ideas. First, that the state mainly
rules through a hegemonic process that operates through institutions and culture
in a way which universalizes what are, in reality, sectional interests and values.
Second, that change can be promoted through creating counter hegemony. This
can be achieved through the development of 'organic intellectuals' from within
the oppressed class whose job it is to promote the principles and aspirations of the
subordinate social group.

There is considerable overlap in the writings of Freire and Gramsci (although
there are differences). Peter Mayo (1999) and Margaret Ledwith (2001) have
explored their ideas in some detail and in the context of community development
practice. In particular there are direct relationships between the working of the
hegemonic process, cultural invasion, naïve consciousness and the individualized
imposition of personal boundaries. The Freirian process of developing critical
consciousness can be linked to Gramsci's ideas of organic intellectuals building
counter hegemony.

Freire's thesis that people learn through action is also supported, albeit in different contexts, by the work of Knowles (1998) and Rogers (1983). What is
necessary, however, is an understanding of how this learning process takes place
in practice. This can be understood as working through a 'Reflection–Vision–
Planning–Action cycle' (RVPA). This is illustrated in Figure 19.1.

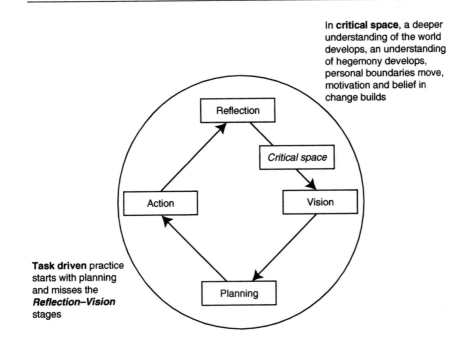

In **critical space**, a deeper understanding of the world develops, an understanding of hegemony develops, personal boundaries move, motivation and belief in change builds

Task driven practice starts with planning and misses the **Reflection–Vision** stages

Figure 19.1 Reflection–Vision–Planning–Action cycle

There are many ways to apply the above cycle to practice. A common approach is through the *Training for Transformation* programme (Hope and Timmel 1996) that has been used in southern Africa and Asia and mirrors similar Freirian inspired work in Latin America (see also a rewriting of *Training for Transformation* for Ireland by Sheehy 2001). In this approach to community-based practice the worker identifies critical themes within the community through listening surveys based upon unstructured conversations. The information from these surveys is then linked to concepts of need (see Maslow 1970 and Max-Neef *et al.* 1990). The analysis of the survey can be used to identify generative themes that link economic causes of problems, to wider issues that include power relationships, culture, gender, and so on.

The generative themes are then represented in codes. A code can be a photograph, drawing, poem, song or diagram. The purpose of the code is to enable focused group discussion. The worker, as facilitator, poses questions which help the analysis of the code. For example, what is happening in the representation? Why did it happen? Has this happened to you? What other problem does this relate to? What is the cause of this problem? What can we do about it? (Sheehy 2001). In responding to these questions the group reflects on their life experiences and explores what a better life for themselves, family and community would look like.

In this process of moving from reflection to vision (through what I call critical space) an understanding of social and cultural processes will be gained. That is people see how hegemony operates and what this has meant to them in terms of creating their own boundary situations. People begin to redefine, to paraphrase C. Wright Mills (1959), a 'private trouble as a public issue'. As critical understanding develops, a thoughtful and more complete worldview develops.

In *Liberation Through Consciousness Raising*, Hart (1990) identifies five principles that outline what she calls 'enabling conditions' for this consciousness raising work to succeed. These are:

- the learning group needs to be representative of an oppressed or marginalized group;
- the social experience of the group needs to be relatively similar;
- the learning group needs to develop on the basis of equality;
- there must be motivation to critically reflect on subjective experience;
- the learners have to be able to create some distance between developing theory and personal experience.

Once a vision of how life can be improved has been developed, ideas and the commitment to action flow naturally. Further learning then takes place to develop the knowledge and skills required to implement change. Because this process is based on reflection and the development of new knowledge, social action programmes are essentially learning organizations. Ideas around learning organizations have been developed by a number of people, for example Peter Senge (1993). In addition, social action is based on the successful development and support of a community-based leadership. Leadership in this context needs to be developed both in terms of 'strategic' leadership to make things happen as explored by Senge, and 'transformatory' leadership that 'moves (people) towards higher and more universal needs and purposes' (Bolman and Deal 2003: 200).

Examples of social action

An example of social action in practice is Photovoice. This is an international organization that works in local communities. It originated in Ann Arbour, Michigan, where homeless street people were given disposable cameras to record their world (Wang 1998). From the pictures, conversations and people's life stories were developed, the photographs acting as codes in the Freirian sense. The resulting exhibition was used to make issues of the 'invisible homeless', a visible and hot issue to be tackled. In this process the homeless people themselves moved from being objects in need of welfare provisions to subjects exploring and promoting their own agenda. The learning included a basic understanding of photography, the ethics of photographing 'people in need', developing knowledge about local power systems, to the range of social and confidence-building skills required to complete the project. Photovoice projects have been run on sexual health issues in

Australia, homeless people in London, HIV-positive women in Congo, street children in Vietnam and refugees in Nepal.

A further example is the neighbourhood houses that have developed in Australia from the 1970s. A particular house, quoted by Foley (1999), delivers a wide range of activities for women including adult education, playgroups, a consumer and tenancy programme, community and environmental projects, discussion and self help groups. Foley identified the following outcomes arising from involvement in house activities: a place for companionship and support, learning through participation leading to new personal knowledge, skills and self confidence, learning through conflict (both interpersonal conflict and community action) and critical learning through exploring and working on women's issues. He suggests that the house operates as a 'liberated space' within which women can reflect upon experience (again being subjects in control of their learning rather than objects to be taught predetermined knowledge), and are able to theorize the position of women within Australian society and to plan and take action on identified issues.

A third example is the Adult Learning Project based in Edinburgh. The project's aim is to implement in an inner city, working class community, the principles and practices of Freire alongside a Gramscian analysis. Galloway describes the project's objectives as 'a commitment to politicise the curriculum, construct learning programmes grounded in the struggle for cultural equality, develop the use of dialogical learning methods and build an authentic relationship between learning and cultural action' (1999: 226). Initially, project workers and local residents undertook co-investigations to explore critical issues around politics, gender and ethnicity, the inner city environment and culture. From this information new learning programmes were developed. Galloway describes these programmes as making a link between 'the cognitive and affective domains of learning ... to create a basis for counter hegemony' (1999: 233). In practice a range of learning programmes on politics, history, Scots and Gaelic language explored how power and dominant culture operated in the local community.

These learning programmes led to a range of local actions. For example, the history groups both wrote and performed plays celebrating radical movements and individuals from Scotland's past. The democracy groups actively campaigned on local issues around school closure, traffic and on wider issues such as water privatization. The music groups promoted traditional Scottish songs and organized performances. As a direct result of the critical insight gained from the learning programmes, many individuals implemented major changes to their lives and created 'spin-off' organizations.

Learning tools for social action

As the above examples demonstrate, the success of social action is based upon an effective learning process. Clearly, given its Freirian roots, traditional banking methodologies are inappropriate. Learning strategies are therefore mostly derived from a combination of Freirian popular education and Participative Rapid Appraisal (PRA) tools (see below). Social action initiatives tend to draw on a range of these learning tools according to local circumstances. It is worth, however, briefly discussing the background of the popular education and PRA approaches.

A critical aspect of popular education is its rejection of mainstream institutions as elitist and as a part of the process of domination. Instead, popular education starts within the experience of the participant and draws on various aspects of local popular culture. Recognizing that written and academic discourse are not natural forms of learning for most oppressed social groups, popular education utilizes a combination of poetry, storytelling, song, art, photography, drama, dance, puppetry and mime. In doing so local cultural values are respected (but not necessarily unchallenged) and the world is demystified in accessible and relevant forms. As Proulx (1993: 39) comments, it is through the process of popular education that 'working class adults recognize their life and their values'.

During the 1980s and 1990s it became increasingly obvious to Non-Governmental Organizations operating in Asia and Africa that the standard top down approach to development usually failed to work. This is also true of community-based work in the UK, as evidenced by the current push by government to promote community involvement in social inclusion and regeneration initiatives. The old methodology was that the outside experts held the answers and the local community was the problem. The current perspective is that external structural processes are the problem and that experts can work with local people to find solutions. To do this new local and external knowledge has to be critically developed to identify how change should take place. Carolyn Jones identifies the changes of emphasis that have taken place as from:

dominance	to	*facilitation*
closed approach	to	*open* approach
tedium	to	*fun*
individual views	to	*group* discussions
verbal	to	*visual*
absolutes	to	*comparing*
averages	to	*diversity*

(Jones 1996: 13)

A new body of learning and analytical tools have been developed to promote this knowledge creation process. Rapid Rural Appraisal methods offered a starting point but it was realized that greater effort and improved techniques were required both to fully involve local people and to explore their local experience. The result was a body of processes and techniques called PRA programmes that have spread rapidly due to their success. By the year 2000 PRA was in use in over 100 countries (including the UK). It is used in urban as well as rural contexts and in a range of settings from economic development to environmental sustainability and social programmes. In the UK it has been used in anti-poverty work, promoting health and wellbeing, urban development, urban literacy, gender, race and agriculture (Chambers 2002).

Although there are some theoretical differences between PRA and the Freirean approach, the former often draws heavily on Freirean methodologies to involve people in a critical dialogue to explore local issues and solutions. An example of the fusion of the two methodologies is the REFLECT approach (Archer and Cottingham 1996). The handbook developed by Actionaid and used increasingly in the UK as well as Asia outlines a range of Freirian inspired learning methods. For example, health issues are examined through graphical body mapping. Wellbeing ranking and matrices explore the relationship between food, health and illness. Socio-political themes, social networks and power relationships are identified and analysed using chapatti diagrams (also known as Venn diagrams), organization matrices and human resource mapping. Life in communities is explored through developing timelines, transect walking, village mapping and developing socio-cultural calendars. Such techniques are linked to the mainstream Freirean and popular education methods of listening surveys, drama, dance, song, and art. As well as developing critical knowledge through the application of these learning techniques, numeracy and literacy skills are increased as a by-product of the process. These methods work equally well with children and adults.

Phnuyal (1997), in exploring the link between Freire, popular education and PRA, summarizes the interrelationship through the following ideals:

- Each person has the capacity to learn and participate and has the right to do so.
- Education processes cannot be neutral; either they help to 'domesticate' people or help to liberate them.
- If education is to have a liberating outcome, the process itself needs to be participatory and liberating.
- 'Knowledge' cannot be imposed upon learners, rather an environment needs to be created for everybody to explore, analyse and synthesize.
- Real liberation is possible only through popular participation and a key to popular participation is popular education.
- Liberation needs to be conceived as both a process of transforming the self and a process of creating a new society.
- Changes are needed in both individual behaviour and social power relations.

Conclusion

Marion Young (1992) argues that to organize for change it is more effective to think in terms of five faces of oppression. These faces are the exploitation of labour, marginalization of groups which constitute a growing underclass, powerlessness through social divisions, cultural imperialism through the universalization of one group's culture as the norm, and violence through the fear and actual use of systematic oppression. Social action is about creating radical if limited change in these areas, through the development of a critical learning and knowledge creation process linked to an action programme.

Traditionally, radical change has been discussed in terms of a Marxist analysis. Indeed, Freire's methodology and the popular education movement were born out of a modernist Marxist approach towards fighting for social justice and liberation. With the current debate surrounding post modernism, the Marxist meta-narrative has been subjected to sustained criticism. It is difficult to deploy an effective analysis of the current political issues surrounding militarism, human rights and ecological disaster simply as the struggle between the bourgeoisie and the proletariat. Clearly there are more elements at play than that.

Baudrillard (1994) and Lefebvre (1995) argue that the globalized commoditization of an international mass culture has devalued debate and political action. 'We are all consumers now' is the cry (although this clearly ignores the dispossessed who cannot consume and who no longer count, if they ever did). However, there is also what is called 'resistance post modernism' (Lather 1991). Notwithstanding its modernist origins, the methodology of popular education that underpins social action fits comfortably here. It gives us a way of seeing how to promote social change within a post modernist cultural setting. For example, Stuart Hall rightly points out that once people engage in conscious reflection and dialogue there is 'a proliferation of new points of antagonism, new social movements of resistance organized around them, and, consequently, a generation of politics ... a politics of health, of food, of sexuality, of the body' (1994: 7).

The value of social action is that it assists individuals and groups to develop a critical understanding of both their current situation and the potential for change. Transformative learning through social action is therefore a challenging process that involves internal struggles against learnt cultural norms and the external dominant culture. Furthermore, many of these struggles will fail unless the object of change is realistic and therefore need to be limited in scope and ambition. Success comes from understanding the local, and possibly global, context of the action and this can only be achieved through the successful application of a critical reflective learning process.

References

Alvarez, S. (1990) *Engendering Democracy in Brazil: Women's Movements in Transition Politics*, Princeton: Princeton University Press.

Archer, D. and Cottingham, S. (1996) *Reflect Mother Manual*, London: Actionaid.

Baudrillard, J. (1994) *In the Shadow of the Silent Majorities*, London: AK Press.

Bolman, L. and Deal, T. (2003) *Reframing Organizations: Artistry, Choice, and Leadership*, San Francisco: Jossey-Bass Wiley.

Burton-Jones, A. (1999) *Knowledge Capitalism: Business, Work and Learning in the New Economy*, Oxford: Oxford University Press.

Chambers, R. (2002) *Relaxed and Participatory Appraisal*, Brighton: IDS University of Sussex.

Dewey, J. (1935) *Liberalism and Social Action*, New York: G.P. Putnam's Sons.

Foley, G. (1999) *Learning in Social Action*, London: Zed Books/NIACE.

Freire, P. (1972) *Pedagogy of the Oppressed*, Harmondsworth: Penguin.

Galloway, V. (1999) 'Building a pedagogy of hope: the experience of the Adult Learning Project', in J. Crowther., I. Martin and M. Shaw, (eds) *Popular Education and Social Movements in Scotland Today*, Leicester: NIACE.

Habermas, J. (1974) *Theory and Society*, London: Heinemann.

Hall, S. (1994) 'Brave new world', *Socialist Review* 21, cited in P. McLaren and C. Lankshear, *Politics of Liberation: Paths from Freire*, London: Routledge.

Hart, M. (1990) 'Liberation through consciousness raising', in J. Mezirow (ed.) *Fostering Critical Reflection in Adulthood*, San Francisco: Jossey-Bass.

Hoare, Q. and Smith, G. (eds) (1971) *Gramsci: Selections from the Prison Notebook*, London: Lawrence and Wishart.

Hope, A. and Timmel, S. (1996) *Training for Transformation* Vols 1–3, Zimbabwe: Mambo Press.

Jones, C. (1996) *PRA in Central Asia: Coping With Change*, Brighton: IDS, University of Sussex.

Illich, I. (1971) *Celebration of Awareness*, London: Calder & Boyas.

Illich, I. (1973) *Deschooling Society*, Harmondsworth: Penguin.

Imel, S. (1999) 'How emancipatory is adult learning?' in *Myths and Realities* No. 6, ACVE.

Knowles, M. (1998) *The Adult Learner*, Burlington: Butterworth-Heineman.

Lather, P. (1991) *Getting Smart: Feminist Research and Pedagogy with/in the Postmodern*, New York: Routledge.

Ledwith, M. (2001) 'Community work as critical pedagogy; re-envisioning Freire and Gramsci', *Community Development Journal*, 36, 3: 171–82.

Lefebvre, H. (1995) *Writings on Cities*, Oxford: Blackwell.

Maslow, A. (1970) *Motivation and Personality*, San Francisco: Harper and Row.

Max-Neef, M., Elizalde, A. and Hopenhayn, M. (1990) *Human Scale Development: An Option for the Future*, Santiago: CUPAUR.

Mayo, P. (1999) *Gramsci, Freire and Adult Education*, London: Zed Books.

Peters, M. (2003) 'Education policy in the age of knowledge capitalism', *Policy Futures in Education*, 1, 2: 361–80.

Phnuyal, B. (1997) *Commemoration of Paulo Freire*, PLA Notes (Education Action 9), Reflect.

Proulx, J. (1993) 'Adult education and democracy', *Convergence*, 26, 1: 34–42.

Rogers, C. (1983) *Freedom to Learn*, Columbus: O.H. Merrill.

Senge, P. (1993) *The Fifth Discipline: Art and Practice of Learning Organisations*, New York: Random House.

Sheehy, M. (2001) *Partners Companion to Training for Transformation*, Dublin: Partners Training for Transformation.

Taylor, M. (2003) *Public Policy in the Community*, Basingstoke: Palgrave.

Wang, C. (1998) 'Photovoice: involving homeless men and women of Washtenaw County, Michigan', *Health Education and Behaviour*, 25, 1: 9–10.

Weber, M. (1948) 'Class, status and party', in H. Gerth and C.W. Mills (eds) *Essays from Max Weber*, London: Routledge and Kegan Paul.

Wright Mills, C. (1959) *Sociological Imagination*, Oxford: Open University Press.

Young, M. (1992) 'Five faces of oppression', in T. Wertenberg (ed.) *Rethinking Power*, New York: University of New York Press.

Chapter 20

Work and learning

Implications for lifelong learning in the workplace

Hitendra Pillay, Lynn Wilss and Gillian Boulton-Lewis

In the context of globalization and the 'knowledge economy' the interest in lifelong learning in paid work has increased both in terms of formal programmes of study as well as informal learning processes. In this chapter the focus is on workers' perspectives on learning at work and their implications for lifelong learning – a neglected dimension in the literature. If workers do not see learning at work as central to their job then developing a culture of lifelong learning in the workplace faces an uphill task. This account draws on empirical work with two different groups of workers. Whilst the majority of those interviewed did hold integrated conceptions of work and learning there were marked discrepancies in relation to age. Older workers were more likely to hold perceptions of work that would be challenging for developing a lifelong learning culture at work. Also, practical obstacles for participating in work-related learning exist, which need to be considered, and universities could have a role in tailoring their curriculum to address these difficulties.

Lifelong learning and work

Lifelong learning can be interpreted in many ways and consequently one needs to adopt a particular perspective to guide discussion. According to the OECD (1996), lifelong learning means more than just adult education, it includes all learning that occurs from the cradle to grave in different settings. Other definitions include reference to the development of human potential throughout life (Peck 1996); learning that is formal, non-formal and informal across the lifespan (Candy *et al.* 1994); and learning that supports and contributes to the development of a knowledge-based economy (Australian National Training Authority 1999). Continuous learning or learning that occurs in the workplace is often subsumed under the rubric of lifelong learning. Garrick and Clegg (2001) explain lifelong learning in the workplace as engagement in study programmes that may constitute modular courses, self-paced learning and informal processes such as mentoring and apprenticeships. As the name suggests, lifelong learning has no end and continues after compulsory education and post university through continuing professional education, further formal study and through self-directed learning (Candy *et al.* 1994).

For the purpose of this chapter, we describe lifelong learning as that which occurs over the span of one's working life. In recent years there has been a significant shift in how business is conducted in many workplaces. We see an emerging trend with job flexibility which has been enhanced by the introduction of ICT. There has also been a parallel shift in employment conditions and we now have full-time, part-time or casual workers. The chapter initially examines lifelong learning generally as it occurs in workplaces today and then discusses findings from a study into older and younger workers' conceptions of work and of learning at work. The findings of the study also capture the types of learning these workers undertook throughout their working lives. The results are examined in terms of the implications they hold for lifelong learning and work.

Lifelong learning in contemporary workplaces

Since the 1990s, globalization, international competition and new technologies have become integral to business and work practices. As a result, employers experience pressure to place greater time and investment in educating and training employees. The shift is attributed to the emergence of the new economy (Jentzsch 2001) and new industries based on knowledge creation (Takeuchi 1998). Other factors that have contributed to learning becoming a key issue for growth and development include changes in markets for goods and services which require new organizational structures, processes and skills; the centrality of knowledge to social and economic progress; the rapidity of organizational and workplace change; and more active ageing (Gallagher 2001; McKenzie 1999). These conditions have contributed to knowledge becoming central in the workplace and the necessity for workers to become knowledgeable or, what some regard as 'knowledge workers' (Cormican and O'Sullivan 2003). According to Clarke (2004), knowledge is now regarded by some as overriding economic capital, labour and raw materials and as the prevalent means of production.

In 1997, the Australian Bureau of Statistics (ABS 2001) reported that 74 per cent of workers undertook some form of learning at work and that demand for on-the-job training peaked at 20–24 years and subsequently declined with age. On-the-job or structured workplace training has, in the past, generally involved relatively small amounts of time. By contrast, formal education often involves full-time participation over a semester or longer and the likelihood of participation is below 10 per cent beyond age 35. Thus, short-term workplace training may be a more attractive option for workers who want to maintain a competitive edge in their professional expertise – a disposition central to lifelong learning as it ensures continuous up-skilling and knowledge building (Gallagher 2001). Given that changes in organizational processes are regarded as continual, positioning lifelong learning within the structure of work would seem to be imperative.

Recognizing the intensity of uptake of education and training by workers, concepts such as continuous learning have emerged. As this evolved it was evident that in order for continuous learning to become sustainable there had to be a profound shift in how we view learning from the early years and not just during the working years of our lives. The lifelong learning construct was considered broad enough to capture the entire shift necessary to create a learning society rather than just a learning organization (Gallagher 2001). Garrick and Clegg (2001) contend that life-long learning encompasses all workplace learning. It is reasonable to assume that workplaces will increasingly become learning orientated and that such learning will be intentional as well as unintentional or informal. Eraut (2004) argues that informal workplace learning occurs in a variety of settings and takes into account learning from other people and contexts that are purposively formal yet are rarely structured with learning in mind. Further to this, Evans and Kersh (2004) believe the formal and informal learning at work can be interrelated in various ways. While we recognize that this is not a new phenomenon, we contend that it constitutes an important form of learning at work and is therefore a vital component of workplace lifelong learning.

Learning in the workplace is driven by work activities and also results from outcomes of work. This often occurs as organizations seek to expedite work processes and to ensure product quality and increased quantity; it also results from organizational competition. According to Lave and Wenger (1991), who advance the perspective of situated learning, the workplace is an important site for learning and is one in which, for example, novices can progress in a community of practice through co-participation with more experienced others. Barnett (2002) argues that work and learning increasingly overlap in current economic and industrial conditions; this can have distinct advantages. For instance, learning in the workplace can ensure sustained work practices (Billet 2001). Eraut (2004) found that the following four main types of work activity give rise to learning: participation in group activities, working alongside others, tackling challenging tasks and working with clients. Learning as a collective phenomenon where workers learn from others and in groups is also recognized by Hager (2004). He believes that workplace learning incorporates social, cultural and political dimensions. Learning is also embedded in processes such as formal learning, listening, observing, reflecting, practising and refining skills, trial and error, giving and receiving feedback and asking questions. While learning that results from such activities at work may be serendipitous, various processes have been established in workplaces to ensure purposeful and ongoing learning. Eraut (2004) found workers learn from manuals, reference books, documentation, and protocols. It is also apparent that technology, such as Inter- and Intranet, supports learning as does mentoring. While much of the learning that occurs at work involves practical and physical activity, it also involves intellectual activity and conceptualization. It should also be acknowledged that many workers not only experience and participate in learning at work, many also undertake work-related courses within formal institutions. Fuller and Unwin (2003) consider that learning in multiple contexts constitutes an expansive approach to learning.

Workers' conceptions of work and learning at work

Much of the current literature on workplace learning focuses on management and policy makers' perspectives on learning. Our study captures workers' perspectives on learning and work, the integrated nature of the two constructs and implications of this for lifelong learning. In light of the emerging centrality of learning in the workplace and the influence this may have in developing lifelong learning habits for individuals, we investigated workers' conceptions of work and learning at work over a three year period. This study involved two cohorts: over 40 and under 40 years of age (Boulton-Lewis *et al.* 2004; Pillay *et al.* 2003a; Pillay *et al.* 2003b) with 18 from a medical service industry and 19 from a transport/rail industry. Medical service workers included project managers, education officers, administrators and security officers. Transport/rail industry workers included a regional operations manager and railway terminal manager, operations co-ordinators and train drivers. Both organizations had undergone considerable restructuring in recent years and associated with this were policy and cultural changes and new management personnel. While this meant opportunity for workers to develop a wider range of competences and knowledge, it also resulted in downsizing of staff and the loss of some senior managers. The focus of the research was to investigate individual workers' learning throughout their working life. We examine the findings and discuss possible links between individuals' conceptions of learning and work and lifelong learning.

The study adopted a phenomenographically inspired approach and distilled a list of categories from the data, describing each conception which represents the different ways in which people experience a phenomenon, in this case, of learning in the workplace and of work. A conception is explained as being dependent on both human activity and the world that is external to an individual and encompasses 'the meanings and understanding of phenomena' (Svensson 1997: 163; Morgan and Beaty 1997). It assumes that each conception logically subsumes and builds on the conception below it (Richardson 1999) and indicates that the conceptions are relational. For example, workers who were classified at a higher-level conception often also expressed one or more conceptions at a lower level such as work also being a job.

The methodology involved data collection from workers in their workplaces. This not only enhanced understanding of the culture of the workplaces involved but it is an important consideration when conducting a study that is based on qualitative processes. This method contributed to the ecological validity of the study (Burns 2000). The participants were also observed at random periods which allowed construction of a profile of tasks and actions that were performed in each workplace. Information from other sources such as artefacts and documents were also used to help construct an overall picture of the workplaces. Interviews were semi-structured and questions were based on current literature as well as workplace training and learning initiatives. The interviewer probed relevant points as they arose to clarify meaning. Some of the questions that were asked were:

- Tell me about your past work experience including training.
- Describe your job to me.
- What does work mean to you?
- What are the important competencies you need to carry out your job?
- How did you learn these competencies?

The correlation between workers and their conceptions can be seen in studies in epistemology and conceptions of learning which suggest that individuals' beliefs about knowledge and learning influence how they learn (Biggs 1999; Marton 1998; Schommer 1994). Extending the findings of these studies, it can be argued that if workers do not consider learning as part of their conception of work they may fail to adopt an integrated approach to learning and work (Hammer 1994; Pillay *et al.* 1998). Thus, it may be difficult to convince workers to subscribe to the emerging workplace cultures including lifelong learning. We assert, therefore, that the nature of conceptions held by workers will influence how they approach learning within their work and, ultimately, impact on the processes of knowledge creation for themselves, in their organizations, and their involvement in lifelong learning.

The categories of conceptions of work identified in the study are summarized in Table 20.1. Further details including supporting quotes and full descriptions of the categories can be found in Pillay *et al.* (2003b). The four conceptions of work are described and structured hierarchically as follows: *work as a job, work as a challenging experience, work as personally empowering,* and *work as an important part of life.* The hierarchical structure is consistent with other studies (Boulton-Lewis *et al.* 2000; Marton *et al.* 1993) in conceptions.

Table 20.2 presents a summary of conceptions of learning at work: *acquiring skills to survive, on-site observing and experiencing, taking formal courses, a continuous lifelong process* and *changing as a person.* Again we believe there is a hierarchy in the categories with

Table 20.1 Conceptions of work, and variations by older and younger workers

Conception	Key descriptors	Older workers (N)	Younger workers (N)
1 Work as a job	• Focus on money • Sees it as survival • Provides a sense of security • Just something one has to do	18	4
2 Work as a challenging experience	• Experiencing new things • Finding better processes • Willing to accept the challenges of work but not let it impact on personal life	4	3
3 Work as personally empowering	• Opportunity for self development • I can make a difference	12	7
4 Work as an important part of my life	• Part of life experience • Work means everything to me • I define myself by my work • I have a responsibility to achieve my work objectives	5	2
Totals		39	16

Table 20.2 Conceptions of learning at work, and variations by older and younger workers

Conception	Key descriptors	Older workers (N)	Younger workers (N)
1 Acquiring skills to survive	• Learn on a need to know basis • Trial and error • Following set guidelines • Learning just happens without you knowing • Makes my job easier	–	–
2 On-site observing and experiencing	• Nothing beats experience … I started as a cleaner • Get someone to show me one-to-one how to do it • See others and learn • I learn because it's like a hobby	11	6
3 Taking formal courses	• Values formal training such as the Cert IV trainer course • The nexus between theoretical and practical education • Casual introduction to computers made me enrol in formal courses	19	5
4 A continuous lifelong process	• Continuously searching for new information – on and off the job • Take opportunity of slow periods to learn about new equipment • Learning never stops • Self taught • Used to take books home to read	8	5
5 Changing as a person	• Made me an entirely different person • Feeling satisfied and content with the work	1	–
Totals		39	16

acquiring skills to survive as the lowest. This lowest category was held by almost all the workers but was not the sole conception held by any of them.

Learning through the working life

Table 20.3 summarizes the education and training for workers during the third year of the study. It differentiates between older and younger workers and by organization types. The following account details how many undertook personal initiatives to acquire formal qualifications through a Technical and Further Education College (TAFE) or university course, or participated in work-based training. We also include a brief summary of two workers' notable career path and associated learning in each workplace and later we explain some of the obstacles to further study that workers described.

Table 20.3 Age, workplace, and level of education for workers

Age	Workplace	NFQ	WBT	TAFE	Degree
>40	Rail	5	4	2	2
<40	Rail	9	9	–	1
>40	Medical	1	3	1	6
<40	Medical	2	7	2	2

NFQ: No formal qualifications
WBT: On the job, work-based training
TAFE: Technical and Further Education

In the rail industry 14 of the 19 workers had no formal qualifications. Of these, 13 said they had undertaken non-accredited work-based training and five workers combined work-based training with further formal qualifications, two at TAFE and three at university. Two of these five held managerial positions. The progress they made throughout their working life suggests a strong lifelong learning disposition. One of these described his career path beginning from his days as an engine cleaner at 18, to locomotive assistant, driver, line manager and trainer. Along the way he studied for a Bachelor's degree in Natural Science, a university Diploma in Health and Safety and he is currently working towards a Masters degree in corporate management. He also participated in work-based training that included learning about fuel efficiency and computing skills. He stated his preferred approach to learning was observing others at work and he is aware that 'I suppose I'm a lifelong learner'. He was conscious of the changes to work practices occurring around him which he explained as follows:

> Gone are the days when you would jump on a locomotive and drive. Now we are always assessing the information, computer information. Computer skills, they are things I've learned since I joined (rail company).

He also stated that there was a need for 'constantly updating skills'. Essentially, learning, whether it was by means of formal courses, at university or work, had occurred throughout this worker's working life.

In the medical service there were more workers with formal qualifications. Of the 18 workers, eight had at least an initial degree, one had undertaken part of an MBA, two were enrolled in a PhD (one completed), three had TAFE qualifications, most had some work-based training and three had no formal qualifications. One of the managers in the hospital started as a qualified graduate physiotherapist, he went on to do an MBA, and subsequently he obtained a PhD. This worker also participated in on-the-job training and learning from colleagues at work. He explained this as occurring over a large part of his working life when he stated as follows:

I think in the ten years I've been here, I've learnt a different level of knowledge as I've changed jobs. I've gone into a different echelon of demand and learnt a few more things. I think the biggest thing is to meet people and for people to know where I come from, as in how I operate and how they operate [and] the last two years have really strongly been reliant upon my ability to learn in the workplace . . . I see that as a positive because it's real life . . . informal mentors also tend to help you learn on the job.

Learning was associated with life events as well as needing to know information and skills to do his job. This may be attributed to technology infiltrating workplaces as well as tasks that were previously part of specialist sections, such as cost centres, being devolved to managerial levels. He described this as 'life skills and a couple of defining moments and then I think the industry that I work in has actually pushed me too [to learn].'

There seemed to be a general consensus among all workers that methods of training in the workplace had changed over time. One train driver believed that this was due to increased technology as simulators became part of the training process and partially eliminated the prolonged apprenticeship model of learning to drive a train. Another driver felt that training methods were now more efficient as they were more structured compared to the training he experienced as an apprentice. A graduate trainee in the transport company stated that she tried to use the skills she learnt at university in her work: 'while I was at uni. there was no practical experience ; . . but now I go back into the text books . . . now I'm like "Wow" it can be used'. Another transport worker started a degree which she said gave her a basic understanding and motivated her. However, she added that the degree was too long and that she preferred short courses that were offered through private colleges. These findings have implications for training initiatives and continuous and lifelong learning.

Implications for lifelong learning

The results of this study indicate that many of the older and younger workers held conceptions of work and learning at work that are compatible with the notion of lifelong learning. For example, regarding work as *challenging, personally empowering* or *an important part of my life* suggests a willingness to engage in work as well as the processes associated with work to improve one's capacity. Workers also reported feeling a responsibility to achieve work objectives. These traits imply self-direction and an underlying need to increase knowledge about work. Most of the conceptions of learning at work also indicate a willingness by these workers to participate in formal or informal learning. Positive views of work and learning associated with work that these conceptions entail, parallel with De la Harpe and Radloff's (2000) view of a lifelong learner, that is, one who possesses persistence and a positive view of the value of learning.

When considering the older workers' conceptions of work compared to the younger workers' conceptions of work an important distinction is apparent. The lowest conception, *work as a job*, was held by 18 older workers and only four younger workers. As stated earlier, those who mainly regard work as a job may not connect with work-based training or initiatives associated with lifelong learning. Consequently, engaging older workers in training could prove to be a challenge for trainers, institutional course developers and proponents of lifelong learning. In terms of learning at work, observing others seemed to be a commonplace occurrence which has the potential to result in informal learning for these workers. This is an opportunistic and unstructured way to learn at work which has been recognized as still forming part of contemporary workplaces (Eraut 2004; Hager 2004). Garrick and Clegg (2001) explain that informal learning that occurs at work constitutes a part of lifelong learning. In the study reported here, eight older workers and five younger workers acknowledged that for them learning at work is a lifelong process. Further to this, almost half of the workers undertook learning that was associated with work. We believe that this may indicate an emerging trend for workers today.

For about a quarter of the workers in this study, courses at TAFE or university have provided the knowledge and skills for self-fulfilment or advancement. As stated above, many workers had undertaken some form of work-based training and a small number had undertaken formal courses throughout their working lives. The rail worker who indicated that he was in fact a lifelong learner recognized the need to constantly upgrade skills and that the emergence of technology in the workplace was a driving factor (Virkkunen and Pihlaja 2004). The medical worker who participated in formal work-related courses during his working life believed that the industry he worked in encouraged him to do so. McKenzie (1999) maintains that being encouraged to learn is an important part of lifelong learning. This worker recognized the need to be knowledgeable with each change in role he undertook and it is reasonable to argue that he was indeed a knowledge worker (Cormican and O'Sullivan 2003). It was also apparent, however, that becoming a knowledge worker can involve some difficulties.

Some described the difficulties involved in work-related learning as including shift work, heavy workloads, family pressures and the need to acquire the prerequisite skills for further study. We believe that this holds implications for the structure of learning in the workplace and in formal courses. Yet, at the same time, if one-quarter of the sample could manage further formal study against such odds then we suggest that more workers in such industries might also be able to undertake further work-related learning. This holds implications for course developers who need to consider factors such as the availability, structure and content of courses to match workers' abilities, timeframes and other commitments. One worker described her university course as being removed from the workplace while another stated that short courses were preferable. Continual and lifelong learning requires sustained engagement which in turn requires motivation and reinforcement. This study indicated that many workers were motivated and were engaging in learning and, for some, short-term training was the preferred option. This may be because it is readily reinforced in the workplace, which provides motivation for further learning. These findings suggest that universities and work organizations should develop closer ties and incorporate field placement more widely in an effort to bridge the gap between theoretical knowledge and practical work-based knowledge. Additionally, more short-term, on-the-job structured training or the development of flexible short-term courses within the higher education sector would be viable alternatives for workers to participate in work-based lifelong learning.

The increasing workplace-based training and other formal training undertaken by workers in this study suggest a potential market for university and courses within industry. Instead of selling education degrees as a product in themselves there is a potential for designing programmes as ongoing professional development and articulating these with TAFE and other courses. Such an approach would support the lifelong learning aspiration noted by the workers. The findings from our study point to challenges to TAFE and university courses, the advocates of lifelong learning and developers of work-based courses. Curriculum models should allow workers to adapt to new skills and knowledge through continual and lifelong learning. We suggest that these models may need to be introduced early in life to foster a natural acceptance and adaptation to learning.

References

Australian Bureau of Statistics, (2001) *Year Book Australia, Education and Training. Special Article – Education and Training Australia's Workers*, Canberra: Commonwealth Government of Australia (ABS Catalogue number 1301.0).

Australian National Training Authority (1999) *National Marketing Strategy for Skills and Lifelong Learning: Literature Review, Final Report*, Brisbane: ANTA.

Barnett, R. (2002) 'Learning to work and working to learn', in R.Reeve, M. Cartwright and R. Edwards (eds), *Supporting Lifelong Learning*, Vol. 2, London: Routledge Falmer.

Biggs, J. (1999) *Teaching for Quality Learning at University*, Open University Press/SHRE, Buckingham: UK.

Billet, S. (2001) *Learning in the Workplace: Strategies for Effective Practice*, New South Wales: Allen & Unwin.

Boulton-Lewis, G.M., Marton, F., Lewis, D. and Wilss, L.A. (2000) 'Aboriginal and Torres Strait Islander university students' conceptions of formal learning and experiences of informal learning', *Higher Education*, 39: 469–88.

Boulton-Lewis, G.M., Pillay, H., Wilss, L.A. and Rhodes, S. (2004) 'Work, learning and change: older and younger workers', *Lifelong Learning In Europe*, IX, 2: 84–93.

Burns, R.B. (2000) *Introduction to Research Methods*, Frenches Forest, Australia: Pearson Education.

Candy, P., Crebert, G. and O'Leary, J. (1994) *Developing Lifelong Learners through Undergraduate Education* (Report to the NBEET), Canberra: National Board of Employment, Education and Training.

Clarke, N. (2004) 'HRD and the challenges of assessing learning in the workplace', *International Journal of Training and Development*, 8: 140–56.

Cormican, K. and O'Sullivan, D. (2003) 'A collaborative knowledge management tool for product innovation management', *International Journal of Technology Management*, 26: 53–67.

De la Harpe, B. and Radloff, A. (2000) 'Informed teachers and learners: the importance of assessing the characteristics needed for lifelong learning', *Studies in Continuing Education*, 22: 169–82.

Eraut, M. (2004)' Informal learning in the workplace', *Studies in Continuing Education*, 26: 247–73.

Evans, K. and Kersh, N. (2004) 'Recognition of tacit skills and knowledge', *Journal of Workplace Learning*, 16: 63–74.

Fuller, A. and Unwin, L. (2003) 'Learning as apprentices in the contemporary UK workplace: creating and managing expansive and restrictive participation', *Journal of Education and Work*, 16, 4: 407–26.

Gallagher, M. (2001) 'Lifelong learning: demand and supply issues–some questions for research', paper presented at The Business/Higher Education Roundtable Conference, on *The Critical Importance of Lifelong learning*, Sydney, July .

Garrick, J. and Clegg, S. (2001) 'Stressed-out knowledge workers in performative times: a postmodern take on project-based learning', *Management Learning*, 32: 119–34.

Hager, P. (2004) 'Lifelong learning in the workplace? Challenges and issues', *Journal of Workplace Learning*, 16: 22–32.

Hammer, D. (1994) 'Epistemological beliefs in introductory physics', *Cognition and Instruction*, 12: 151–83.

Jentzsch, N. (2001) 'The new economy debate in the U.S: a review of literature', Working Paper, No. 125/2001, April. Freie Universitat Berlin: John F. Kennedy Institute.

Lave, J. and Wenger, E. (1991) *Situated Learning: Legitimate Peripheral Participation*. Cambridge: Cambridge University Press.

Marton, F. (1998) 'Towards a theory of quality in higher education', in B. Dart and G.M. Boulton-Lewis (eds) *Teaching and Learning in Higher Education*, Australian Council for Educational Research, Camberwell: Victoria.

Marton, F., Dall'Alba, G. and Beaty, E. (1993) 'Conceptions of learning', *International Journal of Educational Research*, 19: 277–300.

McKenzie, P. (1999) *How to Make Lifelong Learning a Reality*, Monash University, ACER, Centre for the Economics of Education and Training (CEET) and Australian Council for Educational Research (ACER), Victoria.

Morgan, A. and Beaty, L. (1997) 'The world of the learner', in F. Marton, D. Hounsell and N. Entwistle (eds) *The Experience of Learning: Implications For Teaching and Studying in Higher Education*, Edinburgh: Scottish Academic Press.

OECD (1996) *Lifelong Learning for All*, Paris: OECD Publications.

Peck, B.T. (1996) 'European lifelong learning initiatives', *Phi Delta Kappan*, 77: 645–47.

Pillay, H., Boulton-Lewis, G., Lankshear, C. and Wilss, L.A. (2003a) 'Conceptions of work and learning at work: impressions from older workers', *Studies in Continuing Education*, 25: 95–11.

Pillay, H., Boulton-Lewis, G., Wilss, L.A. and Rhodes, S. (2003b) 'Older and younger workers' conceptions of work and learning at work', *Journal of Education and Work*, 16: 427–45.

Pillay, H., Brownlee, J. and McCrindle, A. (1998) 'The individuals' beliefs about learning and nature of knowledge on educating an intelligent workforce', *Journal of Education and Work*, 11: 239–54.

Richardson, J.T. (1999) 'The concepts and methods of phenomenographic research', *Review of Educational Research*, 69: 53–82.

Schommer, M.A. (1994) 'Synthesising epistemological belief research: tentative understandings and provocative confusions', *Educational Psychology Review*, 6: 293–317.

Svensson, L. (1997) 'Theoretical foundations of phenomenography', *Higher Education Research and Development*, 16: 159–71.

Takeuchi, H. (1998) *Beyond knowledge management: Lessons from Japan*. Online. Available at http://www.sveiby.com/articles/LessonsJapan.htm (accessed 10 July 2002).

Virkkunen, J. and Pihlaja, J. (2004) 'Distributed systems of generalizing as the basis of workplace learning', *Journal of Workplace Learning*, 16: 33–43.

Chapter 21

Making a space for adult education in mental health

The Outlook Project experience

Fiona Dowie and Matthew Gibson

People with mental health problems are the learners at the focus of the Outlook Project's brief to provide educational opportunities for this marginalized group. Drawing on the experience of the disability movement the authors argue that care in the community for people with mental health problems is not so easily achieved without structures and attitudes in communities changing too. In addition, the attitudes of mental health service users and the professionals that work with them also have to be challenged. Negotiating a space between different professional interests is a necessary and difficult process but essential if adult educators are to help students regain some degree of autonomy and control over their everyday lives.

Introduction

Our treatment of people with mental health problems has changed dramatically and no more so than in the last fifty years. Historically, the 'ship of fools' (Foucault 1967) took the insane to far away shores, later asylums separated criminals from the insane for the first time and, more recently, the introduction of psychiatric drugs in the 1950s meant that patients no longer needed to be incarcerated within large institutions (Barham 1992). New day hospitals enabled treatment in the community and legislation was delivered over the following forty years which paved the way for 'community care'.

By the 1990s it was apparent that the quality of care offered to people moved into the community from hospitals was inadequate. The former Health Minister, Frank Dobson, announced that the system had failed and that stigmatization had led to under-resourcing of services. The small number of largely unsupported people living in the community who were deemed a danger to themselves and others had led to a crisis of confidence in the system. A revision of community care policy and increased funding were pledged (BBC 1999). Although many people working in this policy context recognized the failings of the system, especially the lack of resources, they were also aware that new opportunities had arisen for a large number of people who had previously been silenced and segregated. There were voices to be heard and experiences to be shared.

What are the community care experiences of people who use mental health services? Have recent developments in mental health and disability legislation empowered them? More fundamentally, have attitudes changed as dramatically as the institutions? What of the role of adult education in engaging with this socially isolated and stigmatized section of society? This chapter will address these questions by locating mental health work in the current policy discourse on disability; it will then discuss the work of the Outlook Project and examine opportunities for educational engagement. First, we would like to present two cameos of experiences of living with mental health problems in the community and make connections with wider social structures and influences.

The following cases are intended to illustrate the human experience of community care – they are not particularly dramatic but, in our view, they illustrate the everyday nature of people's lives we encounter. Bob and Kirsten are composite representations of real cases.

Bob's case

Bob had been admitted to hospital suffering from depression. He became a patient at a day hospital which offered therapeutic groups, treatments and activities designed to equip him to live independently in the community. After discharge from the day hospital, his contact with other people was reduced and he found it difficult to maintain a structure to his life. At 55, Bob found the prospect of work, training and education daunting. The voluntary organizations offering these services were unable to provide the medical and emotional support he needed. Shattered confidence and fear of exposure led him to avoid these opportunities. The stigma associated with mental health within the community and in the media impacted on his daily life. Bob's social contact was mostly with professional workers. Before his illness, he had been a successful professional in his field. His new status as a patient entitled him to prescribed levels of care but support into education or employment was limited and the learning and work environments were rigid and lacking in understanding.

Kirsten's case

At 39, Kirsten was living in her own flat and had strong social networks in place. As a teenager she had experienced some periods of hospitalization. Over the years, Kirsten tried to access employment and further education but found limited support and understanding in either of these settings. She joined a few community groups and studied short-term adult education classes. She also did some voluntary work for a local charity. Although she enjoyed the courses and received certificates for them, she felt they were of value to nobody but herself, leading to nothing further. Her main motivation for study was to meet people and to learn new things.

Care in the community?

It could be argued that both Bob's and Kirsten's experiences reflected deficits in their character or abilities. This would, however, be misleading because it ignores the rigidity of institutional provision and the reality of the working environment. The market economy continues to push education providers to operate as businesses where courses can be 'purchased'. In a context of limited support, understanding and flexibility, students who have mental health problems are more likely to drop out and be left with a sense of personal failure. Very few repeat the experience or complain to the institution and so the process continues unchallenged.

Bob's experience of stigma increased his sense of social isolation, reinforcing feelings of shame and guilt. Language is a powerful tool that can assist oppression and the widespread use of mental health terminology in the media ranges from informative and descriptive to offensive, scare-mongering and demonizing. It is useful to think of this in terms of the process of hegemony which filters dominant values that in turn marginalize individuals and groups who do not fit into the dominant paradigm of 'normality' in society. The 'spontaneous consent of the masses' (Gramsci 1971) is in fact the result of a process that favours dominant social groups and their cultural practices, and one way this occurs powerfully is through media representations of the mentally ill.

Research by The Glasgow Media Group (Philo 1996) into press and television treatment of mental health showed that headlines relating to it tended to be those involving violence. Forty per cent of those interviewed linked mental health with violence and cited the media as the source of their beliefs.

> We have shown here that the media images which stigmatize mental illness can also have a persuasive and damaging effect on users of services and on their immediate social relationships ... Our research also has implications for social policy. There is such a climate of ignorance and fear around the subject of mental illness that policy initiatives such as community care must be accompanied by a major information campaign to challenge dominant images and beliefs.
>
> (Philo 1996: 112)

If the 'community' people enter into holds such prejudices we need to ask what does it mean to be 'in the community'? Simply leaving a hospital behind does not necessarily enable people to regain control of their own lives. It does not ensure equal access to opportunities or challenge discrimination and stigma. Assumptions are made about the caring nature of the 'community', but community is a problematic term that can hide more than it reveals. Community can include inequalities of power and processes of exclusion as much as inclusion. A process of 'integration' into communities where attitudes are not challenged can lead to people being isolated, stigmatized, marginalized and abused. What is the role of adult education in this context? How should we engage with people educationally to extend their autonomy and control, individually and collectively?

Understanding mental health as a disability

The Disability Discrimination Act (DDA) describes the meaning of disability and includes people with severe and enduring mental health problems.

> a person has a disability for the purposes of this Act if he has a physical or mental impairment which has a substantial and long-term effect on his ability to carry out normal day-to-day activities.
>
> (HMSO 1995: Chapter 50, Part 1, Section 1-(1), Page 1)

The inclusion of mental health, which had been formally outside the definition of disability, is useful because it gives a status and recognition to this area of work. How disability is interpreted is, however, the key issue and the distinction between the medical and social model of disability illuminates the significance of this point.

The medical model (Oliver 1993) indicates the way in which 'professionals' can take responsibility and power away from the individual and limit their ability to make choices because of the way services process people. The experience of the disability movement has been particularly useful in highlighting links between the personal experience of disabled people and the structural oppressions of

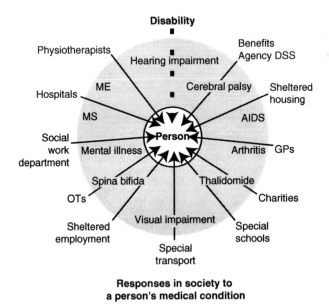

Figure 21.1 Medical model of disability

society. If educators are to avoid replicating similar roles and processes then they need to make their purpose explicit. If not, duties may be transferred from the 'professional' in the institution to the 'professional in the community without changing the power relationship' (Finkelstein 1993: 15).

Oliver suggests that:

> organizations run by non-disabled people ... operate within a framework which assumes that disabled people cannot take control of their own lives [and that] people who run organizations for rather than of disabled people operate within the medical rather than the social model of disability which locates the problems faced by disabled people within the individual rather than being contingent upon social organization.
>
> (Oliver 1990: 114)

In contrast, the social model of disability (Oliver 1983, Figure 21.2 below) developed by UPIAS (The Union of the Physically Impaired Against Segregation (1976) identifies links between the structural oppressions of society and the individual experiences of disability. This model challenges the educator to look at the barriers to engagement in education. Defining society rather than the individual as 'disabled' and therefore problematic is a useful starting point for looking at how disabled people are discriminated against.

Figure 21.2 Social model of disability

The social model highlights the need for educators to challenge disempowering professional practice and discrimination in society in order to build a framework of provision which is inclusive. This process is not easy and includes challenging the attitudes and values of workers, institutions and fellow learners. We now turn to look at our experience at Outlook to learn from it.

The Outlook Project

The Outlook Project began in 1991 in response to community care legislation. It was recognized that the educational needs of mental health service users who were moved from institutions into the community were not being met. Outlook was to provide a 'stepping-stone' into existing educational provision, creating an understanding and supportive environment for such individuals. Outlook students could access free courses and services and experiment with a range of subjects, building both skills and confidence in group settings. The project could also provide a means for people to express their learning needs within Outlook and, through the project, to other learning providers. The context in which Outlook operates includes psychiatric services, social work and education, which creates both tensions and opportunities in our work (see Table 21.1).

The policy context in relation to mental health is one of the closing of institutions, bed reduction in hospitals and a move towards community-based mental health provision. The adult education context is underpinned by the contested concepts and policies of lifelong learning, active citizenship and social inclusion; with an emphasis on creating opportunities for people to engage in employment-orientated, individualized activities. These activities can be seen to develop skills and knowledge and encourage individuals to play a greater role in society, developing their social capital and becoming economically active in their community.

If, however, the mainstream in which people are to be socially included remains rigid and inflexible, marginalized groups will remain excluded. With social inclusion policies in place, there is a danger that excluded groups will be perceived as choosing not to participate or that non-participation is the result of individual deficits. Both medical and educational professionals identify the student/learner as an individual and tend to ignore the collective dimension in the learning experience. Within this context, the Outlook Project creates a space for educational engagement for people who continue to use mental health services or who have finished treatment and use Outlook as a step towards rebuilding their lives.

Our initial engagement with individuals is often through health or social workers who have responsibilities for their care, treatment and risk assessment. Outlook is a voluntary option with a clear educational purpose and extensive negotiation with professionals from these fields is necessary to make this purpose clear. Our priority is to enable students to express their educational desires, free from the confines and limitations of assumed capabilities and their diagnosis and identity as a patient. Sayce asks us to examine our agendas as workers and be

Table 21.1 Outlook and other service providers

Service	Psychiatric services	Social work	Education providers	Outlook project
Identity of client	Person as patient with psychiatric illness.	Person as individual with a range of social difficulties.	Person as individual with specific support needs and possible separate provision.	Person as student with a range of educational interests facing barriers to this process.
Power structure	Diagnosis; medication; medical records; hospital provision; cut patient provision; substantial intervention in people's lives.	Legal requirements for treatment and detention under Mental Health legislation. Care plans.	Exclusive or separate provision; inflexible curriculum; limited support and training for staff.	Prior knowledge of the student's use of mental health services; negotiation; progression; voluntary option; student Forum.
Tensions (opportunities/constraints)	Changes to day care services and move to community based provision; referral system; medical information; support; judgements on capabilities; institutionalization.	Care plans v. voluntary options; support role; legal responsibilities; heavy case loads.	'Inclusive' rhetoric; relevant training; mainstream provision; 'communities of interest' and separate provision; limited input into joint planning processes; health promotion.	Pressure to 'track' students and provide statistics on progression; insecure funding; add-on provision; responsibility for all mental health work; mainstream or exclusive education providers; commitment to inclusive education.

aware that 'professional attempts to steer people away from their goals can result in them feeling unheard' (2000: 234). We need to challenge professional tribalism, not least in our own discipline, to create a culture in which the voices of our students are central.

Shifting identities: patients and citizens

Adult education is ambivalent in that it can be either a system for reproducing inequalities and discrimination or a means of challenging them. In our particular area of work it might be seen as a form of 'soft' therapy or it can be used as a tool in the process of changing and challenging inequalities of power. In order to make this choice we need to be clear about our purpose, the roles we adopt and the limits on what we can do. Outlook workers have no medical training and do not dabble in diagnosis or cure. We cannot offer an alternative to psychiatric treatment but neither do we have to subscribe to its model and assumptions as unproblematic. We cannot offer emotional support to students, nor try to fill the role of counsellor or therapist. This would be potentially dangerous and unsafe for all concerned.

Our work is informed by the radical tradition of adult education which views its purpose as the pursuit of freedom and democracy, the discovery of identity, and ultimately the ability to act against the oppression of the dominant hegemonic forces in society (Thompson 1980). From this position, the role of adult educators is to ally themselves with people using mental health services and to provide them with opportunities to renegotiate a degree of autonomy and control over their lives in areas where it has been missing. This exploration involves identifying and transforming power relationships. It is an 'adult education of engagement' (Jackson 1995) that means a shift from patients as passive recipients of services to students as critical and active participants. In this context it is about regaining (or acquiring for the first time) a voice.

> Voice provides a critical referent for analyzing how people are made voiceless in particular settings by not being allowed to speak, or being allowed to say what has already been spoken, and how they learn to silence themselves.
> (Aronowitz and Giroux 1991: 110)

This is not a linear process and some people remain patients for the rest of their lives. They may, however, through the exploration of their potential to be active citizens, move from a place of enforced silence to a place of apparent voice.

The experience of the disability movement can inform this process for users of mental health services. Patients can experience almost complete disempowerment from the moment they come into contact with the psychiatric system. This experience resonates with that of disabled people as described by Barton (1996). The voice of the patient is rarely heard. Complaints are often dismissed as merely the patient's perception of events. This reinforcement of the invalidity of voice due to diagnosis can eventually lead to silence.

> A significant feature of this oppression of disabled people is the way in which their voice has been totally excluded both from decisions affecting their own lives and from the wider political arena.
>
> (Barton 1996: 179)

To the student, engagement with another profession can involve making the same assumptions about the process involved. In a medical setting the voice of the professional is usually dominant. It is important, therefore, to make the distinctive nature of the adult education setting clear to the student. In our experience the initial task is to value the educational possibilities of the users' experiences and to create learning opportunities which reinforce the democratic nature of adult learning. One of the roles of adult education is to re-connect to the power that lies within people, a process which can be liberating for many, for example, by having a voice in creating course curricula.

Supporting the voice of students may also involve challenging their expectations about educational settings and the role they have. Prior engagement with medical professionals may have required individuals to passively impart detailed personal information on a regular basis. As symptoms and medication have become the facets of their identity most inquired after, students may expect to be asked to discuss this information in educational groups. This reinforces a circular process of unequal power relations and to break through this process adult educators need to consciously and overtly give power back to students as a first principle. This is problematic as many students may find it less challenging to remain passive and to be 'taught' by the expert. Most of their engagement with professionals, both medical and other, will place them in the role of passive recipients of intervention. This context means that they will be receiving contradictory messages in different parts of their lives as they move between the closed medical/support environment and the more open educational/learning environment.

In Outlook we start with students on the basis that their engagement is voluntary and we offer an adult education service. We begin with an initial guidance session, designed to encourage the student to bring his or her desires and experiences to the project. Suggestions and ideas may form the basis of future courses or the student may be given information on existing providers. Project workers will discuss barriers to participation and educational support needs. The most appropriate action is then negotiated with the student. Educational guidance is an ongoing process where students' changing interests and new ideas inform the programme offered. All Outlook courses are run in community settings. This familiarizes students with venues, making links to other providers which students may want eventually to progress on to and enabling engagement with other activity in the community. Figure 21.3 (below) details a range of elements in the process that can enable participants to determine their identity. This process is an iterative one that is never finished. It is also necessary to re-build boundaries which have been eroded through earlier experiences. Once it is established that students are not expected to discuss their health and that the focus of groups is on subjects and learning, it becomes easier to adopt the identity of student rather than patient. Initial guidance enables students also to discuss relevant support needs and mechanisms for identifying services Outlook is unable to offer e.g. home visits or accompanying to classes.

We cannot, however, ignore the fact that as people move between the educational environment of Outlook and the mental health environment, life histories follow them from professional to professional. The process can involve progress and regress. Nevertheless, it is our experience that democratic discussion and decision making can enable people whose opinions may not have been valued or given credence, an opportunity to develop their voice both individually and collectively. Over time this can enable individuals to regain a sense of their own identity, confidence and voice. This happens in different ways and on many levels including involvement with constituted groups, discussion-based courses, our Student Forum representing the student body, video and other awareness-raising tools, employment, extended learning and eventually leaving Outlook behind. This is not always a straight, even path and there are always opportunities for students to access psychiatric services when necessary.

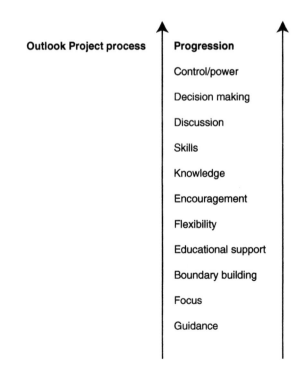

Figure 21.3 Shifting identity: from patient to student

The process depicted above is neither straightforward nor rapid. People who use mental health services are constantly moving between different worlds where they are regarded differently. Redefining identity is complex and difficult, and consequently the process is an ongoing one that involves students acquiring multiple identities.

Conclusion

Amongst the issues we face is the conflict of views of the purpose of education, both from educators and from health professionals. There is a view that working amongst this excluded group is a specialist field, despite the prevalence of people with mental health issues in the population (one in four in Scotland) (Scottish Association of Mental Health). This is multiplied amongst particular groups when poverty, ethnicity, unemployment and gender are factored in. There is also the lack of personal barriers of students coming from an experience of professionals having unfettered access to medical histories. There is the issue of short-term uncertain funding of provision which does little to assist forward curriculum planning and organizational limitations in sharing power with students in a local authority provision. We also need to be critical of 'mainstream' adult education provision and challenge its exclusive nature, rather than channelling people into it, potentially setting them up to fail.

Education is about changing lives. When this is the basis for our work then the outcome of this should be seen not only in the learning group, but also in the wider context of people's lives. Clearly linking personal experience to the wider public arena begins a process of politicization where students begin to think critically about the actions which are taken in relation to themselves. We would contend that the role of adult education in this context is to create the space for people to build a secure identity, find their voice and talk back to power.

References

Aronowitz, S. and Giroux, H. (1991) *Postmodern Education*, Minneapolis, Minnesota: University of Minnesota Press.

Barham, P. (1992) *Closing the Asylum. The Mental Patient in Modern Society*, Harmondsworth: Penguin Books.

Barton, L. (1996) 'Citizenship and disabled people – a case for concern', in J. Demaine and H. Entwistle (eds) *Beyond Communitarianism: Citizenship, Politics and Education*, Basingstoke: Macmillan.

BBC (1999) '£510m boost for mental health care', www.news.bbc.co.uk/1/hi/health/22945.stm, 13 October.

Finkelstein, V. (1993) 'The commonality of disability', in J. Swain, V. Finkelstein, S. French and M. Oliver (eds) *Disabling Barriers – Enabling Environments*, London: Sage and Open University Press.

Foucault, M. (1967) *A History of Insanity in the Age of Reason*, London: Tavistock Publications.

Gramsci A. (1971) *Selections from Prison Notebooks*, London: Lawrence and Wishart.

HMSO (1995) *Disability Discrimination Act 1995*, Norwich: The Stationery Office.

Jackson, K. (1995) 'Popular education and the state: a new look at the community debate', in M. Mayo and J. Thompson (eds) *Adult Learning, Critical Intelligence and Social Change*, Leicester: NIACE.

Oliver. M, (1983) *Social Work with Disabled People*, Basingstoke: MacMillan.

Oliver. M, (1990) *The Politics of Disablement*, Basingstoke: MacMillan.

Oliver. M, (1993) '"Conductive Education": If it wasn't so sad it would be funny', in J. Swain, V. Finkelstein, S. French and M. Oliver (eds) *Disabling Barriers – Enabling Environments*, London: Sage.

Philo, G. (1996) *The Media and Mental Distress*, Essex: Longman Limited.

SAMH 'What are Mental Health Problems?', www.samh.org.uk.

Sayce, L. (2000) *From Psychiatric Patient to Citizen: Overcoming Discrimination and Social Exclusion*, Basingstoke: MacMillan Press.

Thompson, J. (1980) *Adult Education for a Change*, London: Hutchinson.

UPIAS (1976) *Fundamental Principals of Disability*, London: The Union of the Physically Impaired Against Segregation.

Index

Adam, B. and van Loon, J. 61, 66
Adams, F. and Horton, M. 52, 56
Adorno, T. W. 48
Altheit, P. and Dausien, B. 39, 47
Alvarez, S. 208, 216
Appleby, Y. viii, 9, 196–206
Archer, D. and Cottingham, S. 215, 216
Archer, L. 82
Arlin, P. K. 128, 129, 137
Aronowtiz, S. and Giroux, H. 237, 240
Arter, P. 131, 132
Aspy, D. and Roebuck, F. N. 97, 106

Baker, C. and Freebody, P. 140, 145
Ballard, B. and Clanchy, J. 143, 145
Ball, S. 163, 168
Baltes, P. and Brian, O. G. 137
Bamber, J. viii, 7, 82–93
Bamber, J. et al. 82, 92
Bamber, J. and Tett, L. 82, 92
Bandura, A. 148–9, 156
Bardsley, M. et al. 44, 47
Barham, P. 230, 240
Barnett, R. 227
Bar-On, R. 120, 124, 125
Barton, D. and Hamilton, M. 197, 205
Barton, L. 237–8, 240
Baudrillard, J. 216
Baumann, Z. 66, 175, 180
Baxter-Magolda, M. B. 129, 137
Beck, U. 41, 47
Belenky, M. F. et al. 33, 38, 129, 137
Bennett-Goleman, T. 33–4, 38
Bernstein, R. J. 48, 56
Biggs, J. 8, 83, 92, 93, 110, 115, 127–8,
    130–6, 137
Biggs, J. and Collis, K. E. 129, 137

Biggs, J. et al. 110, 115
Billet, S. 220, 227
Blaxter, L. 116, 125
Bloom, B. 97
Boal, A. 52, 56
Bolman, L. and Deal, T. 212
Boud, D. 21, 22
Boughey, C. viii, 8, 138–45
Boulton-Lewis, G. M. viii, 9, 129, 131–3,
    135–7
Boulton-Lewis, G. M. et al. 221–2, 227
Bourdieu, P. and Waquant, L. 162–3
Bourgeois, E. et al. 71, 73–5, 80–1
Boyd, R. 35, 38
Brandt, T. and Clinton, K. 198, 205
Brookfield, S. 18, 22, 30–31, 36, 38, 55–6,
    85, 93
Buiys, J. 201, 205
Burbules, N. and Burk, R. 30, 38
Burns, R. B. 221, 227
Burton-Jones, A. 209, 216
Bynner, J. and Parsons, S. 198, 205

Candy, P. et al. 76–7, 81, 218, 227
Cassazza, M. ix, 8, 146–57
Cassazza, M. and Silverman, S. 146, 156
Castells, M. 174, 176, 180
Chambers, R. 52, 56, 215, 216
Clarke, J. 198, 206
Clarke, N. 219, 227
Coffield, F. 4, 10, 41, 47, 202, 206
Collins, M. 51, 55, 56
Commins, M. L. et al. 18, 22
Connolly, B. 49, 55
Cooper, D. and Subovsky, G. 76, 81
Cormican, K. and O'Sullivan, D. 219, 226
Coule, C. 49, 56

Cranton, P. 34–35, 38
Crowther, J. ix, 3–4, 9–10, 71, 81, 168, 169, 171–81
Crowther, J. *et al.* 10, 52

Davenport, J. 15, 22
De Keyser, L. 175, 180
De la Harpe, B. and Radloff, A. 225, 228
Delphy, C. and Leonard, D. 161, 169
Dewey, J. 207, 209, 216
Dickie, J. 179, 180
Dirkx, J. 35, 38
Doring, A. *et al.* 153, 156
Dowie, F. ix, 9
Dowie, F. and Gibson, M. 230–41
Duffy, K, and Scott, A. 49, 56
Dunlop, C. and Nesbit, T. 73, 81
Durkheim, E. 64, 99
Dweck, C. and Sorich, L. A. 95, 99, 101, 106

Eccles, J. 118, 125
Edwards, R. ix, xiii, 7, 10
Edwards, R. and Usher, R. 58–67, 62, 67
Ekstromm, D. and Sigundsson, H. 49, 56
Elias, D. 35, 38
Elliott, E. S. and Dweck, C. 151, 156
Ellsworth, E. 57, 67
Entwistle, N. 141, 145
Entwistle, N. and Ramsden, P. 109–10, 114–15
Eraut, M. 220, 226, 228
Erikson, E. 17, 22
Evans, K. and Kersh, N. 220, 228
Evison, R. x, 8, 22, 94–107
Evison, R. and Horobin, R. 96, 106
Evison, R. and Ronaldson, J. B. 98, 106
Ewert, G. D. 49, 54, 56
Eyerman, R. and Jamieson J. 171, 174, 178, 180

Featherstone, M. 58, 67
Fenwick, T. 46, 47
Field, J. 40–1, 47, 59, 67
Field, J. and Leicester, M. 22
Fine, B. and Green, F. 165, 169
Finger, M. 173, 177, 180
Fingerette, H. 24
Finkelstein, V. 234, 240
Flavell, J. 18, 22
Flecha, R. 52
Fleming, T, x, 7

Foley, G. 171, 173, 180, 208, 212, 217
Foucault, M. 49, 62, 64, 67, 230, 240
Fraser, N. and Horneth, A. 169
Freire, P. 24, 31, 36, 52, 207, 209, 210, 216, 217
Frosh, F. 46, 47
Fry, W. F. 103, 106
Fuller, A. and Unwin, L. 220, 228
Furedi, F. 40, 47

Gallacher, M. 219, 220, 228
Galloway, V. 213, 217
Gamarnikow, E. and Green, A. 165, 169
Gardner, H. 118, 125
Garnick, J. and Clegg, S. 218, 220, 226, 228
Gee, J. P. 139, 142, 145
Geisler, C. 140–1, 145
Gergen, K. J. 16, 22
Gewirtz, S. 166, 169
Gibbs, G. and Coffey, M. 115
Gibson, M. x, 9
Giddens, A. 40, 47
Gilchrist, R. *et al.* 84, 93
Gilroy, P. 175, 180
Gogtay, N. *et al.* 18, 23
Goleman, D. 8, 10, 118, 119, 125
Goodwin, T. x, 8, 117, 125
Goodwin, T. and Hallam, S. 117–26
Gould, R. 24, 33, 38
Gramsci, A. 56, 178, 180, 207, 210, 232, 241
Gray, D. 83, 93
Greeson, L. E. 113, 115
Griffin, C. 6, 10

Habermas, J. 7, 24–5, 39, 38, 48–57
Hadfield, M. and Haw, K. 167, 169
Hager, P. 220, 228
Hall, S. 216, 217
Hallam, S. xi, 8
Hamilton, M. xi, 9, 196–206
Hammer, D. 222, 228
Harris, C. 49, 56
Hart, M. 212, 217
Hartree, A. 15, 22
Harvey, D. 58, 67
Heath, S. B. 139–40, 145
Heap, J. 140, 145
Hoare, Q. and Smith, G. 210
Holford, J. 171, 180
Holland, D. and Lave, J. 204, 206

Holst, J. and 172, 181, 217
Holt, J. 96, 106
Herriot, P. *et al*. 103, 106
Hope, A. and Timmell, C. 42, 56, 211, 217
Horkheimer, M. 56
Horkheimer, M. and Adorno, T. W. 49, 50, 57
Hull, G. and Schultz, K. 197, 205, 206
Hutchings, M. and Archer, L. 84, 93

Illleris, K. xi, 7, 15–23
Illich, I. 207, 209–10
Imel, S. 208, 217

Jackson, K. A. 237, 241
Jackson, S. 163, 169
Jentzsch, N. 219, 228
Johnson, M. 104, 106
Johnson, R. 176, 180
Johnston, R. 171, 180
Jones, C. 214, 217
Jones, K 295, 206
Jung, G. 34–5

Kane, L. 171, 180
Kant, I. 48
Kegan, R. 32–3, 38
Kember, D. and Gow, L. 113, 115
Kilgore, D. 172, 181
King, P. and Kitchener, K. 28, 33, 38
Kintansas, A. and Zimmerman, B. J. 152
Kirby, A. 102–3, 106
Klein, M. 46
Klein, N. 176, 181
Knowles, M. 15, 23, 210, 217
Koestner, R. and McClelland, D. C. 118, 125
Kohn, A. 97, 99, 106
Kolb, D. 85, 87, 93
Kovan, J. and Dirkx, J. 177, 181
Kuhn, T. 24

Labouvie-Vief, G. 128, 130
Lather, P. 216, 217
Latour, B. 198, 206
La Valle, I. and Blake, M. 117, 126
Lave, J. and Wenger, E. 16, 23, 220, 228
Law, J. 198, 206
Lazarus, R. S. 120, 126
Lea, M. and Street, B. V. 140–1, 145
LeDoux, J. 119, 126

Ledwith, M. 210, 217
Lefebre, H. 208, 216, 217
Lemert, C. 58, 67
Lillis, M. T. 83, 92, 93
Lindblom-Ylanne, S. *et al*. 114, 115
Locke, E. A. and Latham, G. P. 148, 151
Longworth, N. xi, 9, 182–95
Longworth, N. and Davies, W.K. 185
Lyotard, J. F. 59–65, 67

McGivney, V. 116, 126
McKenzie, P. 219, 226, 228
McWilliams, E. 64, 67
Marcus, G. E. 198, 206
Markus, H. and Ruvolo, A. 118, 126
Martin, E. and Balla, M. 111, 116
Martin, H. and McCormack, C. 174, 181
Martin, I. 3, 6, 11, 171, 181
Martin, R. J. 105, 106
Martinez, P. and Munday, F. 116, 126
Marton, F. 109, 116, 222, 228
Marton, F. and Booth, S. 109, 116
Marton, F. and Saljo, R. 110, 116
Marton, F. *et al*. 111, 116, 222, 228
Marx, K. 49, 51, 55–6, 161, 169, 178, 216
Maslow, A. 211, 217
Matuštík, M. B. 48, 56
Mayer, J. D. and Salovey, P. 118, 126
Mayer, J. D. *et al*. 120, 126
Mayo, P. 210, 217
Meade, R. and O'Donovan, R. 175, 181
Mediatore, S. S. 201, 206
Mehan, H. 140
Merriam, S. and Caffarella, R. S. 130
Metfessel, N. S. *et al*. 97, 106
Meyer, J. 86, 93
Mezirow, J. xi, 7, 24–38, 48, 49, 52, 53, 54, 55, 57, 173
Mezirow, J. and Associates 36, 38, 53, 57
Moll, L. 202, 206
Mooney, G. 167, 169
Moore, N. 176, 181
Morgan, A. and Beaty, L. 228
Morrow, W. 145
Morrow, R. A. and Torres, C. A. 49, 56
Murphy, M. xi, 7
Murray, C. 166, 169
Murray, H. A. 118, 126

Nashashabi, P. 162, 169
Newman, M. 173, 181
Nichols, M. 86, 93

Nietzsche, F. 60
Niks, M *et al.* 201, 206
Norris, S. P. 131, 137
Nyhan, B. *et al.* 195

O'Donnell, D. 49, 57
Oliver, M. 179, 181
Osborne, M. *et al.* 189, 195
O'Sullivan, E. *et al.* 31, 38

Padmore, S. 203, 206
Parsons, T. 49
Pascual-Leone, J. 128, 129, 137
Peck, B. T. 218, 228
Perry, W. G. 129
Peters, J. 36
Peters, M. 209, 217
Philo, G. 232, 241
Phnuyal, B. 215, 217
Piaget, J. 8, 18, 127–9, 133–7
Pillay, H. xii, 9
Pillay, H. *et al.* 218–29
Pintrich, P. R. 149, 156
Pitt, K. 199, 206
Plato 184, 195
Plewis, I. and Preston, J. 162, 169
Plumb, D. 55, 57
Porges, S. W. 94, 107
Pressley, M. 152, 156
Preston, J. xii, 9, 161–70
Proulx, J. 214, 217
Purcell, R. xii, 9, 207–17

Rackham, N. and Morgan, T. 98, 106
Raelin 83
Ramsden, P. 132, 137
Reason, P. 83, 86, 93
Revans, W. R. 87, 93
Richardson, J.T. 207–17
Riegel, K. 128–9, 132, 137
Rikowski, G. 65, 67
Rogers, A. 15, 23
Rogers, A. and Illeris, K. 15, 23
Rogers, C. 210, 217
Ronaldson, J. E. and Evison, R. 98, 107
Rorty, R. 55–6
Rose, J. 167, 169
Rossiter, M. 83, 91, 93
Rudnick, P. 176, 181
Ryan, J. 49, 56

Salovey, P. and Mayer, J. D. 118, 124, 126
Samuelowicz, K. and Bain, J. D. 111, 116
Samuels, A. 43, 47
Sato, C. 199, 206
Saxena, M. 204, 206
Sayce, L. 235, 237, 241
Scheff, T. J. 94, 99, 107
Schommer, M. A. 221, 228
Schon, D. A. 85, 93
Schuetze, H. G. and Slowey, M. 75, 81
Schuetze, H. G. and Wolter, A. 84, 93
Schuller, T. *et al.* 206
Schunk, D. H. 147–8, 156
Schunk, D. H. and Schwartz, C.W. 151
Schutte, N. S. *et al.* 120, 126
Seeley Brown, J. S. and Duguid, P. 83, 93
Senge, P. 212, 217
Sennett, R. 40, 47
Shayer, M. and Adey, P. 18, 23
Shayer, M. and Wylan, H. 128, 137
Sheehy, M. 211, 217
Siegal, H. 24, 34, 38
Silverman, S. vii
Simpson, M. L. and Nist, S. L. 153
Sims, L. and Woodrow, M. 92, 93
Skeggs, B. 162–3, 167–8, 170
Skocpol, T. and Fiorina, M. 167, 169
Slaski, M. and Cartwright, S. 120
Socrates 30
Sroufe, L. A. 101, 107
Stanley, L. 41, 47
Steele, C. M. *et al.* 103, 107
Street, B. V. 145, 197, 206
Stroanch, I. and MacLure, M. 62, 66, 67
Sumner, J. 49, 56
Sutherland, P. xii, 4, 8, 11, 18, 127–30,
    132, 134–5, 137
Svensson, L. 221, 229

Takeuchi, H. 219, 229
Talbot, G. 153, 157
Taylor, M. 207, 217
Taylor, R. *et al.* 72, 81
Tett, L. 82, 93
Thompson, E. 101
Thompson, J. 165, 167, 170, 175, 181,
    237, 241
Thorndike, E. L. 118, 126
Thorpe, M. *et al.* 22
Tobias, R. 168, 170
Torbert, W. 83, 86, 90
Touraine, A.174

Treleaven, L. 83, 90, 92, 93
Trigwell, K. xii, 8, 108–16, 114
Trigwell, K. *et al.* 109, 112, 116
Trigwell, K. and Prosser, M. 111–12, 114, 116
Trigwell, K. Prosser, M. and Taylor, P. 111, 116
Trigwell, K. and Richardson, J. T. E. 110, 116
Tuckman, B. and Jensen, N. 105, 107
Tusting, K. 205, 206

Usher, R. viii, xiii, 7, 10,
Usher, R. and Edwards, R. 58–67
Usher, R. *et al.* 67, 177, 181

van Etten, S. *et al.* 151, 156
van Rossum, E. J. and Schenk, S. M. 111, 116
Varela, F. J. *et al.* 100, 107
Villa, D. 30, 38
Virkkunen, J. and Pihlaja, J. 226, 229
Volbrecht, T. 79, 81
Volbrecht, T. and Walters, S. 72–3, 81

Walters, S. xiii, 71–81, 83
Walters, S. and Etkind, R. 78, 81
Wang, C. 212, 217

Warkentin, R. W. and Bol, L. 152, 156
Watters, K. 162, 170
Weber, M. 49, 50, 64, 208, 217
Weiner, B. 118, 126
Welton, M. 50–2, 55–6, 171, 176, 181
Wenger, E. 172, 181
West, L. xiii, 7, 39–47
Wheen, F. 177, 181
Whelan, J. 179, 181
Whipp, J. *et al.* 49, 56
Wildermeersch, D. and Jansen, T. 172–173
Wilss, L. xiii, 9
Winne, P. H. 152–3, 157
Winnicott, D. 42, 47
Wolff, P. 79, 81
Wong, C. S. and Law, K. S. 119, 126
Woodley, A. *et al.* 116, 126
Wray, M. and Newitz, A. 163, 170
Wright Mills, C. 3, 7, 11, 211, 217

Young, M. 215, 217

Zimmerman, B. J. 148, 156
Zimmerman, B. J. and Kinsantas, A. 152
Zimmerman, B. J. and Martinez-Pons, M. 152
Zimmerman, B. J. and Schunk, D. H. 147